Introduction to
MUSIC

Ronald Pen, Ph.D.
University of Kentucky

An American BookWorks Corporation Project

McGraw-Hill

New York St. Louis San Francisco Auckland Bogotá
Caracas Lisbon London Madrid Mexico City Milan
Montreal New Delhi San Juan Singapore
Sydney Tokyo Toronto

Ronald Pen is Professor of Music at the University of Kentucky. He received his B.A. at Washington and Lee University and continued graduate work at Chicago Music College of Roosevelt University. He earned an M.A. in Music Composition from Tulane University and completed his Ph.D. at the University of Kentucky. Professor Pen's current research interests concern Appalachian traditional music and popular music studies. His articles and reviews have appeared in newspapers, magazines, and academic journals.

Introduction to Music

18 DIG/DIG 12

ISBN 0-07-038068-6

Library of Congress Cataloging-in-Publication Data
Pen, Ronald.
    Introduction to music / Ronald Pen.
      p.   cm.
    "An American BookWorks Corporation project."
    Includes index.
    ISBN 0-07-038068-6
    1. Music appreciation.   I. Title.
    MT6.P3916   1992
    780—dc20   91-30282
                                       CIP

Preface

While the appreciation of music is natural to all humans, a deeper understanding of the aspects of sound that shape music and a broad perspective on music's cultural and historical context can yield a more exciting and satisfying listening experience. This volume approaches music appreciation from this dual point of view, providing a solid foundation of the elements of music and a survey of historical periods. It is designed to be used both as a core text around which a course can be structured and as a text supplement for initial study, reference, and review.

For flexible use in a variety of courses, the text is not coordinated with a specific set of listening excerpts and does not contain analyses of specific works. Instead, conceptual information is presented that can easily be applied to listening examples. Explanations of the elements of music, although succinct, make possible through carefully chosen analogies and metaphors an intuitive grasp of those sometimes difficult concepts.

Chronologies of events and musicians preceding each of the history chapters provide orientation and perspective. For easy reference, the names of the musicians and composers are indented at two levels, not to evaluate their contributions but to indicate their relative importance to the narrative. Special chapters on world and popular music reflect current musical direction. A thorough glossary of terms summarizes definitions and descriptions given in the text.

Ron Pen

CONTENTS

Part I: Listening Techniques

CHAPTER 1

Introduction to Listening

Never before in the history of humanity has music been such a pervasive force within our culture. Because of the explosion of electronic sound reproduction, music has become a prominent feature of our daily life. We constantly listen to music within a variety of settings that are both functional and recreational. In this first chapter we shall examine the basic questions pertaining to our personal relationship with music—the questions of who, what, when, where, why, and how.

Who Listens to Music?

Everyone listens to music: people in transit plugged into Walkman-style tape players; commuters in traffic tuned into their car radios; city crowds riding up and down in elevators, enveloped in the muted murmur of Muzak; teens on the street or at the beach "grooving" to their portable cassette decks; vast rock audiences assembled in arenas to hear their favorite bands; couples bathed in the warm glow of romantic music at a candlelit dinner; and concertgoers gathered in orchestral halls, absorbed in the sounds of a symphony. It is music that provides the pulse that directs and reflects the tempo of our daily lives, music that has the power to alter, however subtly, our moods and attitudes. Nearly every aspect of our day-to-day existence is somehow affected by the sound of music.

What is Music?

Music is sound ordered in time—or, from another perspective, time measured by sound. Music originates with a sound source—a composer or performer who organizes and creates the sound using some form of instrument. The sounds then travel through the air as sound waves until they reach a listener. The listener takes in the sound waves through the ear. At this point, the sound becomes a stimulus that is received by the brain and interpreted as music.

Music as Language

Music is a language, a form of communication. It can elicit emotional responses and provoke thought, but it cannot signify concrete things or ideas in the manner of nouns, verbs, and adjectives. Music is an abstract language whose meaning is dependent upon the relationship between the creator and the listener. Meaning in music is also dependent upon social and historical context. Without study and familiarity it would be difficult for an Australian aborigine to make sense of a Schubert string quartet. Likewise, similar study and prolonged acquaintance is necessary for a twentieth-century Italian to comprehend a Roman ecclesiastical chant of the seventh century. Music is a highly affective language, but it conveys only the music itself, and communicates only to those who are familiar with its social and historical context.

Music and Noise

Noise is the antithesis of music. If a listener perceives order in sound, the sound is usually referred to as music. Sound that seems to lack organization or coherence is commonly labeled noise. Ultimately, the distinction between music and noise is determined by the personal judgment of each individual listener. That is why social and historical context are so important to the perception of music. If a listener is not aware of the style, form, and social setting inherent in a foreign or temporally removed music, he is liable to dismiss the sounds as mere noise. The purpose of a course or a text in music appreciation is to open the reader's ears and mind to the magically communicative powers of music from many times and in many places.

When Do We Listen to Music?

By merely turning the switch we can have music whenever and wherever we want today. However, before the age of electronic technology, music was used in very special and sometimes rigidly defined situations. Music was employed to solemnize a ceremonial event such as the coronation of a king, to ritualize a sacred event such as a wedding, or to accompany entertainment such as a square dance. The impact of music was much stronger because it only occurred in special circumstances for a select group of people in a one-time-only performance. Before electronics, all music was live, and the listener had to travel to a certain location that was specially designated for musical use. Then the listener had to concentrate on the music, knowing that he or she would never be able to hear those sounds repeated. The music would unfold during time and then it would dissipate into thin air, remaining only as a memory in the mind of the listener. Today, however, we are surrounded by music wherever we go, and if we want to hear a tune again, all we have to do is press the rewind button. Currently, every type of music is available anytime and anywhere, which is good. On the other hand, since music is no longer rare and inaccessible, we often take it for granted, failing to hear what we are listening to.

Why Do We Listen to Music?

Why do we listen to music? The answer to that question could be as simple as "we listen to music just because we like it." However, the answer can also be more complex because we listen to music in a variety of different ways that satisfy specific needs at certain times. The pleasure attained by attending an orchestra concert is different from the enjoyment engendered by hearing a jazz trio in the background at a fine restaurant. Music produces a feeling of euphoria in both situations, but it does so by appealing to different levels of listening.

Levels of Listening

There are essentially three levels at which we listen to music: those of background mood enhancement, thought association, and analytical perception. During the few seconds that it takes to hear a melody unfold, we will probably experience a great number of thoughts. Some will be directly related to the music, some will merely be provoked by the music and, finally, others will be entirely extraneous to the music. Although the music progresses in an orderly fashion through time, our mind frequently jumps from one level to the next, from one thought to the next, in a seemingly disconnected way. The only continuous thread binding all these disparate thoughts together is the music itself.

Background Mood-Enhancement Level

When we listen passively, simply allowing the music to wash over us, we are using it as background sound to enhance our mood. At this level, music has the power to alleviate our boredom and provide a feeling of emotional contentment. Muzak piped into the dentist's office or soft music played on the radio while one is working makes unpleasant or uncomfortable occasions more tolerable. At the background level we use music merely to help make ourselves feel better.

Thought-Association Level

At the thought-association level we use music to stir memories or stimulate patterns of thought. During this dreamlike state our mind either associates the music with certain personal memories directly related to the music, or it creates fantasy images corresponding to the contour of the sound. The conjunction of music and memory is a very strong union, and the proper music can trigger vivid recollections in each of us. Using this force, composers sometimes deliberately play upon our associative listening in order to represent a story or convey a concept. This associative style is known as program music.

Analytical Level

At the analytical level we concentrate on the music itself. Our ear perceives and interprets musical aspects such as rhythm, form, melody, or dynamics. At this level we also make critical judgments concerning the quality of performance or formulate aesthetic decisions about the effect of the composition. Music aimed primarily at the analytic level is referred to as absolute music.

How Do We Listen to Music?

Everyone listens to music—it seems to be as instinctive as eating and sleeping. Listening to music is such a natural activity that we seldom question the process through which we make sense of the sounds we hear. How do we listen to music? Everyone listens to music in a unique and personal way. We might say that music is created three separate times in the listening process. First, the composer creates the music and notates it; second, the performer re-creates it through his or her personal interpretation; and, finally, the listener creates it yet again, hearing just what he or she wants to hear of the original composition. In a sense, each individual listener in an audience may have a personal interpretation of what he or she heard despite the fact that they all perceived exactly the same sound source.

Our first musical perceptions and value judgments are formed in early childhood. As we grow older our musical understanding evolves and becomes more complex. Each musical activity serves to heighten our awareness and strengthen our ability to participate actively in music. Thus, our "musical taste" seems to be in a perpetual state of change and development. As we learn more about music, we begin to hear even more in the music. There is no right or wrong way to listen to music—but experience and education can provide an expanded perspective that makes our enjoyment more acute and our comprehension much more profound. The question of how we listen to music is central to this text. Through an examination of the basic elements of music and the historical and stylistic contexts for music, the reader will develop a more intimate and fulfilling relationship with the art of listening.

Music pervades almost every aspect of our daily life. Since electronic reproduction has made it so readily available, we are likely to take it for granted, on many occasions not taking the time really to listen. In an attempt to understand our relationship with music, we have examined the basic questions of who, what, when, where, why, and how.

Although everyone listens to music, each person does so in a unique and personal way. Each individual's approach is affected by three levels of listening: background, associative, and analytical. Through experience and education it is possible to deepen one's comprehension of music and thus attain more pleasure from listening to it.

Part II: The Elements of Music

CHAPTER 2

Introduction to the Elements of Music

Pick up a bottle and drop it on the floor—a sound erupts. A musician draws a bow across a violin string—a sound emerges. The crashing-bottle sound would be characterized as noise; the violin tone would be described as music. "Noise" and "music" are value judgments applied to the sounds according to cultural and personal context, but both sounds can be described and analyzed in the same objective terms.

The bottle crashes. The event takes a certain length of time—the time that it takes for the sound to begin and end. The bottle crashes. It has a particular range of frequencies, of high and low sounds, that reach our ear. The bottle crashes. It has a unique sort of sound, a tone color, that distinguishes it from the impact of a metal can. The bottle crashes. It has a certain dynamic level, a volume level that starts in silence, swells, and returns to silence. Duration, pitch, timbre, and dynamics— these are the elements of music that are common to every sound.

The Basic Elements of Sound

Imagine yourself seated by a pond, its surface smooth as glass, without a breath of wind to stir the surface. As you toss a pebble into the middle you notice a series of lovely concentric ripples that radiate outward from the impact. That pebble—the source of agitation—causes geometrically regular waves to move through the medium of water according to certain patterns that can be calculated by the science of physics. Similarly, agitated by a sound source, sound waves move through the medium of air in a way that can be quantified by the science of acoustics. As our eyes perceive the order of the waves on the pond, so do our ears comprehend the order of the sound waves. The basic elements of sound—duration, pitch, dynamics, and timbre—all correspond to the size, shape, and speed of those sound waves.

Duration

The Concept of Time

The concept of time is inseparable from the concept of music. In our day-to-day life we measure time in seconds, minutes, hours, and days. These are absolute values, useful in terms of synchronizing our activity with others, but they do not really tell us anything about the quality of the time that has passed. For instance, how long does an hour feel when it is spent grinding away at homework as compared with that same hour spent luxuriously dining out at a wonderful restaurant. Music occupies real time—it takes up actual seconds, minutes, and hours, but, more importantly, it addresses the concept of psychological time—the perceived tempo of life. Through music we experience the various speeds and intensities of life, ranging from suspended animation in which time seems to stand still, to dizzying and breathtaking climaxes at which time rushes at a frantic tempo. Through the enchantment of music, a lifetime of experience can be condensed and incorporated into a musical composition that occupies very little real clock time.

Music is, by its very nature, transient and ephemeral. Other arts are concerned with the measure of space and are essentially permanent. A painting can be viewed in its totality at once and then admired for hours at a time. Architecture lasts for centuries, literature may be read and reread, but music, like dance, unfolds through time and then disappears. Music, dance, and drama, all rendered by performers through time, are labeled performing arts, to distinguish them from the fine arts (painting, sculpture, photography, architecture) which exist in their totality and have no mediator between the artwork and the viewer.

Time and the Importance of Memory

As music unfolds during time, it is only through our memory that we are able to make sense of the sequence of sonic events that constitutes the music. The listener's comprehension is determined by memory—his or her ability to relate sounds heard in the past to sounds occurring during the present. Meaning in music is revealed through the interaction of past, present, and future sounds. Only the composer and performer know beforehand how the sounds heard at the beginning of a composition will lead to the conclusion of the work. Therefore, the composer relies heavily on form, ways of repeating and varying material, so that the listener is able to follow the musical progress of a work.

Levels of Duration

The element of time permeates every level of music from the brief duration of a single note to the expansive breadth of an entire symphony. Each individual note (like a point in space) defines a moment of time—the time it takes that note to emerge from and return to silence. On a larger scale, notes that are grouped together in context establish rhythm, and rhythm defines the flow of the music through time. In chapter 3 we will explore the specific techniques through which musicians incorporate the concept of time into music.

Pitch

As you watch the ripples in the pond you see that they move at a certain speed or frequency. The frequency observed in a sound wave, called *pitch* by musicians, determines how high or low the sound is perceived by a listener. A scientist is able to measure the frequency precisely and express the quantity as waves, or cycles per second (cps). A musician would describe that number of waves per second as a pitch named according to letters of the alphabet. For instance, the note A located in the middle of a piano keyboard corresponds to a frequency of 440 waves per second. A sound that seems high in pitch would have a large number of waves per second. Conversely, a low sound would consist of a small number of waves per second. Humans have a wide hearing range that extends up to approximately 16,000 cyles per second and down to approximately 15 cycles per second.

Pitch and Instruments

Each musical instrument has a specific range of frequencies that its sound is capable of encompassing based on the physical structure of that instrument. The length or thickness of strings, the width or length of tubing, and the size and tightness of a drum head all dictate the range of pitches the particular instrument can produce. For instance, one of the interesting features of the piano is the wide span of pitches that it can produce, ranging from the highest note C (4,186 waves per second), to the lowest note, A (27 waves per second).

In producing these pitches, each instrument conforms to laws of acoustics and physics. Therefore, the technique of performing on the instrument is directly related to the physical structure of that instrument. For instance, in a string instrument such as a violin, the length of the string dictates the pitch. A shorter string length produces a higher pitch, a higher frequency. Thus, if you pluck the third string of a violin that is in tune, the note A (440 cps) will sound. By placing a finger on a point midway up the string you divide the string length in half. Thus, upon plucking that half of the string, you achieve a higher-pitched sound (880 cps) that happens to be exactly twice the frequency of the whole string (440 cps). Likewise, on brass or woodwind instruments, by opening or closing holes with your fingers you make the tube length longer (lower-pitched) or shorter (higher-pitched).

Musical Tones and Noise

Musical sounds, called *tones*, consist of a single pitch, of constant frequency with regularly occurring vibrations. For instance, the flute plays distinct tones analogous to the regular waves caused by the pebble tossed into a pond. *Noise*, on the other hand, has no definite pitch; it consists of irregularly occurring frequencies. Unlike the flute tone, a cymbal crash sounds more like noise. The cymbal produces an irregular collection of pitches that might be compared to the scrambled profusion of waves created when a handful of pebbles is tossed into the pond.

Dynamics

Dynamics is the element of music concerned with the relative loudness or softness of a sound. To illustrate dynamics, let us return to the pond for one final analogy. If we toss that same proverbial pebble into the pond, waves will radiate forth from the point of impact. However, instead of a pebble, this time let us toss in a rather large rock. Instead of ripples spreading serenely across the surface, we now see large waves crashing outward from the rock's impact. The size of the wave, the *amplitude*, indicates the magnitude of the source of agitation. Similarly, the size of a sound wave indicates the dynamic intensity of the sound source. Small waves issue forth from a quiet sound source and large waves emanate from a loud sound.

Measurement of Dynamics

Scientists and musicians have different systems for measuring and indicating levels of dynamics. A scientist calculates sound intensity using a unit called *decibels* (dB). In this system, zero decibels indicates a sound at the threshold of audibility while 120 dB registers at the threshold of pain. While this is a wide range, in actuality, few instruments play as softly as 20 dB and most instruments play within the range of 40 dB to 80 dB. Whereas scientists calculate dynamic intensity in very specific terms based on a complicated logarithmic formula, musicians indicate intensity level in a more intuitive and interpretive way. The musician's system uses abbreviations of Italian words that mean soft, medium, and loud to represent approximate volume levels. Thus, *p* (piano) indicates a soft sound, *m* (mezzo) means moderate, and *f* (forte) indicates a loud sound. Although musicians do not think in terms of decibels, we can approximate a correspondance between the Italian terms and dB. Thus, forte = 80 dB and piano = 60 dB.

Musical Use of Dynamics

Musical expression is dependent upon the use of dynamics. We naturally associate quiet with sorrow and introspection, and loudness with joy and celebration. Through dynamics in music we can suddenly evoke these moods and just as suddenly alter them, engaging the listener in drama through contrast, or building tension through subtle shading of volume levels. The same passage for violins can be ominous and threatening at one volume level and yet exultant and buoyant at another dynamic intensity—that is the power of dynamics. Composers create dynamic contrast in their music through three different approaches: instrumental technique, combination of instruments, and distance between the performer and audience. These techniques, employed singly or in combination, offer a wide range of expression.

Instrumental Technique

The individual performer can vary his volume by changing the pressure or force with which he plays his instrument. With string instruments, the pressure and velocity brought to bear on the bow alter the volume. With wind instruments, changing the speed of the airstream affects the dynamic level—the faster you blow, the louder the sound you achieve. Finally, in the case of percussion instruments, the force and the material with which you strike the instrument determine the intensity of the sound. For instance, a snare drum hit with a wooden stick would have a louder sound than the same drum struck by wire brushes. Performers are capable of producing a wide range of expression on their instruments through sensitive control of pressure and velocity.

Combination of Instruments

Composers may also control dynamics through the combination of instruments. The addition or subtraction of instruments may increase or decrease the sound, but it does so in a fairly subtle way according to a geometric curve. Layering another trumpet on top of a solo trumpet does not simply double the volume. Another complication involved in building volume by combining instruments is the alteration that takes place in sound quality or timbre. Obviously, adding a trumpet to a violin section would make the sound louder, but it would also completely change the tone color. Even the addition of more than one violin to a solo violin changes the timbre slightly, and produces a slightly out-of-phase chorus effect.

Distance Between Performer and Audience

The last means of controlling volume is through the spatial relationship between the sound source and the listener. An increase in distance between the music and the audience lowers the intensity level while a decrease in distance contributes greater "presence," more volume. This approach is used less frequently because of the established architecture of performance halls. There are, however, some situations in which this means of volume control is highly effective, such as in churches with organ pipes located in both front and back, or in stereos with channel separation.

Timbre

If two different instruments, a flute and an oboe, play exactly the same note at equal volume, we can still distinguish between their individual sounds. This perceived sound characteristic that allows us to distinguish between instruments is called *tone color*, or *timbre*. Timbre in music is analogous to the various shades of paint available to an artist. A composer colors his sound by arranging his music for various instruments or combinations of instruments in order to provide contrast and drama, or to highlight the formal structure.

The particular timbre of each musical instrument is directly related to the way in which that instrument vibrates or creates vibrations in the air. In *string instruments*, such as a violin, the strings vibrate when they are either plucked or agitated by a bow drawn across them. *Wind instruments*, including the brass, reed, and double-reed families, sound when the column of air inside them vibrates. Brass instruments, such as a trumpet, produce sound through the "buzzing" of the performer's lips. Reed instruments, such as a clarinet, excite the column of air through the vibration of a cane reed attached to a mouthpiece. And double-reed instruments, such as an oboe, produce their sound through the friction of two cane reeds held together by wire or string. *Percussion instruments*, such as a bass drum, produce vibrations when the skin head is struck. *Electronic instruments*, such as a synthesizer, derive their vibrations from the motion of a speaker cone. In each case, the vibrations cause sound waves to move through the air until they are perceived as musical tones.

Fundamental Tones and Overtones

When an instrument sounds, it produces a single basic vibration that dominates the sound. This vibration forms the recognizable pitch known as the *fundamental tone*. However, in addition to the fundamental, there are other vibrations present that are not as loud as the fundamental. These secondary vibrations, called *overtones* or *harmonics*, are not heard as separate tones because they are masked by the fundamental, but they do enhance the character or timbre of the sound. When you adjust the tone control of your stereo you are actually controlling the timbre of the sound by adding or subtracting overtones.

Wave Shapes

Just as the frequency of the wave determines its pitch, the particular shape of the wave determines its tone color or timbre. A very pure tone produced on a tuning fork and containing only the fundamental pitch, can be visually represented by a simple shape called a *sine wave*.

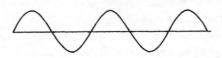

On the other hand, the complex wave generated by an instrument such as a bassoon contains a fundamental and various overtones, and resembles this figure.

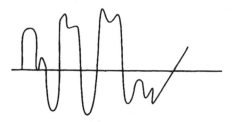

Noise, which contains a great number of different fundamentals, as well as many different overtones, has a wave shape resembling a solid bar.

The richness of the tone color is visually reflected in the complexity of the wave shape.

Wave shapes have an important new application in musical electronic technology. Instead of relying on musicians to perform on instruments, recording engineers can now use a synthesizer to simulate any preexisting timbre by merely matching the wave shape. Tone colors will sound identical if their fundamental and overtone structures are the same, and that relationship is visually represented by corresponding wave shapes.

Sound may be considered music if order is perceived, or noise if only chaos is discernable. Sound, whether it is perceived as music or noise, can be objectively described and analyzed in terms of four distinct categories. These categories—duration, pitch, dynamics, and timbre—form the four basic elements of music. In defining each of these elements we discovered an acoustical basis for musical description and application. It is through manipulation of time, pitch, dynamics, and timbre that music has the power to condense a lifetime of experience into a composition that lasts but a relatively short time.

CHAPTER 3

Music as the Measure of Time

In the previous chapter we formulated some basic assumptions concerning the relationship between music and time. We noted that music is a measure of time, and we also observed that it exists in psychological time as well as in real clock time. Musical events occupy a certain length of time that can be measured in terms of seconds and minutes, but those same sounds also affect our perception of how slow or fast time seems to move. In this chapter we shall examine the specific temporal materials and techniques that composers employ in measuring and manipulating our sense of time.

Beat

In everyday clock time the smallest unit of measurement is the second. The second is a consistent and regular measurement—each second is exactly as long as the second preceding it and the second following it. The second is also an absolute and unchanging division—a second always moves at exactly the same speed, and it always takes exactly the same number of seconds to form one minute. Seconds may seem to move faster or slower relative to our state of mind but, in actuality, each second is exactly the same as every other second.

In some ways a musical beat is very similar to the second of a clock. A beat is the smallest basic unit of measurement in musical time. A beat is a consistent and regular measurement—each beat is exactly as long as the beat preceding it and the beat following it. However, a beat is not an absolute and unchanging division. Beats do not always move at exactly the same rate of speed. In this way, musical time deviates from clock time. A second is fixed and unchangeable, but the speed of the beat, the tempo, may be altered by the musician. In our day-to-day life we can not do anything to alter the steady procession of seconds steadily ticking away. In music, however, the composer can condense or expand the tempo of the music, the perceived tempo of life, by altering the basic tempo of the beat. In that way, music can create the impression of an escape from the reality of an unyielding passage of time.

The beat is usually the easiest aspect of music for the listener to identify and appreciate. We sense the steady pulse of the beat as physical movement and, in fact, frequently respond physically by tapping our feet or clapping our hands. In dance, the rhythm of the dancer's movements are related directly to the force of the beat. When the beat is stated explicitly, as by drums in a rock song, we sense that beat as a compelling physical presence that is propelling us through time at a certain speed. At other times, however, the beat may be only implicit or even hidden, producing a feeling of floating through time. Our sensation of movement through time is largely controlled by the manipulation of the beat.

Tempo

Tempo is the rate of speed at which the beat moves—the basic pace at which the music unfolds. We generally associate fast tempi with excitement, and our own pulse and heartbeat may quicken in sympathy with the music. Likewise, we often relate slower tempi to feelings of calmness and repose, and we can feel our minds and bodies relax in response to the music. A piece of music is not necessarily locked into just one tempo or mood, however, and a composer is able to build and release tension by altering the tempo at will within a single composition.

Tempo Indications

Tempo indications are always provided in a piece of music so that the performer knows how fast or slow the piece should be performed. Usually these tempo indications take the form of descriptive Italian terms, but tempi may also be designated using the more accurate system of metronomic indications. Whichever system is observed, it is essential to have some sort of tempo indication so that the composer may convey his or her desired rate of speed to the performer.

Descriptive Terms

Just as the Latin language once provided an international means of communication for people of diverse cultures and languages, so Italian became a common language for musical description. Musicians across the world may not know how to wish someone good morning in Italian but, through the universal use of Italian musical terms, they are able to communicate with one another despite language barriers. The terms listed below represent a wide range of tempo indications, but it is important to note that these are only approximate speeds. The terms themselves are relative and open to interpretation by the individual performer.

Italian Term	English Translation	Metronomic Marking
largo	very slow, broad	40–60
larghetto	very slow, slightly faster than largo	
grave	very slow, solemn	
lento	slow	60–66
adagio	slow (at ease)	66–76
andante	moderately slow (walking pace)	76–108
moderato	moderate	108–120
allegretto	fast	
allegro	fast (cheerful)	120–168
vivace	lively	
presto	very fast	168–200
prestissimo	as fast as possible	200–208

Other Italian words are used in conjunction with the terms listed above to qualify and describe the tempo in still more detail. These words include:

Italian Term	English Translation
assai	very
meno	less
molto	much
non troppo	not too much
più	more
poco a poco	little by little

Thus, an expression like *allegro assai* means "very fast" and *allegro non troppo* means "not too fast."

These terms denote the tempo but they characterize the mood of the music as well, telling us not only how fast the beat moves but also what attitude or frame of mind is associated with that speed.

Metronomic Markings

Tempo may also be indicated by a metronomic marking that specifies the exact number of beats occurring in a minute. For instance, a metronome marking of ♩ = 60 means that sixty quarter-note beats take place in a minute. Therefore, each beat has a duration of exactly one second. This speed is approximately equal to the Italian term *larghetto*. While this system is more accurate than the use of Italian terms, in performance musicians seldom adhere to the metronomic markings exactly. The final decision about the actual tempo for performance is ultimately made by the individual musician, based on his or her conception of the music and sensitivity to the acoustics of the performance site.

This metronomic system of notating tempo evolved in conjunction with the invention of the metronome by Dietrich Winkel (ca. 1812). Winkel's metronome was a machine that used a double pendulum to create a clicking sound at regular intervals. By adjusting the weight at the upper end of the pendulum, the speed of the pulse could be increased or decreased to accommodate various tempi. Even without a metronome it is easy to determine the exact tempo of a work—the only equipment you need is a watch with a second-hand. Simply tap along with the beat and count the number of beats in fifteen seconds, and then multiply that number by four. The product will be the number of beats per minute.

Accelerando and Ritardando

Up to now, every aspect of musical time that we have discussed has been dictated by the beat. However, music is seldom completely dominated by inflexible adherance to the beat. A composer wanting to speed up the pace of his music can do so either by changing the tempo suddenly or by reducing the value of the note (such as using eighth notes instead of quarter notes). These approaches to tempo change are sometimes effective but hardly subtle. The first technique jumps suddenly to a new speed, and the other approach instantly doubles or quadruples the momentum. However, by deviating from the beat and accelerating gradually, the composer is able to achieve expressive tempo change. This gradual increase of tempo is indicated by the Italian term *accelerando*. A similar sort of decrease in speed is called *ritardando*. Through the use of accelerando and ritardando, musical rhythm can be as supple and elastic as a rubber band.

Meter

Each beat occupies the same length of time but not every beat is exactly equal in terms of stress. In actual practice, beats are arranged into small groupings of accented and unaccented beats in much the same way that words are composed of accented and unaccented syllables. These groupings, consisting of an accented beat followed by one or more unaccented beats, are called *measures*. A series of measures organized in a repeated pattern is called *meter*. We have already observed that music is the measure of time. It is through meter, patterns of measures that consist of strong and weak beats, that we measure that passing time.

Duple Meter

The most basic meter consists of a measure of two beats—an accented beat followed by an unaccented beat. This meter, called duple meter, would be counted *1* 2 *1* 2 *1* 2 with an accent on the first beat of each measure. That first accented beat of the measure is referred to as the downbeat.

Triple Meter

Triple meter consists of measures that begin with an accented downbeat followed by two unaccented beats. Triple meter, counted *1* 2 3 *1* 2 3 *1* 2 3 has a lilting dancelike feel that is strongly associated with the waltz.

Quadruple Meter

Likewise, quadruple meter consists of measures with four beats—a stressed downbeat followed by three weak beats. Quadruple meter is often referred to as *common meter* or *march time*.

Rhythm

So far, we have divided time up into small units called beats, organized these beats into groupings called measures, and consolidated regular patterns of these measures into a structure that we labeled meter. We have constructed a musical system that resembles the clock time system of seconds, minutes, and hours. However, music, like life, does not strictly follow the artificially regular divisions of time but, rather, ebbs and flows freely around time. This ordered musical flow is called *rhythm*. In order to indicate rhythm we need to erect a system of proportions that will allow us to express relative durations.

Divisive Versus Additive Time

In notating rhythm, people of the Euro-American tradition chose to make this system of proportional durations *divisive*. The foundation of our rhythmic scheme is the division of a whole into smaller, fractional parts. However, musicians in other parts of the world, including large parts of the continents of Africa and Asia, have a different approach— an *additive* system that builds rhythm by adding together units of time. The basic differences of philosophical approach, manifest in the use of divisive time versus additive time, contribute greatly to the enormous contrasts among our musical cultures. It is little wonder that Americans have trouble understanding a West African drum ensemble, or that an Indian musician finds it difficult to follow a Beethoven string quartet—we have two completely different notions of time.

Rhythmic Notation (Note Values)

Our system of rhythmic notation indicates relative duration of time. Note values, like whole notes, half notes, and quarter notes, do not automatically represent a specific duration. They only symbolize a proportional duration that is based on their relationship to other note values. For instance, two half notes occupy the time of one whole note, so we know that a whole note occupies twice as much musical time as a half note. The five most commonly used note values are represented as follows:

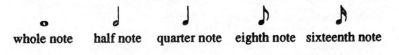

whole note   half note   quarter note   eighth note   sixteenth note

These note values correspond to simple fractions. Each note is exactly half the value of the note to its immediate left and exactly twice as long as the note to its right. The following chart illustrates the various note values and their proportional relationships.

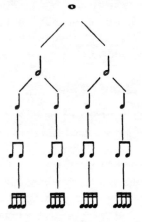

Triplets

All of the relationships indicated on this chart are based on even multiples of two: halves, quarters, eighths, and sixteenths. That is fine when we are notating rhythms that are relatively regular and square sounding, but there are times when this system is just not flexible enough to accommodate the actual freedom of rhythm. There is no such thing as an odd division of a whole note along the lines of a "third note" but, if we wanted to indicate such a rhythm, we could do so with the triplet. A triplet shortens the duration of a note value slightly, and allows you to divide a whole into three equal parts. By joining the three notes together with a curved line (called a slur) and adding a *3* above or below, we can indicate that those three notes should be played during the time that two notes are usually sounded. Similarly, we can use other odd divisions, such as quintuplets in place of four or septuplets in place of six, merely by adding the number above or below.

Dotted Rhythms

Another way of producing rhythmic flexibility is through the use of dotted rhythms. By adding a dot to the right of a note, we increase that note's value by half again its original value. For instance, we already know that a quarter note is equal to two eighth notes. If we add a dot to that quarter note, it would then be equal to two eighth notes plus half of its value (an eighth note), or three eighth notes altogether. Dotted rhythms provide a lilting dancelike feel to music and are used often to indicate the loose "swing" rhythms of jazz.

Relationship of Rhythm and Tempo

So far we have considered the relative durations of note values, but we are still unable to judge the specific durations of those notes. We know that a half note moves twice as fast as a whole note, but does that half note last five seconds or five minutes?

Earlier in the chapter we defined tempo as the rate of speed at which the beat moved. In order to determine the speed or tempo of our various note values, we need to assign one specific note value to match the beat. By knowing exactly how fast that one note value moves, we can determine the speed of the other note values as well. For instance, if there are 60 beats in a minute, and we equate a quarter note with the beat, then we can conclude that each quarter note lasts a second; half notes, lasting twice as long, would each occupy two seconds.

All note values are proportional and move at a rate of speed determined by the tempo. Metronomic markings indicate tempo by equating a specific note value with the beat and then describing how many beats occur in a minute. Thus, ♩ = 120 tells us that there are 120 quarter notes per minute and that each quarter note lasts half a second. Consequently, a whole note lasts two seconds, a half note lasts one second, and an eighth note would last one-quarter of a second.

Rests

Music measures time through sound, but it could not do so without the absence of sound—silence. Similarly, we would not be able to distinguish one day from the next without the presence of night to punctuate and contrast daylight. As night delineates each day, so, musically, is each sound bounded by silence—every sound emerges from, and finally returns to, silence. We notate durations of silence in the same way that we notate durations of sound—through proportional values. The proportional rests are exactly equivalent to the corresponding proportional notes. For instance, a quarter note lasts as long as a quarter rest. The rest values are notated as follows:

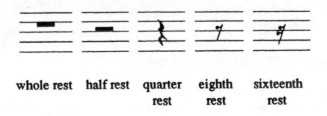

whole rest   half rest   quarter   eighth   sixteenth
                           rest   rest   rest

Meter and Time Signatures

In our previous discussion of meter we found that groupings of strong and weak beats, called measures, were organized into meters, such as duple and triple. Now, through an understanding of the relationship between beat and note value, we can make a final link between tempo and proportional note values, and thereby complete our concept of meter.

Time Signatures

Tempo tells us how fast the beat moves, meter tells us how we group the beats in measures, and proportional note values provide a relationship between beat and duration. Taken as a whole, tempo, meter, and proportional note values can tell us the number of note values, moving at a certain speed, that is contained in a measure. This is indicated at the beginning of a composition (or wherever the meter changes) by a *time signature*. A time signature consists of two numbers, one above the other. The top number indicates how many beats are contained in the measure and the bottom number tells us which note value receives each beat. Thus, in $\frac{4}{4}$ the top number informs us that there are four beats in a measure, the bottom number tells us that each of those beats is a quarter note, and the first beat, the downbeat, is accented. Pictured here are several ways of notating a measure in $\frac{4}{4}$ meter.

Types of Meter

The various types of meter can be usefully classified as simple, compound, asymmetrical, and mixed.

Simple Meter

Simple meter has a top number of 2, 3, or 4, and the beat is divided into two equal parts. The following time signatures represent examples of simple meter:

	duple			triple			quadruple	
2	2	2	3	3	3	4	4	4
2	4	8	2	4	8	2	4	8

Compound Meter

Compound meters consider the basic pulse on two different levels. At the fundamental level, the basic pulse is divided into groups of three. At a higher level of organization, these groups containing three beats may be combined into a pattern of two, three, or four groups per measure. A conductor would beat time at the higher level, but the performers would subdivide each of the conductor's pulses into three beats.

6
8

Fundamental level (three-beat groups)

Higher level (patterns of two)

To form a compound meter you simply multiply the top number of a simple meter by three. These meters are called compound because they have the accented beat of duple, triple, or quadruple meter, but the beat is always divided into groups of three. The following time signatures represent examples of compound meter:

	duple			triple			quadruple	
6	6	6	9	9	9	12	12	12
2	4	8	2	4	8	2	4	8

Asymmetrical Meter

Asymmetrical meters contain an irregular number of beats. They can be subdivided in various groupings of two and three to form exciting meters with surprising accents. For instance, $\frac{5}{4}$ can be divided in the following way:

Mixed Meter

Musicians may change meters as often as they desire. A composition that varies its meter frequently in order to change accents and alter tempo is in what is known as mixed meter. The following is a passage notated in mixed meters:

Music can alter our perception of clock time through the manipulation of sound in time. A composer controls the duration of these sonic events through rhythm, which is the relationship between beat, tempo, meter, and proportional note values. These parameters of tempo, meter, and note value are described and notated in different manners. Tempo, the speed of the beat, is indicated by Italian terms or metronomic markings. Meter is indicated by a fractionlike number that represents the number of beats per measure and indicates which note value is equated with the beat. Finally, proportional note values are indicated by symbols representing various durations of sound or silence.

CHAPTER 4

Music as the Measure of Space

As we have seen, music exists in time and is a measure of time. Music also exists in space, and is a measure of perceived space. Sound waves travel through the medium of air and, therefore, they measure a specific spatial distance—the distance between the sound source and the listener. Sound waves are also a measure of perceived space. In reality, sound waves are not higher or lower than one another but, psychologically, we conceive of them as sounding either high or low, close or distant. Therefore, we can talk about music as being a measure of real and imagined space in much the same way that we previously discussed music in terms of clock and psychological time.

Symbols of Musical Space

Pitches and Intervals

In geometry, a point is the smallest unit, but a point does not really have meaning when considered only by itself. Given two points, however, we are able to make a relationship, and measure a distance in space. Those two points determine the length and path of exactly one line.

Similarly, the smallest musical unit is a single *pitch*. That pitch may occupy time in the same way that a point occupies space, but it cannot indicate a musical relationship in isolation. Given two pitches, sounded either in succession or simultaneously, we have a relationship, and can measure a span of musical space called an interval. An *interval* is the distance in pitch between any two musical tones.

Organization of Intervals

The range of audible frequencies (approximately 15 cps to 1600 cps) has been organized in various ways by different cultures. Think of this audible-frequency spectrum as a fire-engine siren. Like a siren, it has a range of tones bounded by a top and a bottom sound, but with no distinct steps in between. To measure the intervals between tones we would need to organize the audible-frequency spectrum into equidistant steps, comparable to inches on a ruler.

The Half Step

In the Euro-American system the *half step*, or *semitone*, is designated as the smallest interval between tones. It is defined as the distance from one tone to the next adjacent tone. A *whole step* is the distance represented by the combination of two half steps.

The Octave

Twelve half steps comprise a unit of measurement called the octave. The octave as a pitch measurement is based on physical laws. A pitch vibrates at exactly twice the frequency of the pitch an octave below it. For example, the note A (usually notated as a^1), which is the note to which the orchestra tunes, vibrates at 440 cycles per second, while the note A that is an octave higher (a^2) vibrates at 880 cycles per second. Because of this harmonious musical and mathematical relationship, tones that are separated by an octave sound very much alike.

Pitch Names

Pitch is the specific location of a tone in a musical scale as defined by its unique frequency. Each of the twelve half steps within the octave has some form of letter name associated with it. This is confusing at first because we divide the octave into twelve steps but use only seven alphabet letters to name these steps. The tones represented by the white keys of the piano each have a letter assigned to them starting with A and ending with G, at which point the alphabet starts over again for the next octave. These white keys and the notes they represent account for seven steps of the octave, but our octave is divided into twelve steps. The remaining five steps are represented by the black keys of the piano, and are designated by letter names related to the adjacent white keys. If the black key is half a step above a white key it is referred to as a sharp (♯) and if it is a half step below a white key it is referred to as a flat (♭). The keyboard pictured here illustrates the names of the pitches.

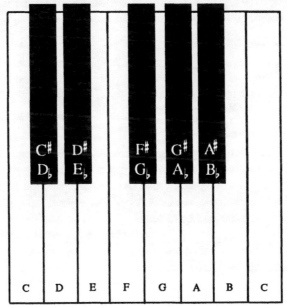

Keyboard with Pitch Names

Pitch and Interval Notation

In written language, symbols known as alphabet letters represent certain sounds that can be combined to form words. Through the use of mutually accepted letters and words, people of the same linguistic culture can communicate thoughts to one another and preserve these thoughts throughout time by notating their thoughts. Written language is one of the most valuable tools in the dissemination and preservation of our culture.

Similarly, musical notation is vitally important to the transmission and preservation of musical culture. Some traditional music, such as ballads and fiddle tunes, is passed on through generations by word of mouth and memory (oral tradition), but extended and complex thoughts can only be transmitted to others and preserved accurately through time by written notation. This is especially the case with art music, in which performers have to interpret the work of a composer.

We have already encountered symbols that represent time values; now we must examine the system for measuring pitch. Fortunately, this is rather simple, since we do not need to learn new symbols. We need only place the time symbols (♩ ♩ ♩ ♪ ♪ ♪) on a series of lines separated by spaces that we call a staff, to represent the pitch names. In doing so, it is useful to conceive of these lines as a graph and the notes as representing points on the graph. The higher the location of the note, the higher the pitch sounds.

Staff and Clef

The staff consists of five horizontal parallel lines that are separated by four equidistant spaces. A symbol called a clef is placed at the beginning of each line to provide the reference point for interpreting each note's position on a line or space. The symbol 𝄞 is a *treble clef* sign and it indicates that the line circled by the spiral represents the pitch G above middle C on the piano (see the chart on page 34). Now that we know that this line represents the pitch G, we can assign the other lines and spaces to consecutive letters of the alphabet by counting forward as we ascend in pitch, and backward through the alphabet as we descend. Remember, we use only the seven letters, A through G, so that when we reach G we need to start the cycle over again with A.

In addition to the treble clef, we use another symbol called the *bass clef* (𝄢) to indicate lower-sounding pitches. In this clef, the two dots following the clef symbol surround the pitch F below middle C. We calculate the pitches in the same way that we did with the treble clef, assigning letter names to consecutive lines and spaces. When the treble clef and the bass clef staves (the plural of staff) are combined, the wide range of pitches that the combination encompasses is called the *grand staff*. Pictured here is the the grand staff with all the pitches indicated. Note that pitches of the lowest octave are indicated by uppercase letters, pitches of the next octave are designated by lowercase letters, and subsequent higher octaves are represented by superscripts.

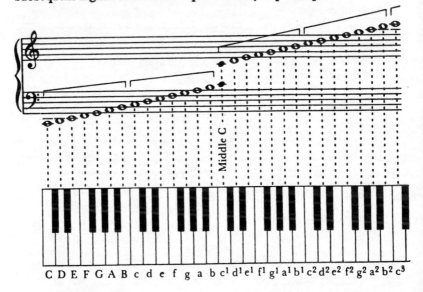

$$C \ D \ E \ F \ G \ A \ B \ c \ d \ e \ f \ g \ a \ b \ c^1 d^1 e^1 \ f^1 g^1 a^1 b^1 c^2 d^2 e^2 \ f^2 g^2 a^2 b^2 c^3$$

Interval Names

An interval is the musical distance between any two pitches. Within any octave, such as the c^1 to c^2 represented on the grand staff, there is the capacity for twelve different sizes of intervals, each encompassing various numbers of half steps. Every interval has a unique, characteristic sound that induces a sense of consonance (repose) or dissonance (agitation) in us when we hear it. Each of these intervals is given a name based on the number of steps between the two tones. As was the case with pitch names (A-G), we assign values to the white keys of the piano but, rather than using letters, we designate intervallic distances by ordinal numbers "second" through "seventh." For example, the interval separating the tones A and C is a third, because it includes three pitch names (A, B, C). Likewise, the interval between the notes C and G is a fifth because it is five pitch names away (C, D, E, F, G)

Interval Quality

As with letter names for pitch, this system uses only seven terms for the twelve possible intervals. Thus, in the same way that we used sharps and flats to modify pitch names, we qualify the numerical terms for intervals by using the terms major, minor, perfect, augmented, and diminished.

Major and Minor

Seconds, thirds, sixths, and sevenths may be either major or minor depending on the number of half steps forming the interval. For instance, the interval from C to E♭ is a third because it includes three pitch names (C, D, E) but the distance from C to E♭ is also a kind of third because it includes the same three pitch names (C, D, E). The interval formed by C and E♭ (three half steps) is smaller than that between C and E (four half steps) so we label the larger third (C to E) a major third and the smaller interval (C to E♭) a minor third. In the same way, the larger forms of seconds, sixths, and sevenths are called major intervals to distinguish them from the minor versions that are one half step smaller.

Perfect, Augmented, and Diminished

Each of the intervals discussed in the preceding—second, third, sixth, and seventh—occurs in two forms—major and minor.

The remaining intervals—fourth, fifth, and octave— occur in only one form, so they are referred to as *perfect* intervals. If we expand or contract the size of a perfect interval by a half step we do not use the terms major and minor but, rather, refer to the expanded form as *augmented* (made larger) and the contracted form as *diminished* (made smaller). For example, the interval defined by the pitches C and G is a perfect fifth (it encompasses the five pitch names C, D, E, F, and G). If we raise the G to G♯ by adding an extra half step, then we would refer to the interval as an augmented fifth. Similarly, if we decreased the size of the fifth by one half step making the G a G♭ , we would call the interval a diminished fifth.

Summary of Pitch and Interval Relationships

Although the system for notating pitch names and interval size may initially seem cumbersome and complex, it springs from the important need for musicians to discuss accurately the relationship between notes—to define space in time. By naming our pitches we define the points in space, and by labeling our intervals we describe the lines that represent the relationships of the points in space. The following chart summarizes and clarifies these spatial relationships. Represented are the various intervals spanning the octave between the note C and the C that is twelve half steps higher. The chart illustrates the intervallic distances calibrated in half steps and indicates the sound quality in terms of relative consonance and dissonance.

Pitch and Interval Relationships

Pitch	Distance	Interval Name	Quality
C	none	unison	pure consonance
C♯	half step	minor second	very dissonant
D	one whole step	major second	dissonant
E♭	three half steps	minor third	mild consonance
E	two whole steps	major third	very consonant
F	five half steps	perfect fourth	pure consonance
F♯	three whole steps	augmented fourth	ambiguous
G	seven half steps	perfect fifth	pure consonance
A♭	four whole steps	minor sixth	mild consonance
A	nine half steps	major sixth	very consonant
B♭	five whole steps	major seventh	mild dissonance
B	eleven half steps	minor seventh	very dissonant
C	six whole steps	octave	pure consonance

Melody

Our method of labeling pitch names and interval distances clarifies the bare facts behind the measurement of sonic space in time. Through this descriptive system we could define the relationship between any two identifiable tones that we might hear in the course of a day. For instance, the "ding-dong" sound of a doorbell chime might well be a major third consisting of the tones C and E. However, music is more than random intervals—it is ordered sound in time, which means that a human is organizing a succession of intervals. This ordered succession of intervals is called *melody*. Because these intervals occur during time, they have durational value and thus, in a melody, pitch cannot be separated from rhythm.

Organization is all-important in a melody. A melody is not a random sequence of tones but, rather, a logical sequence of notes that completes a musical thought in much the same way that a sentence expresses a verbal thought. Unlike a sentence whose message is concrete, the exact meaning of a melody can never be pinned down. Melody communicates an idea, but this idea may be interpreted differently by each listener, and may even be construed differently by the same listener on different occasions.

Melody embodies, more than any other single aspect of music, the marriage of practical craft and artistic magic. There is no single formula for a successful melodic line. There is no analytical study of intervals and rhythm that can explain the emotional impact of a melody. There is no textbook definition that can successfully encompass every melodic type. Ultimately, it is far easier to experience a melody than to describe why the melody creates the effect that it does. Yet, difficult as it is to characterize the extramusical aspects of a melody, it is possible and, indeed, useful to dissect the melody into its component parts and then describe the melodic elements so that we can determine its relationship to other musical aspects, such as harmony and form.

Melodic Contour

Each melody has a broad overall form that we hear as an audible shape resembling a visual silhouette. This characteristic design, determined by the general direction of the pitches, is known as the melodic contour. For example, a melody might start on middle C, ascend gradually to a pitch an octave higher, and finally descend, ending on the same pitch with which it began. Such a contour would be described as a melodic arch. Our first, and most enduring, impression of the melody is generated by the contour.

The contour is the large overall tendency of the melodic gesture, but at a smaller level, our perception of the melody is colored by the sequence of intervals. If the melody consists primarily of small intervals (half or whole steps) then the motion is called *conjunct*. Conversely, if the intervals proceed by leaps rather than steps, the motion is called *disjunct*. Composers frequently contrast melodies within the same piece by casting one melody in smooth conjunct motion and the other melody in a jagged disjunct manner.

Melody Notated with Its Suggested Contour

Melodic Structure

Verbal language has a specific syntax that gives order and coherence to our written and spoken thought. Letters are combined to form words, which are the smallest unit of meaning. These words are then placed in relationships to one another to form phrases and sentences that express thought. Finally, these sentences are linked with one another in a paragraph, so that the culmination of the combined sentences presents a developed concept. The hierarchy of syntax at the word, sentence, and paragraph levels enables us to communicate complex thoughts in an orderly manner.

Music may not express specific and concrete thoughts, but it is still a communicative language. As such, it contains a hierarchy of form similar to that of written language.

Tone, Interval, and Motive

A *tone* is analogous to a letter—both are symbols possessing a sound but having no meaning except when placed in the context of other letters or tones. *Intervals* are analogous to words. As words are combined into phrases, several intervals combine to form a small fragment of meaning called a motive. A *motive* is a short idea that can be used to generate and develop a longer idea or melody. By developing and extending the characteristic idea of the motive, a composer creates the next level of meaning—the musical phrase.

Phrase

A musical phrase presents a single complete musical thought in a way that is analogous to a sentence of verbal language. A phrase is similar to the birth-death cycle of a human life. It emerges from silence to state a motive, it then proceeds to develop that motive through some form of varied repetition and, finally, it closes with a brief figure before returning to silence. This succession of statement, development, and conclusion represents the structure of an entire composition reduced to the microlevel of a single phrase.

Phrase Length. Phrase length is variable, depending on the thought being expressed, but the duration often approximates the cycle of human respiration—the time it takes to inhale and exhale comfortably. In actual practice, this has meant that the average length of a phrase has been about four measures during much of our musical history, so the vast majority of music has been constructed using the four-bar phrase as the basic building block.

Paired Phrases. Phrases often occur in a paired situation in which the first phrase rises in pitch while posing a "question" and the successive phrase returns to the original pitch center, providing an "answer." These paired contrasting phrases, called *antecedent* and *consequent*, often contain similar material (related to the motive) but, as in a conversation or discussion, they usually end with a different concluding gesture.

Cadence. These concluding gestures that complete the sense of a phrase are known as cadences. A cadence is a combination of melodic, rhythmic, and harmonic formulas that converge, leading us to expect a sense of repose. The cadence that ends an antecedent phrase leaves us in suspense because it resolves on a tone that does not correspond to our sense of tonal "home." Such a cadence is referred to as an *incomplete cadence*. A consequent phrase would end with a formula that leads to no further expectation and makes us feel as though we have returned to our tonal home. This type of ending is termed a *full* or *perfect cadence*. Momentum in music is largely conveyed through cadences that either propel us forward by evading our anticipations or satisfy our expectations by resolving musical tension.

Scales and Keys

Before we conclude our discussion of pitch and melody, we need to mention the overall concept of tonal organization that provides a sense of order and direction in melody and invests intervals with meaning. This organizational system of scales and keys, which evolved over hundreds of years, has provided musicians with a means of relating pitches so that they reflect a coherent system, resembling the relationship of stars and planets in a galaxy. Within a scale or key, certain tones have more emphasis, and other pitches revolve about them, bound by gravity, like moons around a planet. A detailed explanation of scales and keys will be found in chapter 7.

We have presented the relationships of pitches as the measurement of perceived space. In measuring this perceived space, tones are separated by a musical distance called an interval in the same way that two points are separated by, or determine, a line. The Euro-American system designates the half step as the smallest interval, and then organizes the entire frequency of audible sound into octaves that each contain twelve half steps. These half-step divisions, called pitches or tones, are provided with names drawn from the first seven letters of the alphabet and are notated on a staff with corresponding lines and spaces. Between each of these twelve pitches are different sizes and qualities of intervals, each of which encompasses a number of half and whole steps. These intervals are characterized as possessing relative degrees of consonance or dissonance, so that when they are combined in melodic phrases, they can convey musical motion through tension and relaxation.

CHAPTER 5

Music as the Measure
of Dynamics

The volume level of our voice reveals a great deal about our emotional state from one moment to the next. During a typical day our speech utilizes a broad dynamic spectrum ranging from soft whispered words of endearment in a romantic setting to full-throated screams at an exciting athletic event. We generally associate the intensity of our dynamic level with the intensity of the situation. Moments of great crisis or exultation are equated with a corresponding climactic dynamic level.

Musically, we also mirror these expressive levels with appropriate dynamics. The crushing climax of a work is often equated with the full orchestra playing fortissimo, highlighted by crashing cymbals and rolling tympani. Likewise, gentle, lyrical passages are often orchestrated for light murmuring strings. Dynamic contrast is an effective barometer of emotional intensity. In addition to its expressive role, however, dynamic shading can also be used to delineate other musical elements such as form, cadence structure, and melody. Dynamic contrast provides an entire musical dimension that brightens color, heightens excitement, and lends shape to formal expression in music.

Methods of Dynamic Control

To achieve dynamic control, three distinct methods may be employed. Individual performers may control intensity through instrumental technique. Composers may regulate volume through combinations of instruments, a technique known as orchestration. And, finally, the distance between the sound source and the listener may be altered by repositioning either the performer or the audience. These methods may be employed independently or in conjunction with one another.

Dynamics Through Instrumental Technique

On a personal level, musicians can alter the force with which they produce the sound. Performers playing string instruments can either vary the pressure exerted on the bow or pluck the strings with more or less force. Brass and woodwind players alter dynamics through the control of wind velocity. Percussionists govern the volume by altering the force with which they strike their instrument. Dynamics in electronic instruments are controlled simply by adjusting the control knob (which alters the voltage and, in turn, controls the dynamic intensity). At this personal level, dynamics are directly related to the sound-producing capacity of each instrument. This dynamic response is inherent in the instrument and can be only partially modified by a musician's performance ability. The instrument may be played louder or softer according to the will of the performer, but the dynamic response is largely predetermined by the nature of the instrument.

Envelope

This characteristic dynamic shape, unique to each instrument, is called the envelope. Although an envelope is heard as a continuous sound, it may be divided into three phases: attack, sustain, and decay. The *attack* is the time that it takes for the sound to emerge from silence and reach the zenith of its dynamic level, the *sustain* is the length of time that the sound maintains that dynamic level, and the *decay* is the time elapsed during the sound's return to silence.

For instance, a piano has an envelope that could be illustrated as follows:

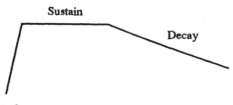

When a finger depresses a piano key and sets the hammer in motion striking the strings and creating a sound, the sound is sharply attacked, sustained only very briefly, and takes a long time to dwindle away into silence if the key remains depressed. The characteristic dynamic contour, the envelope, will remain essentially unchanged despite the volume at which the instrument is played. If the piano key is depressed gently, the hammer will strike the strings with only a small amount of velocity, and the resultant sound will be soft. On the other hand, if the hammers strike the string with a great deal of velocity, the sound will be loud, but the characteristic contour will remain the same.

Because of the mechanical action of a piano, there is little that a performer can do to alter the dynamic envelope. Other instruments, because of their physical nature, possess more or less flexibility in their envelope. Percussion instruments have relatively short envelopes with sharp, precise attacks and decays and very little sustain time. Because of this short envelope, percussion instruments are ideally suited for timekeeping, as they characteristically punctuate silence with short bursts of sound. String and wind performers have more control of their instrument's envelope. The parameters of attack, sustain, and decay are only limited by the musician's breath control or the length of the bow. Electronic instruments, such as a synthesizer, have the most flexibility of any instrument. The musician can exert absolute control over every aspect of the envelope. This can produce many interesting results, such as an inversion of the typical piano envelope with a piano timbre, or the coupling of a percussive snare-drum sound with the distinctive shading of a violin envelope. Through electronics, we can simulate traditional envelopes, but, more importantly, we can also create new and more flexible envelopes.

In short, the envelope is the dynamic history of the rise and fall of each individual sound. By working within the limits of the envelope, musicians are able to effect a wide spectrum of dynamic shading that conforms to the composer's intentions and reflects the performer's personal conception of the music.

Dynamics Through Orchestration

Terrace Dynamics and Instrument Combinations

Until the classic era (1750–1827), dynamic contrast was not notated for individual performers, but was achieved only through combining groups of instruments and voices in various textures. This system is usually referred to as terrace dynamics because the intensity level would suddenly jump up or down in large steps that resembled the terraces of a formal garden. Through terrace dynamics musicians could exert some control over intensity, but the method was complicated because the combination of instruments seriously altered the timbre while the dynamic level was being controlled. This form of dynamic contrast was highly exploited during the baroque period (1600–1750) in the concerto, in which the entire ensemble (concerto grosso) was pitted against a smaller group of instruments (ripieno).

Combining Like Instruments

As we have just noted, dynamics can be achieved through orchestration, but in this technique the change in volume is associated with a corresponding change in timbre. However, if we combine several of the same type of instrument, some new complications occur.

Volume Limitations. Intensity increases at a geometric rate, so that the addition of one instrument to another does not simply double the volume. While two violins will be noticeably louder than just one, it takes about ten violins to double the volume of sound produced by a single violin.

The Chorus Effect. The combination of like instruments also produces an acoustic phenomenon known as the chorus effect, which subtly transforms the timbre of the ensemble sound. Ten violins playing together do not sound the same as one violin that is ten times as loud. With the chorus effect, a number of overtones are generated because each instrument is playing a slightly different pitch at any given second. These overtones fight against one another and produce a range of frequencies that we perceive as a shimmery and rich sound. Musicians can use orchestration techniques to alter dynamics, but in so doing, they modify the timbre as well.

Dynamics Through Distance

If we shine a flashlight into a dark room, we notice that the light originates as a narrow focused beam and then gradually dissipates into a diffuse cloud of light. Sound waves travel in much the same way, emanating in concentrated waves from the sound source, traveling through the air at the speed of sound (1,120 feet per second), and growing softer and more diffuse the farther they travel from their source. Sound waves encounter resistance and disturbance in the air as they travel and, as a consequence, they lose some of their dynamic intensity, or "presence."

Most live music is heard in halls or auditoriums where architects have systematically engineered the acoustics to minimize dynamic differences caused by spatial displacement. There is approximately the same sense of presence in a front-row seat as there is in a seat at the back of the gallery. In addition, auditorium acoustics are designed such that the brass at the back of the orchestra reaches you at the same time as the violins located at the front of the stage, and both do so with very little loss of dynamic level. In very large arenas where presence is more of a problem, electronic amplification is used to overcome the dynamic loss due to distance.

In music from both the late Renaissance to early baroque period and the twentieth century, the element of distance was used intentionally to alter the dynamics. The composer would, for example, position groups of musicians at various points in a large cathedral (such as San Marco in Venice) so that the audience was surrounded by the sound. Thus, certain groups sounded louder or softer depending on their relationship to the audience, and a musical "echo" effect was achieved through dynamic contrast. This technique has also been exploited in various ways during the modern era. Composers have repositioned performers, audiences, and loudspeakers in various configurations to achieve novel dynamic effects comparable to stereophonic and quadrophonic recording techniques.

Dynamic Notation

Unlike the absolute system for qualifying pitch and rhythm, the system for indicating dynamics is a relative one. Instead of employing symbols for a specific decibel level, dynamic notation is relative within a piece of music. In our notational system, dynamics are indicated by Italian terms, usually represented by their first letters. Thus, the basic indication for loud is forte (f), and that for soft is piano (p). Various gradations of these terms are achieved by either modifying f or p with mezzo (mp, mf), meaning moderate, or by adding fortes and pianos together (pp, fff, etc.) to indicate comparative and superlative dynamics. The entire dynamic scale can be represented in the following chart.

Dynamic Level

Softest

Threshold of hearing			0 dB
pppp		as soft as possible	
ppp		extremely soft	40 dB
pp	pianissimo	very soft	
p	piano	soft	60 dB
mp	mezzo piano	moderately soft	
mf	mezzo forte	moderately loud	
f	forte	loud	80 dB
ff	fortissimo	very loud	
fff		extremely loud	100 dB
ffff		as loud as possible	
Threshold of pain			120 dB

Loudest

It is important to remember that the values on this chart are only relative. In relation to the Italian terms, the decibel levels of intensity are simply an approximation. Dynamic notation is useful in indicating a range within the context of the piece, but individual musicians must continually adjust their playing to accommodate such factors as the acoustics of the hall and the performance of their fellow musicians. For instance, a relatively soft instrument, such as a viola, would have to play much louder than a trumpet to produce the same dynamic level. The fine-tuning of dynamic levels, so that no one instrument or group of instruments unintentionally overshadows another, is known as *balance*.

Crescendo and Decrescendo

The Italian expression marks can successfully indicate the volume level of a section of music if the music remains on a static dynamic plane or changes through sudden increments. However, if we want to indicate gradual dynamic change, we use the Italian words *crescendo* (increasingly louder) and *decrescendo* or *diminuendo* (increasingly softer). These terms, often used in conjunction with the symbols $<$ and $>$, need to be associated with a starting and concluding dynamic level. Crescendo and diminuendo can be applied to a short passage of several notes or extended over a large section of music to effect a smooth rise or fall in dynamic level.

Accents

In our daily speech we stress certain syllables and words to intensify meaning in a sentence and to enhance the character of our vocal delivery. Just as we do not speak in a monotone, musicians do not play every note at exactly the same dynamic level. The notated dynamic indications suggest a range, but within that range certain notes are naturally given more emphasis than others, and are stressed because of their rhythmic or melodic importance. This practice of expressive dynamic shading cannot be notated. The personal ability to make subtle distinctions of accent derives from much rehearsal time and a thorough understanding of the music.

Composers may, however, choose to add accent marks if they think these will clarify their musical intentions, or if they wish to accent notes that would not ordinarily be stressed. These accent marks are indicated by the symbol $\bar{7}$ under or above the note head to represent a sharp attack, or by the symbol $\bar{\Gamma}$ to specify a more sustained accent. Accents may also be signified by the Italian word *sforzando* and its usual abbreviation, *sfz*, meaning a loud accent followed by a return to the original dynamic level. Most accents, such as the downbeat of a measure, are already implied by the music, so composers need to apply accent marks only in special circumstances.

Dynamic intensity is a vivid means of musical expression. Through dynamic shading—the contrast of soft and loud volume levels—musical points of drama are articulated and intensified. There are three different approaches to the control of dynamic intensity. First, the performer may exert personal control of the volume level through instrumental technique in accordance with specified musical notation (p, mf, f, etc.) and through individual interpretation. Second, the composer may control the intensity through orchestration by increasing or decreasing the number of instruments. This approach both alters the timbral quality and affects the dynamic level. Third, the distance between the performer and the audience may be altered. This can produce interesting "echo" effects, but it is a difficult approach because the acoustics and rigid seating structure of most auditoriums are not conducive to spatial displacement. Through these approaches used individually or in combination, musicians add vibrant color and climactic excitement to music through the manipulation of dynamic intensity.

CHAPTER 6

Musical Timbre

Timbre, the fourth and final musical element, provides the dimension of color in our musical world. Pitch, duration, and dynamics provide a framework that can be notated in a musical score, but this framework is just a black and white sketch unless the quality of the sound source, the timbre, breathes life into the music. The expressive intent of the music is very closely allied to the timbre. For example, if two contrasting instruments, an oboe and a trumpet, were to perform exactly the same melody, the sound might appear mournful in one case and jubilant in the other. These two very different expressive effects are achieved merely be altering the sound source. That is the mystery and power of tone color.

Timbre is a direct function of the sound source. When we hear a musical idea, it is always presented to us through the medium of some sound source, and it is always associated with some timbre. By orchestrating the sound source, choosing, combining and subtracting sonic colors like a painter adjusting his or her palette, the musician is able to invest abstract musical thought with expressive shades of meaning. Melody and harmony may be notated or analyzed as abstract thought, but they are more capable of imparting musical meaning to an audience when they have been fused with a particular tone color. Timbre is the bond that unites the musician and the audience in the dialogue of musical performance.

The musician has an infinite wealth of timbres from which to choose. Whether their sounds are produced vocally, instrumentally, or electronically, the traditional instruments all have a wide variety of tone colors that may be obtained in different ranges and through various performance techniques. When assembled in various ensembles, the timbral possibilities are practically limitless. The human voice is an amazingly flexible instrument, and musicians are still experimenting with new sonic possibilities elicited through innovative vocal techniques and imaginative combinations of voices.

During the twentieth century, the universe of timbral possibilities has dramatically expanded as a result of technological developments in electronics. Currently, sophisticated generations of synthesizers and samplers can virtually re-create any known sound and, in addition, create new timbres limited only by the chains imposed by human imagination.

Vocal Timbre

The voice is the most natural and expressive sound source. In earliest infancy, we instinctively grasp the art of music by singing and making up songs. The voice is our first and most natural instrument, and song is a heightened form of verbal communication, charged with musical meaning and emotion that supersedes mere words.

Voice Range

Vocal range is the spectrum of tones bounded by the usual upper and lower limits of a singer's voice. In most cases, an amateur singer's voice will be limited to one and one-half to two octaves, while a professional singer will usually span a range in excess of two octaves. A singer's range may be extended through training and practice but, for the most part, the physical dimensions of the vocal cords are the deciding factor. Men have longer and thicker vocal cords than women and, therefore, voices in a lower range.

There are four broad categories of vocal range: soprano, alto, tenor, and bass. The *soprano* voice is the highest female range. The typical soprano would sing as high as a^2 and as low as e^1 (above middle C). The lowest female voice, which is called the *alto* (or contralto), usually extends downward to a, a fifth below the soprano, and upward only to d^2, which is a fifth below the top soprano note. The highest male voice, the *tenor*, has a range that includes g^1 as the topmost pitch and d as the lower limit. Finally, the lowest male voice, the *bass*, has a range spanning from middle C down to G.

To describe range with more accuracy, additional terms are used that provide information concerning sound quality and area of vocal strength within each range (known as *tessitura*). Thus, the *soprano* voice is further described by such terms as *mezzo-soprano* (aspects of both alto and soprano), *dramatic* (powerful voice with low tessitura), *lyric* (lighter), and *coloratura* (virtuosic with an extended high range). The *alto* voice is subdivided into two classifications. The *pure alto* has a low tessitura while the *dramatic alto* has a character similar to the dramatic soprano, but with a slightly lower range.

Similarly, male voices are also further clarified by descriptive terms. The *tenor* voice may be described as *robust, lyric,* or *heroic* — qualities that roughly correspond to the soprano classifications. Finally, the *bass* voice is described as *baritone* (between tenor and bass ranges), *basso cantante* (lyric quality), or *basso profondo* (low powerful range).

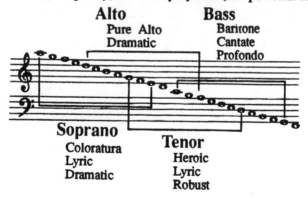

Voice Ranges in Relation to the Grand Staff

Vocal Quality

While we can classify range with a fair amount of accuracy, it is far more difficult to quantify vocal quality or tone color. Because there is no system of measurement, we resort to using vague but colorful adjectives such as "rich," "smoky," or "brassy." Moreover, there is no single universal standard that dictates a desired vocal timbre. Some cultures prefer a more nasal sound while others desire a purer sound in which there is little fluctuation of pitch. The dominant timbre identified with a specific culture or style arises as a result of inbred physical characteristics and through mimicry and training.

The voice is a unique and personal instrument. Each voice is a sonic fingerprint—no two voices are ever exactly alike. Individual sound quality is determined by a number of factors, including vocal cord length, size of various resonant cavities (chest, throat, and sinus), and level of training. Although training can improve *intonation* (the ability to maintain exact pitch), control the expressive use of *vibrato* (a slight wavering in pitch), and develop breath support for pitch and dynamic control, it can only go so far in modifying the basic timbre of the voice.

As in the case of a ballet dancer, the performer is restricted by the personal limitations of his or her own body. Just like the body, the singing voice undergoes a series of changes as it ages. The pure tone of youth becomes deeper and more complex at puberty, and then gradually evolves still more, gaining in harmonic complexity and vibrato as the person grows older. Vocal training can retard the aging process in a singer just as physical conditioning can prolong a dancer's muscle tone, but vocal flexibility inevitably declines with age.

Vocal-Ensemble Timbre

Up to this point, the discussion of vocal timbre has centered on the solo voice. However, when individual voices are combined in various ensembles, another spectrum of timbral effects is available to musicians. With a small ensemble, such as a duo (two voices) or trio (three voices), individual voices are discernable although there is also a definite composite timbre. In large choruses all sense of individual voice quality is lost and only the group sound is perceived.

Ensemble Composition

In forming various vocal ensembles, the variables to consider are the number of performers and the range of particular voices. Although the possibilities range from a duo to a massive choir containing hundreds of voices, the average number of singers in a typical community, university, or church choir generally ranges between twenty and fifty voices. These ensembles may consist of mixed voices containing both male and female singers or they may be limited to a single sex. The most commonly found choral ensembles consist of a mixed choir of sopranos, altos, tenors, and basses (SATB), a female choir (SSA), a men's choir (TTBB), and an all-male (SATB) choir with boys singing soprano parts and the alto, tenor, and bass lines sung by men.

Vocal-Instrumental Combinations

Choirs often perform *a cappella* (without any instrumental accompaniment), especially when interpreting music written before 1600, but various instruments and groupings of instruments are also added to voices to extend the range of timbral possibilities. There is a vast repertoire of music reflecting this combination of voices and instruments, ranging from secular opera to sacred cantatas and masses.

Modern Vocal Techniques

Musicians have not been content merely to retain the traditional sounds and ensembles, however. In the last century choral timbre has undergone an amazing expansion through new singing techniques involving *microtones* (steps smaller than the usual half step of the Western scale system) and *multiphonics* (singing a fundamental pitch and various additional overtones), and through the use of synthesizers to simulate and transform vocal sounds.

Instrumental Timbre

Instruments were developed long ago (prehistoric peoples used bone flutes) to extend the range of sound of which the human voice was capable. String instruments could sustain sounds seemingly without breath, drums could be heard for miles beyond the loudest voice, and certain instruments, such as the piccolo or bassoon, could reach pitches that were beyond the ability of the voice. Singing still colored the general approach to instrumental performance, but it was no longer the sole means of musical expression.

Classification of Instruments

Instrumental timbre is in some respects similar to vocal timbre. As is the case with the voice, each instrument possesses a particular range and tonal quality. However, each instrument is further differentiated according to the way its sound is produced. There are five separate means of creating instrumental sound as opposed to one vocal technique. These five categories are chordophone, aerophone, membranophone, idiophone, and electrophone—scientific names that are based on the way sound is generated.

Chordophones

Chordophones, or strings, include the violin family, the guitar and lute families, and the harp. They produce sound by exciting vibration in a string through any one of three different techniques. First, a string may be *agitated* by drawing a bow across it, as with a violin. Second, a string may be *plucked* as with a harp. Third, a string may be struck as with a piano. Pianos, which contain elements of both string and percussion families, will be discussed later with keyboard instruments.

Basic Features of String Instruments

Chordophones occur in many different forms throughout the world, but there are some basic features that are common to most string instruments.

Attachment Devices. There must be a pair of devices to attach both ends of the string to the body of the instrument. Usually one end of the string is held tight and the other end is fastened to some form of tuning peg so that the string's tension may be adjusted in order to tune the string to the correct pitch.

Shell. Because a string produces very little sound by itself, there will always be some form of shell or body that allows the quiet string vibration to resonate, thereby amplifying the sound.

Fingerboard. There is usually some form of fingerboard under the string to control pitch; different pitches are produced by depressing the string at certain points along the string's length. *Frets*, small metal bars, may be fixed across the fingerboard to make pitch definition more precise.

The Violin Family

The four members of the violin family—violin, viola, cello (violoncello), and bass (double bass)—are the most widely used string instruments in Euro-American art music. They evolved in Italy between 1550 and 1600 and soon thereafter replaced earlier instruments such as the viol family. In the baroque period, composers began writing for the violin family. Violins and cellos were featured solo instruments in sonatas and concerti, the string quartet (a combination of two violins, viola, and cello) became the medium for many chamber works, and the string orchestra (including approximately thirty-four violins, twelve violas, ten cellos, and eight double basses) provided the foundation for the orchestra. Furthermore, violins were widely used throughout the world in folk and traditional music, and are still featured in such styles as Cajun or bluegrass, in which they are more commonly referred to as fiddles.

Violin Range. The violin family encompasses a vast spectrum of pitches extending from the stratospheric e^4 at the top end of a violin's range down to the rumbling E_1 at the bottom of the double bass's range. As with the human voice, the individual instruments divide the spectrum into soprano, alto, tenor, and bass ranges. However, the strings have a considerably wider compass, and there is also more overlap between the ranges of the instruments. The violin provides the brilliant soprano-voiced sound, the slightly larger and more mellow viola lies within the alto range, the rich-timbred cello fulfills the tenor function, and the large double bass provides a resonant bass sound. From piercing violin to growling bass, most of the sound frequency range that is audible to humans is included within the range of the string family.

Violin Design. Although the scale differs, the basic design of the violin is preserved in that of the viola, cello, and double bass. The hollow wooden *shell* supports and amplifies four *strings* of different gauge, which are made of either gut or metal. These strings are fastened to a *tailpiece* at the bottom of the body, and are then stretched over a *bridge* that suspends them above the body. The bridge also serves to transmit the string vibrations to the violin shell. After being stretched over the bridge, the strings then pass over a *fingerboard*, which is attached to the violin body. Because of the height of the bridge, the strings are raised slightly above the fingerboard so that when a finger depresses the string, it rests against the fingerboard and stops the string. This shortens the string length and creates a higher pitch.

At the end of the fingerboard, the strings are fastened to *tuning pegs* that allow the tension of the string to be adjusted. The tighter the string is stretched, the higher the pitch will be. Violin strings are usually tuned a fifth apart to sound the pitches G–D–A–E (from the lowest- to the highest-pitched string), but other irregular tunings (called *scordatura*) may also be used.

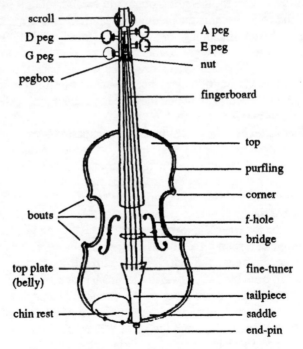

The Various Features of a Violin

Performance Techniques. Although the basic shapes and overall designs of the members of the string family are quite similar, the dimensions and performance techniques vary from instrument to instrument. The violin and viola are held tucked under the chin and extended at a right angle from the body. Because the cello and double bass are so large, they stand vertically, resting on their end pins while being played. The cello is held in place between a seated performer's legs. A double bass performer either stands or sits on a high stool to play the instrument. The violin family is capable of many nuances of expression and shades of tone color. The different performance techniques that elicit these qualities are described below.

Sul Ponticello, Sul Tasto: A string instrument may be bowed close to the bridge (*sul ponticello*), producing a thin and metallic sound, or it may be bowed toward the opposite direction, over the fingerboard (*sul tasto*), producing a softer and warmer tone. With this bowing technique, certain bands of overtones are either muted or enhanced so that the effect is a little like adjusting the tone control on a stereo.

Tremolo: Drawing the bow rapidly back and forth across the strings in short strokes (*tremolo*) produces a shimmery effect at soft volume and an aura of tension or excitement at a louder dynamic level.

Col Legno: Instead of drawing the bow across the strings in order to achieve a sustained sound, a performer can use the back of the bow to strike the strings (*col legno*), thereby producing a dry, distant, percussive sound. This effect is particularly striking when employed by an entire string orchestra.

Pizzicato: A performer may pluck the strings with his or her fingers, without using the bow at all (*pizzicato*), producing a fleshier percussive sound. Pizzicato is often used on the double bass, especially in jazz styles.

Muting: A wooden or metal device clamped on the bridge reduces the amplitude of vibrations reaching the body. The mute produces a softer sound, but it also changes the timbre, making it thin and glassy.

Vibrato: The expressive vibrato of a singer's voice can be simulated on a string instrument by a slight oscillation of the left-hand finger that is forming a pitch on the fingerboard. This vibrato can be controlled to produce narrow, wide, slow, or fast fluctuations in pitch. Vibrato is used to impart warmth to a tone and to heighten expression in a dramatic passage.

Harmonics: Very pure, high-pitched overtones can be produced by lightly touching a string at one of the fraction points of the total string length. For instance, lightly damping the string at the midpoint of the string will produce a harmonic or overtone an octave higher than the pitch of the string. Harmonics can be used to produce striking bell-like tones and eerie thin-timbred sounds.

Double Stops: More than one string may be sounded at once, producing the effect of a chord, or a melody with an accompaniment. Because of the arch of the bridge, this effect is easy to achieve with two strings, but when three or four are to be sounded together they must be played in rapid succession so that they are perceived as arpeggios (broken chords), in which the notes sound successively). Double stopping is used more often as a solo technique to suggest several simultaneous lines of music than as an orchestral effect.

Guitar and Lute Families

While the instruments of the violin family generally produce sound through a bow drawn across the strings, other chordophones, such as the guitar, lute, mandolin, banjo, cittern, and dulcimer, achieve their sound through a plucking technique. Because these instruments are relatively soft dynamically and incapable of sustained sound, they are rarely included in the orchestra, except when their particular effects are called for. However, they are often used individually in chamber ensembles or as accompaniment for singers, and in combination within folk music ensembles called string bands.

The guitar and lute families include instruments that have bodies with flat backs (guitars) or rounded, gourdlike backs (lutes) and a fretted fingerboard. The number of strings varies from instrument to instrument. For instance, the guitar has six strings tuned E–A–D–G–B–E, and the mandolin has eight strings tuned in double courses to the pitches G–D–A–E, like a violin. Because the fingerboard is relatively narrow and the bridge is flat compared to the arched violin bridge, these instruments can easily produce chords as well as single melodic lines. This capability makes them extremely useful in situations that require a portable accompanying instrument. As an electric instrument, the guitar currently enjoys widespread popularity; this will be discussed under the heading of electrophones.

The Harp Family

The harp family, including various forms of harps (troubadour, Irish, and concert harps) and autoharps, zithers, and hammer dulcimers, is one of the oldest forms of instrument. Mesopotamian harps have been documented as far back as 3000 B.C.E. and the Bible is full of references to the instrument in King David's hands.

As a family, harps are distinguished by their lack of fingerboard. The strings are all plucked or strummed in "open" position, which means that the pitch is not controlled by stopping the string as with violins and guitars. Therefore, a harp's range is limited by the number of strings it contains. A concert harp generally has forty-seven strings covering a six and one-half octave span, while smaller harps, such as the Irish harp, have approximately thirty-seven strings. To provide some flexibility, modern harps are equipped with pedals that tighten or release the string tension slightly so that the pitch can be raised or lowered by half steps. This allows the performer to play in various keys and to perform chromatic melodies.

Unlike the guitar and lute family, the harp has found considerable acceptance in orchestral use during the nineteenth and twentieth centuries, particularly at the hands of the impressionist composers who used the harp's pure, liquid timbre to infuse color and light into the orchestral sound. The harp timbre has become closely associated with a special technique, the *glissando*, in which scales and chords are rapidly strummed. This gesture, often used to convey a celestial feeling, has become a cliché that is practically synonomous with the harp itself.

Aerophones

Aerophones, or winds, utilize a vibrating column of air to produce sound that is amplified by a length of tubing. Aerophones are divided into two categories, brass and woodwinds, according to the way that the breath is used to excite the column of air. In brass instruments, sound is created by the vibration of a performer's lips buzzing into a cuplike mouthpiece. Woodwinds set the column of air into vibration through wind directed across a mouthpiece or over one or two reeds. Although brass and woodwind instruments both utilize a column of air contained within a tube, the different means used to cause vibrations in that air produce very different timbres.

Woodwinds

Originally, woodwinds were simply instruments made of wood that produced their tone through air. However, flutes and piccolos are now generally made of metal (usually silver and, in rare instances, gold and platinum), and some modern clarinets and oboes are made of plastic.

Classification. Regardless of whether they are constructed of wood, metal, or synthetic material, instruments are classified as woodwinds if their sound is achieved through one of four distinct sound-production techniques.

Flute Family (*common transverse flute, alto flute*, and *piccolo*): The performer blows across a hole as though blowing over an empty bottle in a jug band.

Flageolet Instruments (*recorders*): The performer blows into a whistle-type mouthpiece where the air is concentrated and directed by a beveled wooden lip.

Single-Reed Instruments (*common B♭ clarinet, basset horn, bass clarinet*): The performer blows over a thin rectangle of cane (called a reed) that vibrates against the lip of a mouthpiece.

Double-Reed Instruments (*oboe, English horn, bassoon*): The performer blows over a pair of reeds that vibrate against each other.

These techniques yield some interesting musical timbres that can be characterized as the "pure" tone produced by the transverse flute, the "woody" sound common to the whistle types, the "reedy" sound of the single reeds, and the "nasal" or "buzzy" sound effected by the double reeds.

Pitch Control. In woodwinds, pitch is directly proportional to the length of the vibrating column of air. Thus, a longer column of air produces a lower pitch, a shorter column of air, a higher pitch. This control of the air column is achieved by opening and closing a series of holes along the tube. To extend the length of the air column, and thus lower the pitch, the holes are covered by the fingers or by pads controlled by small mechanical levers. Conversely, when the performer lifts the fingers or raises the mechanically controlled pads, the length is shortened and the pitch is made higher.

Registers. Pitch in woodwinds strongly affects tone color. Woodwind instruments encompass four separate registers, each register consisting of a portion (usually an octave) of the entire range, and having a specific timbre.

Low Register: In their lowest register flutes and clarinets "speak" very quietly and are easily masked by other instruments. Such terms as "breathy," "thick," "dull," and "dark" are often used to describe this register. The oboe and saxophone are less breathy and sound stronger in the lower part of their range. Bassoons have difficulty playing quietly in their lowest octave because a fair amount of wind pressure is required to make the instrument sound the low notes.

Middle Register: Woodwinds are more frequently played in the next octave, called the middle register. Words like "sweet," "transparent," and "mournful" are used to describe the sound quality within this timbral area.

High Register: The next area of the woodwind range—the high register—is used most frequently. In this register, the woodwind tone is penetrating and can be easily distinguished above other groups of instruments. "Clear," "bright," and "silvery" are terms often applied to this range.

Altissimo: The upper end of the woodwind spectrum, known as the altissimo, can sound shrill, and is best reserved for musical effects that demand a whistling, piercing, or highly penetrating tone quality.

Brass Instruments

While woodwinds are not always made of wood, brass instruments, true to their name, are generally fashioned out of brass. The brass tube, which contains the vibrating column of air, is shaped in different lengths and diameters, and is either straight or coiled depending on the length of the tubing. One end is equipped with a cuplike mouthpiece for directing breath, while the other end is flared into a bell shape to amplify and direct the sound.

Pitch Control. As with woodwinds, pitch is directly proportional to the length of the vibrating column of air. However, instead of extending or contracting the air column by covering and uncovering holes along the shaft, brass players achieve the desired pitch through a combination of lip pressure, breath velocity, and the use of three mechanical valves.

Through lip pressure and control of air velocity, certain overtones of the harmonic series can be generated. Thus, a brass instrument such as the bugle, which has no mechanical means of altering pitch, produces a number of different tones solely through the player's control of his or her *embouchure* (placement of the lips, teeth, and tongue) and the force of exhaled breath. Because the overtones closest to the fundamental pitch are the most easily produced, we often hear brass instruments stressing intervals such as perfect fifths, perfect fourths, octaves, and major thirds. Pictured is the overtone series generated by a fundamental pitch of C.

Overtone Series Based on C

The other technique for controlling pitch involves a *mechanical* approach to extending or compressing the length of tubing. The trombone has a slide or crook that can be drawn in and out to change the length of the vibrating column of air. Other brass instruments, including the trumpet, French horn, and tuba, possess keys or valves that control the flow of air into certain auxiliary lengths of tubing. The control of these valves, used singly or in combination, serves to lengthen the tube, thereby producing a different fundamental pitch. The fundamental pitch can then be altered through the control of breath and embouchure to extract overtones drawn from the new fundamental pitch.

Trumpet Family. The trumpet family provides a brilliant soprano voice that is widely employed in orchestras, chamber ensembles, and jazz and rock combos, whenever a bright and penetrating melody line is desired. The family includes the common B♭ instrument (the instrument is constructed such that the fundamental pitch is B♭), but there are also a variety of trumpets that are manufactured in different keys and sizes, such as the smaller, high-pitched piccolo trumpet. Other closely related instruments include the bugle, the cornet, and the flügelhorn.

Trumpets are constructed with a cylindrical bore (the diameter of the tube is constant) that contributes the characteristic bright timbre. The cornet, on the other hand, is equipped with a conical bore (the diameter of the tube gradually increases) that produces a more mellow sound. Both the trumpet and the cornet are fitted with three valves that allow considerable pitch flexibility. The bugle, however, has no valves, so it is limited to the pitches that can be easily produced from the overtone series, such as the military calls known as taps and reveille. The flügelhorn is essentially a larger version of the cornet, with a warm alto voice similar to that of a French horn.

Because trumpets have a loud and penetrating timbre, they are generally used singly when combined with small jazz and chamber ensembles. In larger instrumental forces, such as a big band or symphonic orchestra, it is common to find a relatively small complement containing four trumpets per section (in comparison to almost sixty strings). Because they are powerful and brilliant instruments, they must be carefully orchestrated to avoid overbalancing the rest of the orchestra. For this reason they are generally reserved for climactic passages or bold and heroic statements accompanied by the rest of the brass.

Compared to the woodwinds, trumpets have a more uniform timbre across their various registers. In general, the tone becomes more brilliant as the higher register is approached, while notes of the lower register sound somewhat ominous. Regardless of the range, trumpet tone color is still consistently recognizable as that of a trumpet. Although register does not seriously affect trumpet tone color, timbral quality can be altered by using various types of mute devices, such as the "cup" and "harmon" designs, that are inserted into the bell of the trumpet. These mutes deaden the vibrations somewhat, reducing the volume level, but they also change the overtone content, thereby modifying the timbre. Jazz musicians rely especially on mutes, such as the "plumber's helper" to create talking and growling expressive sounds.

Trombone. The trombone provides a noble bass-tenor voice within the trumpet family. As is the case with the trumpet, the bore is essentially cylindrical, but unlike the trumpet, the trombone relies on a slide, rather than mechanical valves, to affect the pitch. The slide extends the length of the tubing, thereby lowering the pitch. There are seven slide positions, each of which extends the slide outward from the body in a small increment that produces a pitch difference of a half step. Thus, the slide, in conjunction with the performer's embouchure and breath control, can create all the pitches within the range of Bb_1 to eb^1.

The trombone's wide range enables it to speak with a bright, yet dignified, tenor sound in its upper range, and in a mellow or dark timbre in its lower register. This flexibility enables it to be used as a plodding bass line in support of the harmony or as a soaring, heroic melody figure. Much of the music written for trombone includes passages designed to lend solemnity and dignity to the music, but one gesture particularly associated with the trombone is sometimes used for comic effect. Since the slide can quickly be moved in and out, the trombone can produce a glissando that swoops up and down, smearing across notes, creating a sound that resembles a laugh or the whinny of a horse.

While the trombone does not possess as penetrating a sound as the trumpet, it does have enough power to cut through an entire string section. In chamber music and Dixieland-style jazz combos a single trombone is usually sufficient, while in orchestral and big-band settings in which more sound is needed, there are generally four trombones per section.

French Horn. The French horn possesses a mellow alto-soprano voice whose pastoral quality has made it useful in combination with woodwind instruments as well as with other members of the brass family. Like the cornet, the French horn has a conical bore, which is partially responsible for its warm golden tone; rather than being fully extended, however, the tube has been wound into a spiral with a widely flared bell in order to compress the length of the instrument. Like the trumpet, it is equipped with valves, which allow a musician to produce a full chromatic scale spanning the range from B_1 to f^1.

The French horn is the softest of the brass instruments. When used singly, it will not overbalance a chamber ensemble such as the woodwind quintet (flute, oboe, clarinet, bassoon, and French horn), and when used in an orchestra four horns are usually combined together in the section.

Tuba. Tubas are the bass voice of the brass family. In construction, they closely resemble the French horn, being equipped with a conical bore, coiled tube, wide flaring bell, and valves. Because of their deep timbre and relative inflexibility, they were generally relegated until the twentieth century to a supporting role and seldom entrusted with solo melodic lines in orchestral and chamber music. The tuba and the other members of its family, such as the sousaphone, euphonium, and helicon, are most often used in orchestras, Dixieland-style jazz, and marching bands, in which they outline the harmony in the clichéd "oom-pah" style.

Percussion

Percussion instruments are perhaps the most ancient of all musical instruments. Rhythm is a natural phenomenon of humans and their environment; it is through percussion that we most strongly articulate the rhythms that we perceive in ourselves and the world around us. Every known culture possesses drums, and throughout the world an amazing array of shapes and forms have evolved to meet the specific timbral needs of each style of music. From the kettledrums of the European orchestra to the talking drums of West Africa, percussion instruments have been used both to mirror and to manipulate the pulse of people and the natural world.

Percussion instruments are divided into two families—the membranophones and the idiophones.

Membranophones

Membranophones, more commonly known as the drum family, produce sound when a membrane (drum head) stretched across a form (the drum body) is struck by hand or with a stick. Membranes were once made exclusively of tanned animal skins, but now they are almost always constructed from synthetic material.

Idiophones

Idiophones are instruments whose sound is produced by striking, rubbing, shaking, or rattling the elastic material of which they are constructed. Idiophones contain various types of cymbals and gongs constructed of metal, sundry shakers and rattles made of gourds, and assorted woodblocks and marimba-style instruments fashioned from wood.

These two classes are further subdivided into those instruments that produce a *distinct pitch* (melodic percussion), such as xylophones or kettledrums, and those that produce an *indefinite pitch* (nonmelodic percussion), such as snare drums or cymbals.

Some cultures, such as Native American or West African, construct their music almost entirely for percussion instruments, generally avoiding chordophones and aerophones altogether. On the other hand, Euro-American art music has traditionally relegated percussion to a supportive role, using those instruments to add exotic color to an ensemble, to highlight a strongly rhythmic or dancelike passage, or to heighten a dramatic climax. While percussion is the heart of a good jazz, rock, or marching band, only since 1930 has percussion been treated as an independent voice in chamber and orchestral music. Percussion instruments may possess an ancient lineage, but they are in many ways the embodiment of the new sonic frontier of Euro-American art music. Listed here are a number of percussion instruments in general use within Euro-American music.

Membranophones

Distinctly Pitched
timpani (kettledrums)

Indefinitely Pitched
snare drum
tom-tom
bass drum
bongos
congas
timbales
tambourine

Idiophones

Pitched
xylophone
marimba
vibraphone
celesta
chimes
crotales
bells

Indefinitely Pitched
triangle
temple block
claves (woodblock)
cymbal
gong (tam-tam)
castanets
guiro
maracas (rattles)

Keyboard Instruments

The keyboard instruments—piano, organ, harpsichord, clavichord, carillon, accordian, and calliope—exhibit various characteristics of chordophones, aerophones, and percussion instruments, but their distinguishing feature is a keyboard mechanism that controls the sound production. The keyboard is a device consisting of a series of wooden or plastic keys with white or black surfaces, organized in a pattern of half steps. These keys are operated by some mechanical or electrical action that allows a performer to produce sound merely by depressing a key. Instead of having to run back and forth across the wide range of a harp, a musician seated at the piano has all of the notes within easy reach, and he or she can easily play as many as ten notes simultaneously.

The advantages to keyboard instruments are the relative ease with which a performer can access a wide range of pitches, and the ability to play a number of tones simultaneously. Equipped with a keyboard instrument, a single performer is able to reproduce the whole range and density of an orchestra, and for this reason keyboard instruments have had a thriving career as both solo and accompanying instruments.

Piano

The piano is a happy marriage between a chordophone and a percussion instrument. The keyboard controls an elaborate mechanical system that operates a series of felt hammers, which strike the keys, thereby producing the sound. This sound is sustained as long as the key remains depressed; as soon as it is released a felt damper drops back down and mutes the string. Thus, the piano envelope has the sharp attack characteristic of percussion instruments coupled with the sustain and decay that are more typical of a string sound.

The mechanical action of the piano permits a wide range of expression. The piano's full name is the *pianoforte*; it is so named because the action of the hammers allowed a musician to play both softly and loudly depending upon the force exerted on the keys. This is different from the action of the harpsichord and organ, with which the force exerted on the keys has no effect on the dynamic level of the sound.

Harpsichord

The harpsichord is an ancestor of the piano, but it has a thin, tinkling sound achieved through a plucking of the strings, rather than the variable dynamic effect obtained by the percussive use of piano hammers. Because the keyboard control of the plectra action did not permit dynamic variation, harpsichord builders often added several courses of strings, each attached to a different keyboard, so that groups of strings could be added together (coupled) for a larger sound.

A *clavichord* is quite similar in sound to the harpsichord, but its light hammers strike the strings from below, producing a more delicate and subtle sound than the harpsichord.

Pipe Organ

The pipe organ is really a collection of whistles and reeds—an entire woodwind orchestra—all of which are controlled by a keyboard. These whistles and reeds, located at the bases of cylindrical pipes of different heights, produce higher or lower pitches according to their diameter and length. For instance, thirty-two- and sixteen-foot pipes are used for rumbling bass tones, eight- and four-foot pipes are used for notes in the middle of the keyboard, and the one- and two-foot pipes produce shrill, sharp treble sounds.

The keyboard operates a series of valves that open to allow a wind source to blow through the pipe when a key is depressed. Since the wind source is blowing constantly, the tone will continue to sound as long as the key is depressed and the valve stays open. A pipe organ has at least one pipe for each note of the keyboard (called a *rank*), but generally there are many different ranks of pipes, each with different timbres produced by different materials, and these ranks are activated by as many as five keyboards on the same organ. This vast wealth of different tone colors formerly found on the great organs can only be compared to the diversity of sound available on the synthesizer today.

Other Keyboard Instruments

The other keyboard instruments use similar keyboard control to effect sound. The *calliope* resembles the organ but it uses steam to power the whistles. A *carillon* consists of bells rung from a keyboard. An *accordian* blows air generated by the folds of a bellow through metal reeds.

Electrophones

Electrophones—instruments that generate, alter, or amplify sound through electronics—are the first new development in sound production since the ancient inventions of string, breath, and percussion. Devices such as synthesizers, electric guitars, and digital samplers have radically altered the complexion of current music; traditional limitations of timbral possibility, compositional approach, and dynamic flexibility have been shattered. All of our musical concepts, gently evolved and nurtured through generations, have been challenged by the applications of electronics, and the ever-increasing new technology, coupling computers with digital sound processes, has virtually revolutionized the entire way we make music.

Electronic Instruments that Generate Sound

The earliest usable electronic instruments, such as the *Theremin* and the *Ondes Martenot*, were developed in the 1920s. They were purely experimental in nature and highly limited in ability, but the lure of new sounds drove composers such as Varèse to combine them with traditional instruments. Later, more useful sound generating instruments such as the Hammond organ were developed to "replace" existing instruments like the pipe organ.

Synthesizers. The next large advance in technology produced synthesizers like the vast roomful of RCA equipment housed at the Columbia-Princeton Electronic Laboratory in New York. These early synthesizers generated wave shapes through oscillators (circuits that allow AC current to be controlled at specific frequencies), and then altered the sound of these waves through various devices such as filters that determined overtone content (timbre) and amplifiers that controlled volume. All aspects of the sound were created by electricity and shaped by the control of electrical voltage.

Although this early RCA synthesizer opened up new possibilities, it was cumbersome and difficult to use, relying on punched cards for information. Making use of transistor technology in the 1960s, Robert Moog transformed the concept of the Columbia-Princeton synthesizer into a useful and relatively inexpensive instrument that resembled a telephone switchboard appended to a traditional keyboard. When Moog developed portable synthesizers that were easily affordable, the synthesizer became a household name, finding its way into the mainstream of rock and jazz bands and into commercial recording studios that produced sound tracks and advertisements.

Synthesizer-Computer Combinations. The most recent developments in electronic technology have produced synthesizers that work in tandem with computers to store and retrieve musical information coded as bits of data. Devices such as a digital sampler can absorb actual sound, store it on floppy disks, and then reproduce it either intact or altered through any of the traditional synthesizer functions. Musical software that is currently available enables a musician to perform at the keyboard, play back those sounds with any combination of timbres and dynamics, edit and store those sounds in electronic memory, and then print out publishable music text on a laser printer. Laborious chores that once occupied the composer—copying out individual parts, transposing for various instruments, editing, erasing, and inking in final copies—are no longer necessary. Synthesizers have not replaced the creative process for musicians; all they have done is allow more time and flexibility for the exciting artistic aspects, while reducing the drudgery of repetitive tasks.

Electronic Modification

Making use of electronic technology, microphones, pickups, and transducers convert the acoustical sounds of traditional instruments into electrical energy. In the simplest applications, microphones are used to amplify and record the voice, and pickups and transducers are used to boost the dynamic level of traditional instruments. However, once the acoustic sound has been converted into electrical impulses, it can then be modified electronically. There are a number of devices ranging from phase shifters to fuzz-tone distorters that can be used to alter the natural tone of an instrument. Any instrument can be amplified and timbrally modified, but guitars and bass guitars are most commonly altered because of their featured use in rock and jazz groups.

An exciting innovation in electronic technology is MIDI, an interfacing device that allows the acoustic sound to be converted into digital information that can be communicated to computers and synthesizers. With MIDI, acoustic instruments such as a violin or flute can be played traditionally, but the sound can be directly manipulated by synthesizers and computers to produce any conceivable sound. Thus, a flutist can simulate the sound of a vast choir of human voices merely by playing a single line of melody. The relationship between MIDI, computers, and synthesizers holds the key to the musical future.

Instrument-Family Summaries

String Family

Because of its wide range, the highly expressive timbral quality, and wide variety of sonic possibilities, the violin family has become a featured solo instrument, the backbone of the orchestra and a most important instrument in chamber ensembles. Other chordophones provide color and have found uses outside art music, but the violin remains the dominant string instrument.

Woodwind Family

Unlike members of the string family, the woodwinds possess great diversity of tone color. They contain a wide spectrum of instrumental character, from the mournful feel of the oboe to the jocular nature of the bassoon. This diversity of character, a result of the various sound-production techniques coupled with the distinctive timbral variety produced by different registers, makes the woodwind instruments particularly valuable as melody instruments.

Brass Family

The brass family of instruments has been widely used for thousands of years to effect a bold musical statement that carries across great distance. The brass sound has long been strongly identified with both war and royalty. Even today, the sounds of concert bands, marching bands, and drum and bugle corps produce a stirring martial sensation, and orchestral and chamber use of brass includes fanfares and heroic melodies that reflect on the noble and martial tradition.

Percussion Family

The percussion family has traditionally provided the rhythmic impetus that has charged music with energy and pulse. Although historically these instruments were relegated to a supporting role in orchestral and chamber music, the twentieth century focused attention on the percussion family as an important solo and ensemble medium in Euro-American art music. Percussion is the heart of contemporary music such as jazz and rock and roll.

Keyboard Family

The keyboard instruments are perhaps the most widely used and versatile instruments, because they allow a single performer to simulate the performance of many different musicians. While performers of other instruments are seldom able to play more than one note at a time, a pianist can play melodies and accompaniments of chords and cascades of notes, drawing from pitches spanning the full range of a symphony orchestra. An organist can juggle a number of simultaneous lines, coloring each melody with different timbres, or combining several ranks for a massive sound with the depth of an entire orchestra. The harpsichordist, with an economy of timbre and dynamic variety, can delicately weave four or five melodies into a single exquisite tapestry. The keyboard instruments possess all the interesting timbral variety of the aerophones, chordophones, and percussion families and endow a performer with technical flexibility as well.

Timbre, or tone color, is the musical element concerned with the quality of the sound. Timbre is directly related to the specific sonic properties of sound that can be analyzed according to instrument type and overtone formation. There are five families of musical instruments: chordophones (strings); aerophones (winds) which are subdivided into brass instruments and woodwinds; membranophones (drums); idio-phones (percussion); and electrophones (electronic instruments). In addition, keyboard instruments are in a special class containing features of one or more of the other families. Through timbre, musical expression is directly communicated to an audience—notes on a page are not music until they are brought to life as sound.

CHAPTER 7

Music as the Measure of Harmony

Musical tones may be sounded in succession or they may be sounded simultaneously. The sequential or horizontal sequence of tones is referred to as melody; the vertical concurrence of tones is called harmony. Although music in many world cultures does not stress the concept of harmony, music of the Euro-American tradition emphasizes the delicate balance between the elements of horizontal melody and vertical harmony. In this music, the tension and relaxation of a melodic line implies corresponding harmonic activity. Ideally, attention should be drawn not to the horizontal or vertical texture alone but, rather, to a combination of the two—a texture that integrates features of both.

Consonance and Dissonance

Chapter 4 introduced intervals, the musical distance separating any two tones. Each interval is equated with a degree of consonance (relaxation) or dissonance (tension). An interval that feels unstable, that sounds harsh, that seems to demand resolution, is said to be *dissonant.*

On the other hand, an interval that seems stable, that sounds pleasant, and that seems completely at rest is said to be *consonant*. Through the contrast of consonance and dissonance we are able musically to mirror the drama, the joys and the sorrows, that comprise our lives.

In melody, the sequential progression of consonant and dissonant intervals produces the sensation of movement and the illusion of musical direction. In harmony, a series of simultaneously sounded intervals evokes an impression of motion known as *harmonic progression*. Music seems to move through time, and it is the ebb and flow of tension and relaxation, dissonance and consonance, that defines this movement. A dissonant combination of tones always demands a *resolution* to a consonance. When a musician evades or postpones this resolution, it has the effect of intensifying the drama, prolonging the mystery, and sustaining the listener's attention.

Scales and Key Relationships

A scale, major or minor, is said to be "in" a key, and that key is identified by the tonic or key note on which the scale is built. However, key consists of more than the relationship of the notes of the scale. It also consists of the relationship of the chords that are based on steps of the scale.

Scale

A scale is an ordered succession of tones that comprises the basic organizational structure of both melody and harmony. Scales provide a hierarchical framework for organizing consonance and dissonance within a tonal framework. In Euro-American music a scale generally consists of seven tones, starting on a pitch called the *tonic*, and then progressing by half- and whole-step intervals until the pitch an octave away from the tonic is reached.

Major Scale

The most commonly used scale in Euro-American music is called the major scale. It is formed by a succession of five whole steps and two half steps in the following sequence: two whole steps, one half step, three whole steps, and a final half step. For instance, in the C major scale we start with the tonic note C and then include the pitches that correspond to the pattern of whole step, whole step, half step, whole step, whole step, whole step, half step. These pitches turn out to be the white notes of the keyboard—C, D, E, F, G, A, B, and C.

If we were to form a G major scale, however, we would use a slightly different series of notes. Starting with the tone G as tonic and applying the major-scale pattern of whole steps and half steps we would include the notes G, A, B, C, D, E, F♯, G. Note that we had to use a black key, F♯, to complete the final whole step of the pattern. Similarly, any of the twelve pitches may serve as the tonic note of a scale and, if the sequence of whole steps and half steps is adhered to, a major scale may be formed around any of those notes.

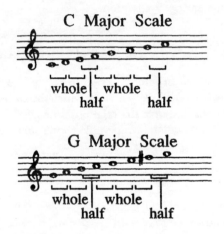

Minor Scale

The minor scale also contains the same five whole steps and two half steps, but they fall in a different order. Merely by shifting that pattern, we arrive at a different-sounding scale that has often been used to express sadness and tragedy rather than the joy and exultation that the major scale often conveys. The minor-scale formula consists of one whole step, one half step, two whole steps, one half step, and two whole steps. Thus, if we start with the note A as tonic, the pitches of the A minor scale would be A, B, C, D, E, F, G, and A. The C major scale is closely related to the A minor scale because they both contain the same pitches, but these pitches occur in a different order. The C minor scale, on the other hand, contains some pitches that are not included in the C major scale because of the different pattern of whole and half steps. The C minor scale consists of the pitches C, D, E♭, F, G, A♭, B♭, and C.

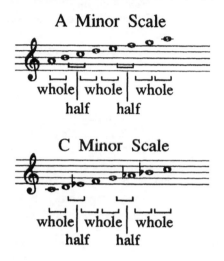

Use of Scale and Key

When we use a scale to organize our music, we are assuming that some pitches are going to be more important than others.

Tonic

The most important note, the tone that begins the scale—the tonic—is usually the pitch that will begin and end a tonal melody, thereby stressing the centrality of that note and the subservient nature of all the other notes in relation to it. The concluding idea of a phrase needs to end with a tonic pitch in order to bring the listener to a complete release of musical tension. This is known as a *full* or *perfect cadence*.

Dominant

Another tone, a fifth above or a fourth below the tonic, is also strongly emphasized. This pitch, called the dominant, is often used to "pose a question" at the end of an antecedent phrase. When used in this way the concluding idea is referred to as a *half cadence*. Much Euro-American music can be thought of in terms of a voyage that leads us from the tonic to the foreign terrain of the dominant, and then back home to the tonic.

Key

While the other ten tones all have unique relationships with the tonic, the seven scalar steps have the closest and most important relationship to the tonic note. The relationship of these scalar notes is referred to as the *key*.

Other Tones

Scale steps other than the dominant also have names that reflect their own relationship with the tonic note and the key. For instance, the scalar pitch that is seven notes away is referred to as the *leading tone*, because the sense of musical "gravity" is so great that it seems to pull us naturally back to the tonic. Likewise, each of the scale steps seems to lead away from or prepare for the return to the tonic. These terms are shown here with their corresponding scale degree.

I Tonic II Supertonic III Mediant IV Subdominant
V Dominant VI Submediant VII Leading Tone VIII Tonic

The seven steps of the scale are not the only notes that can be used in a melody, but they do imply special functions and provide particular melodic focus and movement. For that reason, the scale and its key relationship is the basis of our melodic and harmonic musical organization.

Chords

Whereas an interval is the combination of only two tones, a chord is the simultaneous sounding of three or more pitches. Just as intervals contain a certain degree of consonance or dissonance, chords also possess a quality of relaxation or tension. However, since a chord may contain three, four, or more tones the issue of harmony and discord is more complex.

The Triad

The most basic chord form, the core of our harmonic system, is the triad. A triad is a chord consisting of three notes built on successive intervals of a third. A triad can be constructed upon any note by adding alternating notes drawn from the scale. For instance, in the key of C major, the triad built on C would contain the notes C, E, and G. Likewise, the chord built on the second step (scale degree) of the C major scale, D, would contain the pitches D, F, and A. In each case the note that forms the foundation pitch is called the *root*, the middle tone of the chord is designated the *third* (because it is separated by the interval of a third from the root), and the top tone is referred to as the *fifth* (because it is a fifth away from the root).

Shown here are all of the triads built on steps of the C major scale. (The notation used to label the triads here is explained on page 83).

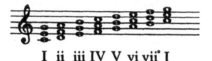

I   ii   iii IV V   vi vii° I

Triads can be constructed on notes of any other scale as well. For example, the triad built on the first note of the G major scale would contain the tones G, B, and D, while the triad based on the first scale degree of A major would include the tones A, C♯, and E.

Tonic and Dominant Chords

In any key, triads based on notes of that key have a relationship with one another. The triad built on the first tone of the scale is called the *tonic*. This chord feels like home, and all the other triads of the key are drawn back home to this triad. In the key of C major the tonic triad contains C, E, and G, and in the key of D major it contains D, F♯, and A, but in both cases the chord functions as home base, and although other chords may lead away from this home base they always return to the stability of the tonic.

The chord built on the fifth step of the scale (G, B, and D in the key of C major) also has a strong relationship with other triads in the key. This triad is known as the *dominant*. The tonic and the dominant have the two most important functions in any key. The tonic conveys a sense of stability and rest while the dominant is charged with a feeling of restlessness that wants to return to the security of the tonic. Therefore, many pieces of music come to a close by preceding the tonic chord with a dominant chord. This closing formula in which a tonic follows the dominant chord is referred to as an *authentic cadence*.

Functional Triadic Notation

Roman numerals are often used, as well as descriptive terms such as tonic and dominant, to label the triads of a key. Uppercase numerals designate major chords and lowercase numbers represent minor chords. Shown here are the triads and the functional harmony terms applied to the C major scale.

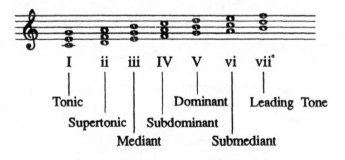

Chord Qualities

Chords may possess one of four distinct qualities—major, minor, augmented, or diminished—depending on their particular configuration of thirds. If we were to hear the triads shown above, for example, we would discover that they do not all sound exactly alike. Some are pleasant and stable; others are more dissonant and restless. This is because of the specific quality of the individual thirds that combine to form each triad (see the discussion of major and minor third intervals in chapter 4). A triad with a major third on the bottom and a minor third above it is called *major*. A triad with a minor third on the bottom and a major third above it is called *minor*. A triad constructed of two major thirds is called *augmented* and, finally, a triad built with two minor thirds is referred to as *diminished*.

Harmonic Notation

In indicating functional harmony a major chord is designated by an uppercase roman numeral (I), a minor chord by a lowercase roman numeral (i), a diminished chord by a small circle superscript (i°), and an augmented by a plus sign superscript (I^{+}). This figure illustrates the four triad qualities.

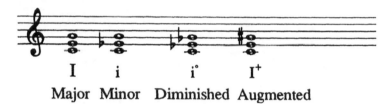

I   i i° I^{+}

Major Minor Diminished Augmented

Triad Qualities and Scales

Every major and minor scale has the same pattern of triad qualities associated with its scale degrees.

Major Scale

In the major scale, the tonic (I), subdominant (IV), and dominant (V) are all major chords, the supertonic (ii), mediant (iii), and submediant (vi) are all minor chords, and the leading tone (vii°) is a diminished chord.

Minor Scale

In the minor scale, the tonic (i), subdominant (iv), and dominant (v) are all minor chords; the mediant (III), submediant (VI), and leading tone (VII) are all major chords; and the supertonic (ii^o) is a diminished chord. No augmented chord occurs naturally in either the major or the minor scale. These scale-chord relationships are summarized here.

Triadic Chord Qualities

Major	(I): Major third on bottom; minor third above
Minor	(i): Minor third on bottom; major third above
Augmented	(I$^+$): Two major thirds
Diminished	(i^o): Two minor thirds

Chord Qualities Associated with Major and Minor Scales

Major Scales	Minor Scales
Major Chords	*Minor Chords*
Tonic (I)	Tonic (i)
Subdominant (IV)	Subdominant (iv)
Dominant (V)	Dominant (v)
Minor Chords	*Major Chords*
Supertonic (ii)	Mediant (III)
Mediant (iii)	Submediant (VI)
Submediant (vi)	Leading tone (VII)
Diminished Chords	*Diminished Chords*
Leading tone (vii^o)	Supertonic (ii^o)

The Importance of Key

The choice of key determines the specific pitches that will be emphasized, the chords that will be featured, and the functional relationship between tones and chords. As if to highlight the importance of key, composers often include the specific key in their title, as in such titles as Sonata no. 2 in E♭ and Symphony no. 9 in D Minor.

Throughout history, musicians have discussed the peculiar qualities and relative merits of the different keys. The ancient Greeks viewed the Dorian mode (similar to the D minor scale) as being suited to noble statements, Beethoven used the key of C minor for dramatic and tragic questions, and the Russian composer Scriabin claimed that certain keys were clearly associated with specific colors. It is true that composers feel more comfortable with certain keys, and that certain instruments are especially well suited to particular keys because of their construction. However, there is no proof that keys themselves contain intrinsic expressive values. Despite all the discussion and experimentation, it is not the key that makes the statement but, rather, the composer. What the composer does with the raw material of the key—the tones and chords—determines the effect of a piece of music.

Chord Progression

A chord progression is a formulaic succession of chords that determines the harmonic direction of a piece of music.

Harmonic Notation

Chord progressions are usually indicated with the roman numeral system described previously because the functions of the chords remain the same regardless of the key. For instance, the progression I–IV–V–I in the key of C major indicates the triads based on C, F, G, and C; in the key of G it indicates the triads built on G, C, D, and G.

Harmonic Rate

Each chord of a progression may be sustained for a variable length of time. A single chord can last anywhere from a fraction of a single beat to the duration of the entire work. The rate of speed at which chords change is called the harmonic rate. In a strongly chordal (homophonic) style like a chorale or hymn tune, the harmonic rate usually consists of a chord change on each beat of the measure, whereas in a blues progression each chord might be sustained for the duration of at least a measure. The speed at which the harmony changes strongly affects our perception of passing time; the more quickly the chords shift, the more quickly time seems to pass.

Blues Progression

One clear example of a standard chord progression is the blues progression. The blues progression is the foundation for most blues tunes from the delta blues of Robert Johnson to the electric blues of Robert Cray. It is also the foundation for a vast number of jazz and rock tunes. This chord pattern associated with the blues can be repeated again and again throughout the work, providing a sense of organization. One cycle of chords in the progression equals one chorus of music or three lines of text. Since the musicians all know where the chord pattern is leading, they are able to structure their improvisation around that pattern, knowing that their fellow musicians are in the same musical place.

Outlined here is a standard twelve-bar blues progression indicating the functional roman numerals, the specific triads in the key of C major, the number of measures that each chord occupies, and the corresponding line of text.

One Chorus of Blues Progression

Measures:	1–4	5–6	7–8	9	10	11	12
Functional Chord:	I	IV	I	V	IV	I	V
Chord in Key of C:	C	F	C	G	F	C	G
Text Phrase:	first	second——		third—————			

Modulation

Modulation is the shifting from one key to another within a piece of music to create tension and variety.

Functional harmony is based on the concept that there is a hierarchy of chords. Although each chord is equally interesting out of context, in a musical composition based on the tonal system of the Euro-American tradition, the tonic chord is always the most important chord. It is the tonic, based on the key note of the key, that establishes a sense of origin and destination. The tonic chord is "home"; the other chords are merely diversions along the way—diversions that provide variety and build suspense, that delay the anticipated return home and the final resolution to the tonic.

In short, simple works that do not contain extended musical development, there is enough variety in one key to sustain the listener's interest. However, in longer works, musicians often resort to more elaborate ways of manipulating the listener's sense of harmony. To intensify further the feeling of tension and resolution, a composer might alter the perception of "home" by temporarily creating a new tonic area—transforming the original key to another secondary key. This process of key change is known as modulation.

Modulation can be abrupt and sudden, changing keys so unexpectedly that the listener has the sensation of being jolted out of complacency. Modulation may also be effected in subtle ways so that the listener senses the change almost unconsciously. However the modulation is brought about, the result produces a sense of "home away from home." Modulation is like a journey from one solar system of chords revolving around its tonic sun to a new solar system populated with its own planet chords.

Extended Chords

So far the discussion of harmony has been limited to triads, those chords containing three notes which are constructed by imposing two successive thirds upon a root tone. However, it is possible to create more complex chords merely by placing additional thirds on top of that same root tone. Chords in which additional third-generated tones are added to an existing triad are known as extended chords. Just as the four qualities of triads have various degrees of tension or dissonance associated with them, so these extended chords have relative degrees of dissonance. However, because extended chords contain more notes than triads, they possess a more complex and dissonant sound. The presence of these additional notes heightens the sense of tension and demands a more dramatic sense of resolution.

Seventh Chords

The first of these extended chords is called the seventh chord because the additional third is a seventh away from the root. In the key of C major the seventh chord built on a root of C contains the tones C, E, G, and B while the seventh chord constructed on the dominant tone G will contain the pitches G, B, D, and F. Because the tension of these seventh chords demand resolution so strongly, they are often used at cadence points to make the resolution seem more complete and final.

Ninth Chords

Other extended chords are built in exactly the same fashion. A ninth chord contains the usual root, third and fifth of the triad with an additional seventh and ninth.

Additionally Extended Chords

Eleventh and *thirteenth* chords also occur, but their complexity and richness of tone are used primarily in music of the early twentieth century and in later forms of jazz.

Extended-Chord Notation

Extended chords are notated with Roman numerals in the same way as simple triads with the added notes indicated by arabic number superscripts (V^7).

Nontertian Harmony

Although tertian harmonic construction (building chords by thirds) has dominated the history of musical harmony, other forms of chord construction have also been used.

Quartal Harmony

Quartal-harmony chords, built by superimposing successive fourths over a root, provide an interesting, somewhat hollow sound that seems ancient yet modern. Unlike tertian harmony, however, the equidistant fourths produce a more static sense of harmonic motion. As with extended chords, the characteristic sound of quartal harmony is heard primarily in music of the impressionist period, of the twentieth century, and in modern jazz styles.

Clusters

Perhaps influenced by sounds of the urban industrial environment, modern composers have employed chords constructed of successive half or whole steps. These chords, referred to as clusters, are so dense that their dissonance does not lead to any particular resolution or release of tension. Listeners usually perceive them in terms of their rhythmic and timbral efects rather than as harmonic gestures. Only a fine line separates clusters from noise.

Harmony is created by the intentional simultaneous production of musical tones. Although many world cultures place little or no emphasis on harmony, our musical tradition has particularly stressed the delicate relationship between the linear aspects of melody and the vertical structure of harmony.

The basic unit of the Euro-American harmonic tradition is the chord and, in particular, the triad, which consists of two intervals of a third superimposed upon a root tone. Other, more complex collections of tones consisting of four or more pitches, called extended chords, are also utilized for coloristic effects. These chords are organized in hierarchical relationships based on keys, and the sequence of chords, known as harmonic progression, provides the impression of musical motion through the tension and resolution contained in the chordal movement. In many ways, our systematic development of harmony is the unique contribution that our musical tradition has made to the totality of world musical culture.

CHAPTER 8

Form: Order in Music

Form is the structural blueprint that determines the particular musical relationships in a piece of music. All the elements of music (pitch, duration, timbre, and dynamics) are aspects of form, but form itself is a much larger concept—an overarching ideal that provides coherence and invests each musical element with meaning relative to the whole work.

While form is an important organizing principle in all the arts, it is particularly critical in music, because music unfolds during time. Our comprehension of music is based on our ability to perceive and recollect passing musical events and create a constantly shifting frame of reference for them. Form is the musical framework that structures statement, repetition, variety, and contrast to provide a meaningful and coherent work of art.

Form as the Organizing Principle

Sift four cups of flour, one teaspoon of salt, one teaspoon of sugar, and one teaspoon of baking soda into a bowl. Make a hollow in the center and pour in one cup of buttermilk. Mix with your hands and add enough additional buttermilk to make a firm but not dry dough. Turn onto a floured board and knead lightly. Shape into a round loaf, place in a buttered skillet and bake at 350° for forty to forty-five minutes. This recipe yields a delightfully fragrant loaf of freshly baked Irish soda bread.

Present four phrases of conjunct melody in the key of G major played by one violin. Add one piano playing a chordal accompaniment in $\frac{6}{8}$ meter, outlining the harmony consonant with the violin melody. Add dynamics that intensify the arch of the melodic line. Contrast with an additional four phrases of conjunct melody performed by the violin in the closely related dominant key area, D Major. Mix with a supporting piano part concluding with a half cadence that returns to the beginning material of the piece. Play at a brisk allegro tempo for ten minutes. This formula yields a sprightly Irish jig for fiddle and piano.

In the manner of a recipe, musical form combines the raw ingredients of pitch, timbre, dynamics, and duration in measured proportion to create a coherent and expressive sound. Without form, sound is merely chaotic noise. Form structures musical material from the micro level of the relationship between one note and the next to the macro level spanning the beginning and ending of a vast symphony.

Hierarchy of Formal Units

Tone and Interval

The smallest unit of formal organization is a single *tone* embodying pitch, timbre, dynamics, and duration. However, this single tone is isolated in time like an atom adrift in space; it has no intrinsic meaning because it bears no relationship to any other sound. Just as two atoms can combine to form a molecule, so two tones can combine to form an *interval*. An interval is the most elementary unit of meaning, describing the simple spatial relationship between two tones.

Motive

The first level of actual expression or musical idea is called a motive. A motive (or motif) is a short, characteristic fragment that may be developed and expanded throughout a work. The motive is the most basic building block of melody and is generally between two and five tones in length, bound together by a strong rhythmic sense. The opening four notes of Beethoven's Fifth Symphony, often characterized as fate knocking, are one of the most famous examples of a motive.

Melody

A utilitarian, if colorless, definition of melody might state simply that it is a succession of musical tones in rhythm expressing a musical relationship. If a tone is analogous to a word, an interval to a simple comparison of two words, and a motive to a clause, then a melody is equivalent to a complete sentence containing nouns, verbs, and modifiers. Melody is a single, complete statement of musical thought. A melody contains tones, intervals, and motives combined into an expressive whole. It is much easier to recognize a melody than to attempt to describe one. Creation and perception of melody is one of the most subjective and magical aspects of music.

Phrase

Melody is generally constructed of several phrases that are punctuated by points of articulation called *cadences*. Phrases are ordinarily four measures in length, are usually structured in pairs, and are based on an antecedent- and consequent-, or question- and answer-, relationship called a *period*.

Period

Within a period, the composer initially states the first phrase, the antecedent, which generally concludes with an incomplete-sounding ending called a half cadence. This half cadence achieves its restless, questioning effect by drawing the listener away from the original tonal area and toward a new and more distant resting point. The antecedent phrase is the equivalent of a verbal question and the half cadence is equivalent to a question mark.

Once the antecedent phrase is stated, the musician then provides a second complementary phrase that "answers" the question. This consequent phrase serves to resolve the tension created by the antecedent and restores the music to its initial state of repose. The final cadence, a full cadence this time, reasserts the original tonality, thus reestablishing harmonic stability.

In analyzing the form and structure of music, it is common practice to use lowercase letters of the alphabet to represent phrases. Thus, a period commonly found in small dance forms might be represented as *aabb*, indicating four phrases with two contrasting ideas. Phrases that are subsequently varied following an initial model are designated by the same letter to show their relationship but are also provided with a numbered superscript to show that they are varied (a, a^1, a^2 etc.). For a more complete discussion of phrases, periods, and melody see page 92.

Section

The next level of musical order combines phrases and periods into a larger whole called a section. Sections, represented in diagram form as capitalized letters to distinguish them from phrases, often consist of two periods. Thus, a "regular" section might contain a total of four phrases subdivided into paired periods that are linked together as a complete thought. Although this standard prototype of a section usually consists of four phrases, it is important to remember that forms are not rigid molds but, rather, flexible models for structuring specific musical ideas. The most interesting artistic expression occurs when the antici- pated formal model is somehow subtly altered, when the musician plays upon our preconceived expectations to lead us to a surprising revelation.

In the hierarchy of forms, sections are the largest *dependent* formal building block. While they contain the completed thoughts of periods punctuated by the repose of full cadences, they are not fully capable of standing alone as a completed composition. Through the manipulation of sections a musician delineates the large architectural perspective of his work. Motives, phrases, and periods might be thought of as detailed views of aspects of an individual room, but sections represent the large conceptual view of the room itself. When we speak of large formal organizations such as binary or ternary forms, we are referring to organization at the sectional level.

Single- and Compound-Movement Works

At the final formal level, sections are combined with one another to create the broadest level of structural organization—either a discrete musical composition or a single *movement* contained within an extended compound movement work such as a symphony or an oratorio. Movements sound like complete and self-contained compositions, because they possess a clearly defined beginning, middle, and end. However, they are not totally independent works because their structure is closely related to the other movements of a multimovement work. Rather than being an isolated entity, they represent certain aspects of a larger picture. To continue the architectural analogy, individual movements of a symphony correspond to individual rooms of a house, and the multimovement symphony to the house itself. Each room has unique dimensions, form, and a specific function, but the rooms could not exist without the overall frame of the house. From the smallest microdetail of motivic construction to the greatest unity of compound-movement form, the musician seeks to articulate his musical expression with perfect architectural clarity so that his ideas may be discerned through listening. Because music unfolds during time, clarity of form is essential to the comprehension of musical ideas as they rapidly pass through the listener's perception and dissipate into the air.

Principles of Musical Organization

At every level of musical organization, form is determined by the balance between unity and variety. Unity and variety are governed in turn by three basic approaches—repetition, contrast, and variation.

Unity and Variety

Unity establishes a sensation of security, stability, and peace, while *variety* invokes a state of change, motion, and adventure. In this way, music is an accurate reflection of our lives: we strive for some sense of unity, for the stability afforded by comforting routines and habits repeated each day, but we also look forward to the refreshing variety of experiences sparked by unanticipated events.

Repetition, Contrast, and Variation

Once a musical idea is stated it can only be repeated in an identical statement, contrasted with a totally new idea, or repeated in varied form. *Repetition* creates a center of focus and breeds a sense of stability, but too much repetition is perceived as boring and ultimately frustrating. *Contrast* provides the motion and drama that sustains interest in a composition, but a work containing too much variety loses its sense of focus and order. *Variation* meshes the coherence produced by repetition with the variety formed through contrast. In variation technique, certain recognizable features of the music are retained while others are transformed. Variation is an especially effective technique because it embodies both unity and variety. Repetition, contrast, and variation all figure in the types of musical form described below.

Types of Musical Form

Strophic Form

Strophic form is a repetitive formal approach in which all the strophes (or stanzas) of text are sung to the same music. The words or text change from one strophe to the next but they are sung to the same melody and harmony. Musically, a strophe usually consists of four musical phrases that correspond to four lines of text. This form, frequently found in blues or in narrative ballads, is often enhanced by the addition of a chorus. The *chorus* (or refrain) consists of one or two repeated lines of text sung with the same melody at the end of each strophe. Strophic form complements the variety of the changing text with the repeated music and, similarly, the constancy of the music is spiced with the varied text.

"O Susanna" by Stephen Foster
An Example of Strophic Form

Strophe:	I come from Alabama with my banjo on my knee, I'm going to Louisiana, my Susanna for to see.
Chorus:	O, Susanna! O, don't you cry for me, For I come from Alabama with my banjo on my knee.
Strophe:	It rained all night the day I left, the weather it was dry, The sun so hot I froze myself, Susanna don't you cry.
Chorus:	O, Susanna! O, don't you cry for me, For I come from Alabama with my banjo on my knee.

In strophic form, the audience's interest is sustained largely through attention to the text rather than by being directed to the musical gestures. Therefore, strophic form is usually associated with music for voice and accompaniment, and is seldom applied to purely instrumental music.

Additive Form

In additive form (represented in diagrams by the letters *A*, *B*, *C*, etc.), the uniform, monochromatic tinge of strophic construction is replaced by the colorful opposition of various contrasting ideas. Additive form, in its pure state, is all variety without unity—exactly the opposite of strophic form. Since things are constantly changing, there is no sense of stability, of perspective from which the changes might be observed. It is as though one were constantly traveling without ever having a home to return to.

While strophic form employs the same music to accompany each stanza of text, additive—or through-composed—song form employs different music for each stanza. In through-composed song the music and the text progress from beginning to end in one seamless unity, with no repetition of text or melody. As the musical material is in constant flux, the organization and coherence of through-composed song are dictated by the ability of the music to portray the ebb and flow of the textual narrative.

Binary Form

Binary form (represented in diagrams as *AB*) is the most basic manifestation of additive form in instrumental music. Two-part, or binary, structure simply presents two contrasting large sections. The musician states an introductory idea and then presents a contrasting second idea. This second idea may contain new melodic material, it may explore a new harmonic area, or it may utilize new rhythmic patterns. There is usually some common thread, such as a rhythmic motive or melodic sequence, that binds the two contrasting sections together, but the essential nature of their relationship is based on contrast.

At the more local phrase level, the "model" binary form consists of a pair of phrases per section (a period), which are then repeated before moving into the contrasting section. This repeating phrase structure is duplicated at the section level with each section usually repeated, so that the global binary structure could best be represented as follows:

Binary Form

Section:	*A*	*A*	*B*	*B*
Phrase:	*ab*	*ab*	*cd*	*cd*

Harmonically, the *A* section moves away from the original tonality to the new harmonic area of the *B* section. The *B* section then begins in the new tonal area before it returns to the initial tonality. While a work in binary form does not return to the initial melodic material, it does come full circle harmonically, so that the listener feels a sense of completion and return to stability. Binary form is often used to frame short dance works, such as fiddle-tune reels and jigs, in which the simple and clear architecture crisply delineates the form of the dance.

Return Form

Return form couples the desire for unity with the desire for variety. Whereas strophic form is dominated by repetition and additive form stresses contrast, return form combines elements of both repetition and contrast into a balanced formal design. Return-form structure may be as rudimentary as a *rounded binary* form ($AB^{1}/_{2}A$), as common as the three-part *ternary* structure (*ABA*), or as complex as an extended *rondo* (*ABACA*), but in each case the basic idea of the initial theme returns at the conclusion of the piece, thereby creating a sense of symmetry and order.

Simple Return Form

Rounded Binary. Rounded binary is a transitional form that combines aspects of both additive and return form. Binary form returns to the harmonic area presented in the opening *A* section, but it always concludes with the thematic material of the *B* section—even in cases in which various sections are repeated (*AA BB AA BB*). However, in rounded binary, the basic two-part structure is altered and enhanced by a return of the opening melodic material of the *A* section. While the *A* section is not restated in its entirety, this short recollection of the opening material provides a sense of unity and return in the composition. Rounded binary form is best diagrammed as follows:

Rounded Binary

Section:	*A*	*B*	$^{1}/_{2}A$
Phrase:	*aa*	*bb*	*a*

Ternary Form. In three-part, or ternary, form, the composer first establishes a musical focus, a "home," for the audience, by presenting the initial melodic material, rhythmic idea, and harmonic scheme in the *A* section. The composer then directs the audience along an extended journey away from home. This journey, the *B* section, presents new thematic material, rhythms, and harmonic areas that contrast strongly with the original ideas presented in the *A* section. When the journey is complete, the composer then returns the audience to the original starting point, the *A* section, which may be either restated exactly as it was in the beginning or recast in a recognizable, yet varied version.

Purely instrumental music has utilized ternary form more often than any other structure, because the clarity and satisfying sense of musical completion inherent in the form naturally induces balance and symmetry. In abstract musical expression—music without the concrete benefit of text to support and direct the activity—ternary form allows a musician to create the drama of interaction and resolution between two contrasting characters. For that reason, many extended works of symphonic and chamber literature develop their musical content within the terms of ternary form.

This frequent use of ternary form is especially prevalent in music composed during the "common practice" period of tonal-dominated music. Works written during the seventeenth through the nineteenth centuries feature clearly marked sectional boundaries, and these borders are defined by tonal-area distinctions. The comparison and contrast of melodic and rhythmic material is sharply etched by a deviation from, or a return to, the original key area. Ternary form is the arena in which the gladiatorial combat of key relationships is enacted. In this "combat," however, the conflict of tonal areas is always resolved by a return to the opening material coupled with a return to the tonic key. Ternary form, shaped by the struggle between a tonic key and a foreign tonal area, is a symbolic representaion of the drama—of the conflicts and resolutions—of human life.

Vocal Ternary Forms. Ternary form is not just applied to instrumental music. Because of its flexibility and heightened sense of resolution, three-part form is also successfully utilized in vocal music with text. Such forms are found in both operatic and popular musical styles.

Da Capo Aria. In opera, the most common form for an *aria* (extended solo song) is the *da capo* structure. In a *da capo* aria, the melodic idea is stated, a contrasting idea is introduced, and then the singer returns to the beginning, completing the work with a final statement of the opening section. *Da capo* (indicated as *D.C.*) literally means "to the head" referring to the "head," or beginning, of a composition. During the final return to the opening, however, the performer adds vocal ornaments that embellish the melody and showcase the performer's singing ability. Thus, *da capo* form would be indicated in a diagram by *A B A'*, to indicate that *A* returned in varied form.

Thirty-Two-Bar Pop Song. Another commonly employed vocal ternary form is the thirty-two-bar pop song form. Represented as *AABA*, a work in thirty-two bar pop song form presents its initial melody in an eight-measure phrase. It then repeats this idea verbatim. Following this second statement of the original melody, the composer interjects a contrasting eight-measure section, called a *bridge*, which presents a new melody stated in a different harmonic area. The cadence at the end of the bridge arouses a sense of unrest that is then satisfied by an exact repetition of the first *A* section.

Thirty-two-bar pop song form is frequently used for popular music of the twentieth century, including Tin Pan Alley–style songs of composers such as Irving Berlin and George Gershwin, songs contained in musical comedy, and jazz arrangements of the swing era that were often based on the harmonic progressions of tunes such as Gershwin's "I've Got Rhythm."

Compound Return Forms

Compositions that use only one of the binary or ternary forms discussed previously are referred to as being in simple form. The pattern may be repeated, but the organizational structure is based on a single model of *AB* or *ABA* form. However, larger works may combine more than one pattern, using various forms at different levels of organization. This type of complex formal arrangement is known as compound form. It is exemplified by the minuet and trio and rondo forms discussed presently, and by multimovement works such as opera, oratorio, and symphony.

Minuet and Trio. The minuet and trio is an instrumental form based on a French country dance that gained popularity in the court of Louis XIV. Today the minuet and trio, or scherzo and trio, is most frequently heard as the third movement of symphonies written during the classic and romantic periods. Other examples of the form include dances in baroque suites, ragtime compositions by pianists such as Scott Joplin, and marching-band pieces by composers such as John Philip Sousa.

Minuet and trio is a compound form because two different formal patterns exist at two different levels of organization. At the primary, or highest, structural level, the combination of a minuet, a contrasting trio section, and a return to the minuet reflects a ternary form. However, at a subordinate layer, each of the three sections is stated in a rounded binary form. At the phrase level the minuet consists of the pattern *aa ba ba*. The second section, called the trio, contains new material, but it is structured in the same format as the minuet section, *cc dc dc*. The third section is a return to the material of the initial minuet. This time, however, the phrases that were originally repeated are now simply stated once, so the return of *A* is best diagrammed as a simple, ternary *aba*.

Minuet and Trio Form

Minuet	Trio	Minuet
A	*B*	*A*
aa ba ba	*cc dc dc*	*aba*

Rondo. Because of the exciting refrain effect of the rondo, this form is used most frequently as a dazzling concluding symphonic movement. A rondo is a compound form, strongly marked by recurring thematic ideas that always return between intervening episodes of contrasting material. Formally, rondo form somewhat resembles the compound ternary form of the minuet and trio, but the concept of contrast and return is further expanded by the presence of additional sections.

At the principal organizational level, rondo form may consist of one of various return designs represented as *ABABA*, *ABACA*, or *ABACABA*. Regardless of which particular design is chosen, in each case the initial thematic material and tonal area represented by the *A* section returns following various contrasting sections. These contrasting sections, known as *episodes*, present new melodic ideas expressed in tonal areas that may explore unusual key relationships. However, no matter how far an episode draws us from home, the initial refrain always returns like an old friend to guide us back to the original tonality and thematic material.

Variation Form

Variation, or processive, form is the union between the polar concepts of unity and variety. In variation form, some elements are retained and explored through repetition while others are transformed by various changes. In this way the boredom of tedious repetition is averted while the unity of organizational repetition is maintained.

Sectional Theme-and-Variation Form

The most common processive form, called theme and variations, introduces a theme (usually in a simple binary or ternary form) and then proceeds to alter certain aspects of that theme during a series of sectional variations diagrammed as $A\ A'\ A''\ A'''$ (the prime indications represent variations of the theme). Although various facets of the material are altered with successive variations, each section generally maintains the harmonic progression and phrase length of the original theme. There is no set number of sections, no preconceived approach to the variation technique but, in general, the variations become increasingly complex and are more remote from the original material as they progress. Often the work will conclude with a final variation that returns triumphantly to the original theme.

Although each original theme suggests its own unique method for varying the material, there are some commonly accepted techniques that have been applied to variation form over the years. Listed here is a partial description of variation techniques that might be applied to a composition.

Variation Techniques

1. Change of harmony while maintaining initial melody
2. Change of key (often from tonic to dominant area)
3. Change of mode (from major to minor)
4. Ornamentation of the melody (trills, grace notes, etc.)
5. Change of orchestration or timbre
6. Change of rhythm
7. Use of different dance rhythms (as in baroque suites)
8. Change of melody while retaining harmony

9. Use of imitation of melodic ideas

10. Use of idea in canon (round form)

11. Change of dynamics (this can accompany change of orchestration or timbre)

12. Change of register (octave displacement)

13. Addition of new countermelodies

14. Inversion of melody (reversing direction of intervals)

15. Retrograde motion of melody (backward)

16. Augmenting or diminishing rhythmic values

In notated art music of the Euro-American tradition, variation form has proven to be a highly effective and popular means for communicating ideas. Variation form has also been an important mode of expression within improvisational styles such as jazz and bluegrass music.

In both of these styles the work begins with an introductory theme statement, the *head*. In jazz the head is often in either *AABA* thirty-two-bar pop song form or strophic twelve-bar blues, while bluegrass often uses the binary statements of fiddle tunes. Following the head, the musicians then improvise ornamented forms of the melody or completely new melodic lines over *choruses* based on the harmonic progression of the original theme.

As with art music, the improvisations tend to grow more elaborate and range farther afield as the work progresses. Then, just at the point where the tension and suspense reach their peak, the musicians return to the head for a final statement of the original theme, thus closing the circle.

Continuous Variation Form

Continuous variation forms maintain a thread of organizing material throughout, but they do not divide the music into discrete sections that are punctuated by clear-cut cadences. Unlike sectional variation, continuous variation does not blatantly state the material to be developed at the beginning of the work. Instead, the developmental material tends to be subtle and obscured, and is hidden away in the bass line or harmony. The listener senses organization in the structure, but it is often difficult to pinpoint the pattern itself. Whereas sectional variation is based on embellishments of a clearly defined melody, continuous variation avoids melodic organization in favor of functional musical ideas that form a foundation for new melody.

Passacaglia. The passacaglia is a continuous musical form that has been in use since the baroque period. Taken from the Spanish word *pasacalle,* meaning a "stroll in the street," the passacaglia consists of a *repeated bass line* over which melodic variations are imposed. The bass line, characteristically eight measures long, is usually repeated continuously without pause between repetitions. Although this bass line is the foundation, the form's thread of continuity, the listener's attention is directed not to the bass but rather to the melodic figurations imposed upon it.

Chaconne. The chaconne, another continuous variation form, features a *repeated harmonic progression* rather than a repeated bass. Since the bass line frequently outlines the shape of the harmony, there is often confusion as to whether a composition is actually a passacaglia or a chaconne. In fact, a work may well be both. The criteria according to which one distinguishes between the two forms are first, the aspect—bass line or harmonic progression—that is emphasized, and second, whether one or the other is repeated strictly throughout the work. However, while such distinctions might be important to music historians, categorization does not affect the beauty of the work—composers frequently write without concern for formal designations.

Combinational Forms

In addition to the four basic formal types—strophic, additive, return, and variation—there are forms that fuse elements of several forms into a new organizational unity. Of these two approaches, the fugue is a continuous form based on imitation and the sonata-allegro form is based on presentation, development and return.

Fugue

In some ways, the fugue, taken from a Latin word meaning "flight," is more a process than a distinct form. It is an approach to imitative development rather than a sectional form defined by return, variation, or strophic repetition.

Exposition. A fugue consists of an opening section called the exposition. During this exposition a melodic theme called the *subject* is introduced in one of the parts. Consequently, the subject is imitated in turn by each additional voice (usually three or four voices in all). After the subject is stated in the first voice, and during the subsequent entries of the other voices, that first voice continues with additional material. If this new material is a strong, identifiable idea that is then also imitated by the other voices in turn, it is called a *countersubject.*

Most often in a "standard" fugue there is an interesting conflict of tonality that is established and resolved during the course of the composition. The first statement of the subject is in the tonic or home tonal area. The second entrance imitates the subject, but is often stated in the dominant key. The third entrance returns to the tonic as originally stated, then the fourth entrance parallels the second entrance in the dominant. With fugues in the minor key the relationship between the subjects is one of minor and relative major keys rather than tonic and dominant—but in each case the subject establishes some tension through its statement in two different tonal areas.

Episode. Following the exposition, in which all the voices make their first imitative entry, a section follows in which the subject does not appear. This section, known as an episode, provides contrast and allows the composer freely to develop new ideas as well as some motives that may be extracted from the original subject. For the remainder of the work, the composer alternates returns to the subject (also known as expositions) with contrasting episodes.

Development. Beyond the initial subject and episode, there is no preestablished format, no rigidly defined form to which the fugue must adhere. Expositions and episodes feint and parry, the voices weave around each other in an intricate web, drawn ever tighter through the rapid imitation of the subject material.

Coda. When the initial subject and episodic material have been exhausted, the work may culminate in a triumphant final presentation of the original subject above a sustained bass note called a *pedal tone.*

The fugue, in the hands of a consummate master such as Johann Sebastian Bach, is a form of infinite delight tempered by absolute logic in which each note is essential and inevitable.

Sonata Form

Sonata form developed during the early classic period and quickly became the dominant form of musical expression for instrumental works such as symphonies, string quartets, sonatas, concerti, and overtures. Sonata—from the Italian word *suonare*, meaning "to sound"—was originally a generic work written especially for instruments. In time, sonata indicated a distinct musical form with a clearly established architecture that reflected an evolving sense of aesthetic purpose that was synonymous with classicism itself.

Origin of Sonata Form. During the baroque period (1600–1770), movements and discrete compositions were unified by a homogeneity of approach. The "affect" or mood created by the work was expected to remain constant throughout the work. In order to provide some contrast, movements were placed in conjunction with one another to create a form such as a dance suite. Within the suite, a fast dance might be presented, followed by a slow dance, and perhaps concluded by another fast dance. Each dance maintained its particular mood and tempo, but the suite, as a whole, contained the contrast of different dance movements.

Musicians during the preclassic period conceived of incorporating the contrasting movements of the suite into a single movement. This single movement consolidating contrasting moods and tempos within itself became the prototype for sonata form. However, it was not until composers began to regard the melodic subjects as musical *themes* capable of *development* that the essence of sonata form crystallized. The contrast presented through the juxtaposition of two dissimilar themes merely sets the stage. It is the function of the development section to develop the relationship between the contrasting ideas—to resolve that contrast. For this reason the development section became the most important part of the sonata form—the arena for the most profound classic and romantic musical expression.

Aspects of Sonata Form. Sonata form's tripartite structure, consisting of an *exposition* section, a *development* section, and a *recapitulation* section, resembles a simple *ABA* ternary form. But, while the statement of the exposition and the return of the recapitulation section suggest a standard return form, the importance of the extended central development section places the form in a class by itself. Sonata form is not simply based on strophic, additive, variation, or return form; it is a combination of all these approaches. It is a unique formal method that creates a forum for the musical embodiment of conflict and resolution.

Sonata form is based on contrast. Drama is the result of contrast. The musical contrasts, expressed by such oppositions as forte versus piano dynamics, orchestral versus solo timbre, legato versus staccato articulation, allegro versus largo tempi, homophonic versus polyphonic texture, and major versus minor tonality, creates the sense of drama in music. Much of the music written within the Euro-American tradition of 1700–1940 is constructed around the dramatic dialectic narrative that introduces two contrasting ideas in an exposition section, develops the dialogue between these two opposing ideas, and culminates in some sort of resolution or synthesis of the ideas in a final section.

In many ways, the dialectic narrative of sonata form is analogous to the drama found in a traditional play, film, or novel. A short introduction sets the scene, informing us about when and where the story takes place. The exposition then introduces us to the cast—the major figures and supporting characters—providing us with some insight into their personal characteristics. The development, the main body of the novel, play, or film, then ensues. Within the development the characters interact: the plot thickens, characters come into conflict, action occurs, tension builds, and a climax is reached. At the climax, the conflict is resolved, the tension is released, and the action stabilizes. Subsequently the denouement—or, in musical terms, the recapitulation—ties together the various loose strands of the plot and resolves the final differences between the major themes or characters. A conclusion corresponding to the musical coda completes the work with a parting gesture.

Structure of Sonata Form. We have seen that sonata form consists of introduction, exposition, development, recapitulation, and coda sections, each of which is invested with a specific purpose. Let us now examine in more detail the specific structure and relationship of these sections.

Structure of Sonata Form

Introduction

An introduction is an optional appendage that may precede the exposition. Although the introduction generally establishes the key and tempo of the movement, in some instances it consists of a short, contrasting slow section that prepares the listener for the brisk tempo of the exposition to follow.

Exposition

Principal Theme. The exposition presents an initial theme or theme group of melodies in the tonic or home key of the movement. These themes are usually couched in a small binary or ternary form and average about sixteen measures of $\frac{4}{4}$ meter. The first theme is generally strongly rhythmic, energetic, and boldly assertive. The essence of the theme should invite and encourage further exploration and development.

Bridge. A transitional passage called the bridge links the first theme group with the second theme group. The bridge material is not strong melodically because its main function is to modulate, to change keys between the tonic of the first theme and the dominant key area (or relative major if the first theme is in a minor key) of the second theme.

Subordinate Theme. The second theme group, stated in a new tonal area, is usually more gentle and lyrical in nature, contrasting with the principal theme in character, key, and melody. As with the first theme, there is no set length or form, though generally the subordinate theme roughly parallels the primary theme.

Codetta. The exposition frequently concludes with a short closing passage called a codetta. This may consist of a new theme that is largely cadential in nature, giving weight to the harmonic formula that terminates the section.

Repeat of Exposition. The entire exposition is then repeated in its entirety. This allows the listener to become familiar with the thematic material to be developed in the next section.

Development

The development is of variable length and form. Usually it is at least as long as the exposition and is in a nonsectional form that stresses the organic development of ideas. The material to be developed is primarily drawn from the themes introduced in the exposition, but new themes or ideas excerpted from bridge material may be used as well.

Although there is no set method for developing the musical themes, composers have used some of the following approaches.

1. *Modulation*: exploration of new key areas; perhaps the most important developmental technique
2. *Alteration of mode*: use of major rather than minor keys and vice versa.
3. *Change of texture*: polyphony, homophony, monophony
4. *Variation of dynamics*: crescendo, diminuendo, abrupt changes
5. *Alteration of articulation*: legato, detached, and staccato approaches
6. *Change of orchestration*: use of different instruments
7. *Contrast of register placement*: displacing themes up or down in range
8. *Variation of rhythms*: triplets instead of duple divisions; augmentation or diminuition of rhythms
9. *Imitation*: repetition of motives; canons or rounds
10. *Melodic manipulation*: inversion and retrograde
11. *Sequence*: repetition of an idea on successively higher or lower pitch levels
12. *Contrapuntal combination of themes*

13. *Fugal treatment*
14. *Change of harmony*: use of different chords to accompany theme

This is only a partial listing of techniques available to composers. Each composition, each theme, suggests its own unique approach to development. The stronger and more complex the theme, the more possibilities may be suggested.

Retransition. The development generally concludes with a retransitional passage whose purpose is to modulate back to the original key area. This is the critical point at which the tension of the development section is to be resolved in the return to the initial theme and tonality.

Recapitulation

Principal Theme. The recapitulation statement of the first theme group is exactly as it was in the exposition. After the developmental exploration of different tonal areas, the return to the original tonic key area is sensed as a triumphant homecoming.

Bridge. The function of the bridge is altered in the recapitulation. The passage no longer needs to modulate between the first and second themes; it now exists primarily to preserve the symmetry of the exposition and to mitigate the change of character posed by the juxtaposition of the two contrasting themes.

Subordinate Theme. When the second theme group returns in the recapitulation it is stated in the same key as the first theme group. If it was originally in the dominant it returns in the tonic; if it was in a major key it returns in the tonic minor. In this way, the conflict, the drama posed by these two ideas, is brought to a final resolution.

Codetta. The small closing formalities close out the recapitulation because there is no repetition of the principal themes now as there was in the exposition.

Coda

The entire movement may conclude with a coda that presents a final emphatic farewell. The coda is usually strongly cadential in character, reinforcing the final tonic-dominant-tonic chord progression. Exceptionally, some composers have extended the coda, incorporating such gestures as new themes, development, and false returns to the exposition as a way of prolonging the suspense of the entire work.

Pictured here is a diagram representing a model sonata form. It is important to remember that this is just a theoretical model. In actual practice, composers alter the form to suit their particular expressive needs. The content determines the form. This is especially true for works rendered in sonata form in which the developmental process seeks to forge a seamless unity from the various contrasting ideas.

Theoretical Model of Sonata Form

Section:	[	EXPOSITION	]
Activity:	Principal theme	Bridge	Subordinate theme
Tonality:	I (or i minor)	Modulates	V (or III major)

Section:	EXPOSITION [	DEVELOPMENT	]
Activity:	Codetta	Various activity	Retransition
Tonality:	V	Changes tonal areas	Modulates

Section:	[	RECAPITULATION	]
Activity:	Principal theme	Bridge	Subordinate theme
Tonality:	I (Tonic)	I	I

Section:	RECAPITULATION	CODA
Activity:	Codetta	Final cadential extension
Tonality:	I	I

Summary

Form is the organizing factor at every level in music, from the smallest detail of interval to the large relationship between movements of a symphony. Every aspect of music—pitch, timbre, dynamics, and rhythm—is structured to delineate the form. It is through form that meaning and coherence are imparted to musical expression.

Form is dictated by a balance between the principles of order and variety. The four basic formal approaches—strophic, additive, variational, and return—serve to establish enough unity to ensure coherence while also providing the right amount of contrast to satisfy our desire for variety.

The table that follows highlights the various single-movement forms commonly used in the Euro-American musical tradition.

SINGLE MOVEMENT FORMS

Strophic Form

A, A^1, A^2, A^3, etc.

Exact repetitions of the musical material are coupled with changing verses of text. Choruses may be added that couple each repetition with a repeated refrain of text.

Additive Form

A, B, C, etc.

Through-composed music in which new ideas are constantly stated without repetition. Most frequently this is found as through-composed accompaniment for nonstanzaic song text, or instrumental continuous-development music of the twentieth century.

Binary Form

AB or *AABB*

An example of additive music that has only two contrasting sections. Although the A and B sections may be repeated, the composition concludes with a final statement of the second section.

Rounded Binary Form

$$A \quad B \quad ^1/_2A$$
$$aa \quad bb \quad a$$

The most rudimentary return form in which the simple binary form is modified by a brief reference to the initial thematic material of the *A* section.

Return Form

$$A\ B\ A$$

Simple ternary form in which the material stated at the beginning returns to conclude the work.

Da Capo Aria Form

$$A\ B\ A'$$

A vocal form frequently used in opera in which the original material returns after a contrasting section. The restatement appears in a varied form with ornamentation.

Thirty-Two-Bar Pop Song Form

$$A\ A\ B\ A$$

A repetition of the initial eight-bar theme before a contrasting section. The initial material concludes the work. Used in pop songs and jazz charts.

Minuet And Trio Form

$$A \qquad\qquad B \qquad\qquad A$$
$$aa\ ba\ ba \qquad cc\ dc\ dc \qquad aba$$

Minuet and trio form is a compound form in that it is ternary at the large sectional level and a rounded binary form within each section. The minuet and trio appears most often as the third movement of a symphony.

Rondo Form

$$A\ B\ A\ B\ A,\ A\ B\ A\ C\ A,\ \text{etc.}$$

Rondo form is a compound return form that features contrasting episodic material interspersed between recurring statements of the initial material. Rondos are frequently used as the fourth movement of symphonies.

Variation

A A' A" A''' etc.

Sectional variation form presents a theme and then varies certain features of that theme while generally maintaining the harmonic structure and phrase length of the initial idea.

Continuous Variation

Passacaglia or chaconne form in which either a bass line or a harmonic pattern is repeated throughout the composition as a foundation for various alterations of the harmonic, melodic, or rhythmic aspects.

Fugue

Voice 1:	Subject-Countersubject		Episode
	I		
Voice 2:		Answer-Countersubject	Episode
		V	
Voice 3:			Subject-Countersubject
			I

Fugue is more a process or technique than a form. A theme or fugal subject is developed in imitation and contrasted with episodic material before the final return of the initial material.

Sonata Form

(INTRODUCTION)	EXPOSITION	EXPOSITION
	Theme 1, Bridge, Theme 2, Codetta	(repeated)

DEVELOPMENT	RECAPITULATION	CODA
	Theme 1, Bridge, Theme 2, Codetta	

Sonata form is a compound developmental form that contrasts an energetic theme in the tonic key with a lyrical theme in the dominant or relative major key. These ideas are explored in a development that reconciles itself in the restatement of the opening material known as the recapitulation.

CHAPTER 9

Song: The Union of Music and Text

There is a special relationship between the spoken word and musical sound. Verbal and musical utterances both enable communication between humans, but they do so on two different planes and through very different languages. The specific and concrete language of the word is in sharp contrast to the directly affective but nonspecific meaning intrinsic to music. However, when melody and text are joined in the medium of song, the union magically acquires the ability to appeal to both the right and left hemispheres of the brain. Communication takes place in a directly intuitive mode as well as through logic-based channels. The felicitous union of verbal and musical language conveys a depth of meaning not available to either language in isolation.

The earliest surviving musical artifacts and the most ancient descriptive musical treatises demonstrate early human awareness of the expressive possibilities of tune and text. The voice is our first instrument—a natural extension of the body. In the accents and intonation of our daily speech we find the incipient rhythms and melodies of our music. There is only a fine line separating the animated call of a tobacco auctioneer or the intensified speech of Gregorian chant from the more

115

developed melody of our songs. Despite protestations to the contrary—
"I couldn't carry a tune in a wheelbarrow!"—singing is a natural and
instinctive expression of the human condition.

Elements of Vocal Music

Rhythmic Relationship

Emotion in speech and meaning in music are both largely controlled by the articulation of rhythm. Rhythm in speech may be discussed in terms of accented and unaccented syllables. The accented syllables receive an agogic stress (emphasis through increased duration) and are also accorded a slight rise in pitch and dynamic level. To demonstrate the importance of stress, try reading the preceding sentence in a monotone without stressing any of the syllables. It will sound peculiarly automated but, more importantly, you will have difficulty understanding the meaning of the words themselves.

Similarly, in a line of melody, certain pitches receive a stress effected by a slight extension of duration and an increase in dynamic intensity. If each note were to receive the same degree of stress, the music would have a boring regularity similar to that of speech uttered in a monotone. Meaning and vitality are imparted to both speech and music through the subtle play of expected and unexpected accents.

Meter

The regular pattern of stressed and unstressed syllables in both verbal and musical expression is known as meter. In verse, meter is described in terms of *feet* (units of stressed and unstressed syllables). These feet are then combined together in a larger unit known as a *verse* or *line*. A common meter found in English verse is *iambic tetrameter*, in which there are four iambs (an unaccented syllable followed by an accented one) in a line. The following example corresponds exactly to iambic tetrameter:

```
x   /   x   /   x   /   x   /
A-round the rough and rug-ged rocks,

x   /   x   /   x   /   x   /
the rag-ged ras-cal rude-ly ran.
```

In music, the meter most frequently employed in Euro-American art music is known as *common time*, or $\frac{4}{4}$. In its most regular form, common time consists of a measure (the unit corresponding to a foot of verse) containing an accented beat followed by three unaccented beats. This measure is then combined in a larger entity called a phrase (analogous to a line of verse). A regular phrase most often contains four measures of common time. Thus, spoken iambic tetrameter is comparable to a musical phrase containing four measures in common time.

Phrase and Strophe

Just as sentences are combined to form a larger cohesive unit of meaning called a paragraph, so single musical phrases, paired with the corresponding line or verse of text, are then combined in a larger whole known as a *strophe* or *stanza*. The most common stanzaic arrangement consists of four melodic phrases with four lines of verse. Musically, these are arranged as two pairs of musical phrases known as antecedent and consequent. Similarly, in text itself, a stanza is usually arranged in two pairs of verse lines, each of which is called a *couplet*.

Cadence

The end of the first antecedent-consequent pair comes to a brief pause called the *midpoint cadence*. The second pair of antecedent-consequent phrases concludes with another pause known as the *final cadence*. These two resting points articulate and give form to the musical expression. Similarly, each couplet of text is punctuated by a cadence, usually represented at the midpoint as a comma, and at the end as a period.

Marriage of Tune and Text

While we recognize and classify regular metric patterns in speech and music, in actual practice we find that realistic speech or naturally expressive music cannot be constrained by simple meter. Exact repetition of a regular meter in text or music would be almost as monotonous as no pattern of accents at all. The great challenge in matching tune to text is to accommodate both the subtleties of spoken language and the musical demands—to match the accents inherent in the text with those implied by the music. This is the level at which the real marriage of the text and tune takes place. Just as a husband and wife need to make compromises with one another to lead a harmonious life together, so must the librettist (writer of text intended to be set for music) and the composer accommodate one another to achieve harmonious song.

Vocal Musical Forms Through the Ages

Instrumental music, because of its generally abstract nature and its functional relationship with dance, has developed various forms and genres that are most idiomatic to instrumental expression. Likewise, vocal music, though it may often be coupled with instrumental music, has developed its own particular forms and genres that accommodate the expressive union of text and music. The presence of text, with its particular structure, demands a response from musical form. The form of the text should shape the form of the music and the textual design should correspond to the contour of the music. In this way the meaning of each is articulated and amplified. For instance, if a line of text is repeated it strongly implies that the corresponding phrase in the music should also be repeated. Thus, the development of vocal music forms is simultaneous with that of musical text forms.

Medieval Period

Medieval Chant

The earliest body of song preserved in notated form is the *Gregorian chant* of the Roman Catholic church. Sometimes referred to as *plainsong* or *plain chant*, Gregorian chant was so named in honor of

Pope Gregory I (r. 590–604) who organized approximately three thousand melodies within the context of Roman Catholic worship. This chant fuses ancient melodies adapted from the oral tradition of Hebraic, Greek, and Eastern sources with liturgical prayers of the early Christian church.

Plainchant is a remarkable fusion of text and tune sublimated to the function of prayer. The Latin text completely dictates the musical rhythm—text and tune rhythms correspond exactly. Likewise, the melodic contour is shaped by the direction of the words. The words are generally set *syllabically* (one syllable per note) so that the text is easily comprehended. Some of the chant is also set *melismatically* (one syllable sustained over several notes) so that important syllables can be ornamented and emphasized.

Traditionally sung *a capella* (unaccompanied by instruments) by male choir, the simple *monophonic* (consisting of a single melodic line) texture focuses attention on the meaning of the words. The music in no way detracts from the text, but rather serves merely to intensify the meaning of the prayer. There are no dynamics or accents other than the natural ones produced in speech, but there are several musical textures that enhance the expressivity of the text. In addition to *unison* singing (all voices singing the melody simultaneously), there are responsorial passages in which a soloist alternates with the choir, and antiphonal sections in which choirs respond to one another.

Secular Medieval Song Forms

Although chant dominated the sacred musical landscape of the medieval period, other song forms were also used in secular expression. Musicians employed musical structures that strongly reflected the text form. The *virelais*, for instance, consisted of a characteristic *Abba* stanza in which *A* is a refrain, *b* is the first line of the strophe (which is then repeated), and *a* is the last line of the strophe (which contains the same melody of the refrain). Another popular literary and musical form was the *rondeaux*, which had an *ABaAabAB* form in which the uppercase letters represent refrains.

Vast numbers of songs were written by secular musicians called *troubadours* (in southern France), *trouvères* (in northern France), and *minnesingers* (in Germany). Nonetheless, Gregorian chant was the single most important song form of the Middle Ages. Since then, chant has continued to exert its influence. It remains a part of contemporary Roman Catholic liturgy, although the original Latin text has been translated into vernacular languages.

The Renaissance

The Renaissance period (1450–1600) can be considered the golden era of choral music. During the Renaissance, vocal music—specifically, polyphonic choral music—was the dominant style of the era. Although sacred music did not dominate musical style as it had in the medieval period, ecclesiastical choral music was still the principal focus for composition. Burgeoning humanist awareness kindled a sensitivity to language and the delicate relationship between music and text. This awareness found expression in the mass and culminated in the exquisite motets of Josquin des Prez and the dramatic word painting of later madrigalists.

The Mass

A portion of the medieval Gregorian chant concerned itself with the central rite of the Roman Catholic church—the reenactment of the Last Supper of Christ as expressed in the breaking of bread and the drinking of wine at the Eucharist. During the Renaissance, unified settings of the various sections comprising the ordinary of the mass became a focus for composers. While various prayers and readings, known as the *proper*, changed on a daily basis, the *ordinary* of the Mass, consisting of the *Kyrie, Gloria, Credo, Sanctus*, and *Agnus Dei*, remained the same from day to day. Since the ordinary could be used on a daily basis, it made sense for composers to lavish care and attention on those prayers that would be sung most often. For this reason, the mass was the single most important large form for musical composition during the Renaissance.

The text of the ordinary established the musical form of the mass. Containing a sequence of five separate prayers, the overall musical form similarly consisted of a multimovement work composed of five distinct yet integrated movements. The threefold repetition of the opening *Kyrie Eleison* (Lord Have Mercy) suggested a tripartite form in a penitential mood. The following *Gloria* (Glory to God in the Highest) was uplifting in character and featured some internal repetition. The *Credo* (I Believe) was an extended statement of faith that required a more declamatory and through-composed style. The final *Agnus Dei* (Lamb of God) was pastoral in character with a tripartite form that reflected back to the initial *Kyrie* structure.

The Motet

The motet was a polyphonic choral form in which the various voice parts were added to a preexisting chant melody sung in the tenor voice. The motet was sacred music, but it was nonliturgical because it was not part of the Mass. Frequently the motet contained a number of different texts underlying each vocal line. This sounds extremely confusing to us today. With so many different texts being sung at the same time, how could anyone possibly comprehend the words or understand what the work meant? We can only conjecture that the musical sense was more important than the clarity of the words, and that the contemporary audience was sufficiently familiar with the words and did not need to follow them explicitly.

Techniques for Relating Music to Text. Gradually the motet, influenced by secular forms such as the chanson, devoted more attention to the relationship between words and music and, in the hands of master composers such as Josquin des Prez, the music reflected the rhythm and sense of the text. Two important means to this end were the use of homophonic texture and word-painting techniques.

Homophonic Texture. This technique, in which all of the voices move together simultaneously, improved the clarity of the text and allowed important declamatory text statements to be contrasted with more florid polyphonic sections.

Word-Painting Techniques. Word painting involved musical representation of text images, such as a rising scale to accompany the word "ascendit" (ascended).

Motet Form. There was no rigid formula or mold according to which the motet was structured. In general, however, motets were distinguished from other forms by the following five characteristics:

1. They were divided into two or three separate sections called *pars* (parts).

2. The dominant texture featured imitative and polyphonic writing for three or more voice lines, with some later use of homophonic texture for special declamatory passages.

3. Motets were constructed upon the foundation of the musical structure imparted by the tenor line which contained a preexisting Gregorian chant.

4. The text was the important organizing feature. This became even more true as humanist concern with language influenced the union of music and words.

5. The form, based on the text, was generally through-composed.

The Madrigal

The dominant secular form of the Renaissance was the madrigal. Since sacred music was a conservative tradition, composers used the madrigal as the vehicle for their more experimental concepts and techniques. As with the motet, there was no single identifiable mold or form, but there were some distinguishing characteristics that separated the madrigal from other contemporary forms.

1. The madrigal text was set in the vernacular rather than in Latin.

2. Composers stressed application of word-painting technique and a heightened sensitivity to text.

3. Bright, dancelike rhythms were often used.

4. The dominant texture was homophonic.

5. The form, based around the text, frequently employed strophic form and sometimes included refrains.

6. The melody was generally in the soprano voice.

The Baroque

Music in the medieval and Renaissance periods was almost synonymous with sacred vocal music—the medieval era was dominated by monophonic chant and the Renaissance by polyphonic mass and motet. During the baroque period (1600–1770), however, all that was to change forever. Instrumental music attained parity with vocal music, and secular music received as much, if not more, attention than sacred music. Still, it was the union of text and tune as embodied in opera that influenced all forms—sacred and secular, instrumental and vocal.

Sacred music is a conservative tradition, and composers in the baroque era still wrote in the Renaissance forms of the mass and motet. However, musicians began to concentrate on new sacred forms such as the oratorio and cantata, which were based on the solo vocal styles popularized by the secular opera.

Opera in the Baroque Period

Opera is a multimedia genre that fuses elements of all the arts: the expressive movement of drama, the singing and instrumental accompaniment of music, the visual artistry of costumes and sets, the plot and libretto of the writer's craft, and the choreography of dance. At the heart of this lavish production, however, is the fragile yet magical union of tune and text.

Monody. Opera developed in Florence, Italy, in the beginning of the seventeenth century when a group of artists known as the Camerata initiated a new style of singing called monody. Monody was solo song, closely patterned after natural speech rhythm and supported by sparse instrumental accompaniment. This new style of singing was soon employed in longer dramatic works based on mythological stories, and, in the hands of composers such as Caccini and Monteverdi, the genre of opera evolved.

Monody was a rather dry and uninteresting singing style. Although perfectly suited to narrative with its clearly declamatory technique, it was somewhat monotonous from the musical point of view. For that reason, Monteverdi alternated sections of monody with songlike passages known as arias. In this way, the two major operatic forms became established. Recitative, based on monody, advanced the story line and arias commented on the action through glorious song.

Recitative. Recitative was through-composed and based entirely on the text. There was no explicit beat; the rhythm was based entirely on the accents of the words. The melodic shape was largely stagnant because the singer maintained a single note for much of the narrative, varying the contour only for emphasis or at cadential points.

Aria. The aria, being reflective rather than narrative, was based on musical considerations rather than those of text. There was no clearly defined text or musical form at first, but by the middle of the seventeenth century, the aria had gradually evolved into a three-part *ABA* form known as the *da capo* aria. In the *da capo*, the first section is repeated at the conclusion of a contrasting second section but, upon its return, the reprise is heavily ornamented, displaying the virtuosic abilities of the singer.

Oratorio

Opera was such a dominant force during the baroque that the drama, form, and vocal styles characteristic of opera strongly influenced other musical genres as well. Oratorio, indeed, was similar to opera, lacking only the elaborate staging and complex secular plots. Designed to replace opera performances during the penitential liturgical season of Lent, oratorio presented all the recitatives, arias, and choruses characteristic of opera, but it did so without the sets, costumes, dance, and acting of the secular stage. Because the drama had to be implicit in the music rather than explicitly portrayed on the stage, composers such as Handel employed every possible musical device to extract the dramatic intensity of the text.

Cantata

In general shape, the cantata is very much like the oratorio. Cantatas are either sacred or secular narratives containing solo arias, recitative, and chorus numbers in an unstaged production. However, the cantata is on a much smaller scale. Whereas a mature oratorio such as Handel's *Messiah* contains fifty-three movements, a typical cantata usually opens with a chorus, proceeds through three arias and three recitatives, and concludes with a final chorus.

Classic Period

The classic period (1750–1828) is most closely associated with instrumental music works. Composers working in a conservative sacred style continued to write masses, oratorios, and anthems, but the most important genres and forms developed during this period include string quartets, symphonies, piano works, and concerti written for instrumental symphonic and chamber ensembles.

Of the vocal music composed during the classic period, there was choral music cast in forms that were relics of the Renaissance, opera that built upon and expanded baroque forms, and art song that drew upon indigenous folk music and pointed toward the next period. More importantly, however, the instrumental music was heavily influenced by vocal style. The gracious and elegant string lines of a Mozart symphony have more than a little in common with his operatic arias.

Opera in the Classic Period

Opera continued to be the dominant form of secular vocal music, but as the century progressed, two different styles emerged: opera seria and opera buffa.

Opera Seria. The older style, known as opera seria, was most associated with the southern Italian city of Naples. In opera seria, numbers of arias are improbably bound together through convoluted plots. The roles of plot, narrative recitative, and sheer musical expression were diminished in favor of virtuosic, heavily ornamented arias that were sung by both females and *castrati* (male singers neutered before puberty to preserve the soprano or contralto range of their voices).

Opera Buffa. The second style of opera, known as opera buffa, grew out of comic scenes inserted in opera seria to provide amusing interludes. These scenes acquired an independent existence, and a form of opera emerged that stressed more natural plots, earthier characters, and comic situations.

Parlando. Singing styles changed to accomodate buffa style. Less emphasis was placed on florid arias, ensemble choruses were emphasized, and a new form of recitative, called parlando was developed.

Parlando featured a syllabically set, speechlike delivery that raced along with an effect not unlike that of a machine gun.

Art Song

Art song, independent vocal compositions not attached to larger multimovement works, received some attention during the classic period. Especially important were the *lied* of Germany, which was to flower during the subsequent romantic era. Art songs tended to be relatively simple works for voice and piano, written in emulation of traditional folk song. Formally, the lied tended to be strophic with two pairs of rhymed couplets in each stanza. Other song structures included rounded two-part form (*ABA*) after the fashion of the *da capo* aria, and five-part song form (*ABACA*) along the lines of instrumental rondo form.

Romantic Period

Literature played a major role in shaping the musical art of the romantic period (1826–1900). The contemporary poetry and prose directly affected musical ideas and attitudes and provided plots for opera, texts for song, programs for symphonies, and structure for tone poems. Although instrumental music was still the favored medium, the solo art song also claimed an important portion of the repertoire, and opera continued to evolve as well.

Lied

The romantic fascination with literature manifested itself especially in the German lied (plural *lieder*) of composers such as Franz Schubert, and in the French *chansons* of composers such as Fauré and Duparc. In these solo vocal works with accompaniment, composers strove for a perfect balance between the solo vocal line and the piano or orchestral accompaniment. Word painting, through which composers attempted to portray specific concrete images through musical terms, was a favored accompaniment device. The art song repertoire is filled with illustrations of word painting, such as the galloping triplets in the piano accompaniment that portray the horse in Schubert's "Erlkönig." The story of the Erlkönig is made explicit through the music as well as the text. The musical narrative of the piano accompaniment is no less important than the tale told through the sung text.

Song Cycles

Lieder were sometimes incorporated into larger collections of songs known as song cycles. A number of songs, each a separate and independent composition, were loosely bound together to form a larger entity on the basis of text source or central concept. Most cycles were organized around the work of a single author, such as Brahms's *Magelone* cycle based on poems by Ludwig Tieck, and Robert Schumann's *Dichterliebe*. Other song cycles were united through a central theme or topic, such as Schubert's *Winterreise* cycle, which depicts encroaching madness.

Opera in the Romantic Period

As literature and drama dominated the intellectual landscape of the romantic period, opera, naturally, was a focus for the large-scale musical expression combining voice and orchestra. The movement was away from the artificial separation of aria and recitative and toward a flowing, seamless unity that ultimately coalesced in the Italian opera of Verdi and Puccini and in the *music dramas* of Richard Wagner. Just as the piano accompaniment became a full partner with the vocalist in lieder, so the orchestra acquired equal status with the singer in opera.

Leitmotif. Through the device of leitmotif, which associated a character or idea with a musical motive, Richard Wagner and other late romantic composers portrayed the operatic drama and narrative simultaneously. In such works, the voice was locked in an intimate embrace with the accompanying music. The vocal melody became simply another voice in the total fabric of the music drama. At the same time that the soloist and text explicated the story, the orchestra presented its own version of the story. The voice, tied to the text, offered a more literal interpretation, but the orchestra, free from the tyranny of the word, could more easily explicate the story on psychological and symbolic levels. The way in which a leitmotif was altered, developed, or combined with other leitmotifs mirrored the unfolding of the drama.

Sacred Music in the Romantic Period

Composers still worked in some of the older sacred choral forms, including oratorios, masses, requiem masses, and extended anthem or motetlike works. These compositions were marked by the drama and grand scale of the romantic period, and were usually intended for large choruses accompanied by full orchestras and organ. Although the text was sacred, these works most closely corresponded to secular style, and they were generally better suited to concert performance than performance in an actual liturgical situation.

Modern Period

The modern period (1900–to date) is a highly eclectic era, drawing influences from other times and cultures. Contemporary sounds are influenced by contemporary styles and trends, but they are also molded by the forms, styles, and sounds of the musical past. Composers of the past century have certainly developed new musical devices and ideals. New technological developments in sound production and reproduction have had a profound impact on musical composition. Much of our modern music may sound new, experimental, and original, but it is still inextricably linked with a chain of tradition forged from a musical past extending back to chant.

The voice is still our primary instrument—and, while there are now many ways of altering, simulating, and enhancing vocal sound, the basic vocal forms and genres have been preserved and developed. Art song may now feature electronic accompaniment rather than traditional acoustic instrumental accompaniment, but the song forms -strophic, through-composed, or sectional—have been maintained. The content has evolved but much of the form remains.

Context

The most important idea dominating vocal music form now appears to be the notion of context. Each text, each musical idea, bears the seeds of its own form. A composer does not attempt to pour the musical or textual material into a preconceived form but, rather, allows the material to shape itself. For that reason, modern art song is most frequently through-composed because it is based on poetry written in free verse rather than strophic or sectional form.

Vocalises

The concrete nature of the word and the abstract nature of music have always made the marriage of text and tune an uneasy, if interesting, union. The conflicting natures of the two languages have led to various compromises to effect a workable relationship. The voice is an instrument, but it is also the source of speech. One interesting modern development, based on isolated examples of the past, has been the liberation of the vocal sound from the confines of the word. Through the use of *vocables* (vocal sounds without meaning) rather than *lexicals* (words), musicians have invested the voice with the freedom of abstract expression. Similar to the nonrepresentational art of abstract expressionism, musical art may now use the voice as an idiomatic musical instrument free from the constraints imposed by text. Compositions written for voice in this style are referred to as *vocalises*, and jazz passages in this style are known as *scat singing*.

Song, the union of text and tune as expressed through the voice, marries two forms of communication—the concrete language of words and the abstract meaning of music. In this partnership it is usually the text that determines the form of the music. Thus, a special set of forms and genres intended for vocal rather than instrumental use developed during succeeding musical periods. While these forms evolved and developed in response to contemporary aesthetic demands, the ideal relationship of tune and text remains a harmonious match between the meter and intonation of the words and the contour and rhythm of the melody.

Part III:
The History of Music:
Periods and Styles

CHAPTER 10

Introduction to Music History

Periods of Musical History

Period	Range	Characteristics
Medieval	600–1450	Sacred music of Christian church; monophonic Gregorian chant
Renaissance	1450–1600	Sacred music; polyphonic choral style; dawning of humanism
Baroque	1600–1750	Drama and text in both sacred and secular music. Homophonic style; development of opera
Classic	1750–1828	Form and symmetry. Rise of instrumental music (e.g., the symphony)

| Romantic | 1828–1900 | Emotional, imaginative approach. Large-scale orchestral works with programmatic intent |
| Modern | 1900–to date | Plurality of approach. Influence of electronic technology and sound reproduction. Postmodern trend makes eclectic use of the past and blurs distinction between traditional, popular, and art music. |

Music functions within three distinct, yet interrelated categories: art, traditional, and popular. Art music *is the "cultivated" music of the Euro-American culture, transmitted though written notation and generally performed in a concert-style setting.* Traditional music *is the folk music of a culture, passed on orally, from person to person, and performed in an informal atmosphere.* Popular music *is created and marketed with commercial intent and disseminated through mass media. All three categories of music exist at the same time and they constantly interact with one another. Although most musical studies focus attention on high art styles and periods, it is important to remember that traditional and popular styles exist simultaneously. Their history is just not so well documented, and until recent times, their music was not preserved in written form.*

Art music is usually divided into six large time periods based on dominant aesthetic ideals and stylistic similarities. These periods are medieval (600–1450), Renaissance (1450–1600), baroque (1600–1750), classic (1750–1828), romantic (1828–1900), and modern (1900–to the present). The art music of these periods will be discussed in the chapters that follow.

Categories of Music

The three categories of music—art, traditional, and popular—have characteristics that clearly distinguish them from one another, as the following sections will show. However, these categories are not mutually exclusive. Composers of art music have often incorporated traditional music characteristics within their works; a well-known example is Aaron Copland's *Appalachian Spring*. Likewise, popular music has transformed art music to serve its own purposes in recordings such as Walter Murphy's "Fifth of Beethoven." Finally, traditional music has also embraced elements of art and popular art as shown in the folk parody "here comes the bride—big, fat, and wide" set to the wedding march from Wagner's *Lohengrin*. Spillover among these categories of music serves to refresh and revitalize each of these styles.

Art Music

Art music is the medium that is most commonly called "classical music." Unfortunately, this term creates a certain amount of confusion because what is called the "classic period" in music (1750–1828) represents only a fraction of the entire history of art music. "High art music" is less ambiguous, but this term also causes problems, because it becomes confused with the general category of "arts," of which music is merely one discipline. It also incorrectly implies that traditional or popular music cannot be artful or artistic. While no term is perfect, the expression "art music" will be used throughout this book in reference to the cultivated masterworks of the Euro-American tradition.

In the Euro-American tradition, art music is written music. It is passed on from person to person, from generation to generation, through a system of written notation in manuscript and published sheet music. It is performed by musicians who interpret the written notation and play what the symbols represent. It is composed by musicians who use the symbols to convey their musical ideas to others. It is the continuous record of Western culture as expressed through music and preserved through written notation.

This written tradition has been crucial to the evolution of art music. Musical notation enables composers both to preserve and to disseminate musical knowledge. Today, we are able to reconstruct the musical past by performing a centuries-old Renaissance motet in the style of the time. We are also able to spread contemporary ideas worldwide through printed scores. The individual musician does not necessarily have to travel—only the written score needs to make the trip for a performance to take place.

In function, art music seeks both to entertain and to enlighten an audience. Most often this takes place in a formal recreational setting such as a concert hall, but art music is also used to accompany ritual and ceremonial events such as worship services and coronations. In each case, however, the composer presents a personal and subjective voice that speaks to an audience. The audience may be comforted or confronted by the composer's personal vision, but if some communication has taken place between artist and audience, then the purpose of the music has been served.

The relationship of audience and performer in art music is well defined. In live presentation, there is usually a stage separating the performer from the audience. The music itself is the bridge, but there is a division between musician and listener that is rigidly maintained through physical distance, custom, and etiquette. Applause is customary at certain times, and relatively formal dress is often assumed for both the performer and the audience. Frequently it is this "cultural baggage" that makes art music seem initially intimidating to listeners nurtured on popular music.

Traditional Music

Traditional music is transmitted orally, rather than in written or printed form as is art music. Traditional music is folk music—music of the people. Whereas art music involves trained composers, skilled interpreters, and a knowledgeable audience, traditional music belongs equally to people of every level of musical ability. One does not need any special vocal training to sing a folk ballad, but to perform a Verdi aria properly requires professional vocal study.

Because traditional music is passed on orally through generations, there is no single "correct" version of a song or tune. Art music, in its written form (not necessarily as it is performed by musicians), presents a single definitive version. There are thousands of variations of the folk ballad "Barbara Allen" but there is only one definitive version of Beethoven's Fifth Symphony. (To serve their personal interpretation, conductors may make slight adjustments of tempo and dynamics in the

Beethoven work, but they also must strictly adhere to the notes and rhythm dictated by the score).

In traditional music, the performer and listener are one and the same. Everyone is an active participant, encouraged to sing or dance along with the music. Traditional music thrives in informal settings—places that are just a part of everyday life. Although it may be performed on stage, it is never completely natural in a setting that creates a barrier between musician and listener. Traditional music is seldom played in concert halls while art music is rarely performed on a back porch.

In contrast to the personal and subjective perspective of art music, traditional music presents an objective view. The writer presents a story or song with little personal intrusion upon the "facts." Likewise, the singer or instrumentalist presents the song objectively, neither adding to nor subtracting from the traditional version. The traditional performer is just one voice in a long line of voices that give expression to a song passed on in a timeless continuity. Improvisation and personal creativity, much prized in art music, are a destructive force in the transmission of traditional music. While folk musicians may certainly write new songs or personalize an older work with improvised ornaments, intentional alterations to existing songs are strongly discouraged by tradition.

Popular Music

Like traditional music, popular music is music of the people; unlike traditional music, however, popular music is intended to reach a large segment of the public and is disseminated through mass media. The success of popular music is measured by how wide an audience it reaches through published sheet music, recordings, radio airplay, and television performances. Art and traditional music reach a relatively small audience during a long period of time; popular music reaches a large audience but is generally heard for only a brief span of time—although some pop songs enjoy a long life as "standards" or "golden oldies."

Performers of art music interpret the composer's intentions through rather strict adherence to the printed score. They are merely the medium through which the composer's voice sounds across the ages. Traditional musicians are emotionally involved in the music, but they perform in an objective style because they see themselves as an extension of community expression rather than as entertainers. Pop musicians stress their personal interpretation of the music, reaching an audience through their individual conception of a song. Here, the song and the singer, the tune and the performer, are joined to entertain a broad spectrum of the listening public.

While certain examples of art music or traditional music might become popular, popular music is designed to be popular. It is consciously constructed to appeal to a large audience, and it is marketed and targeted as such. If art music is associated with complexity, and traditional music with earthiness, then popular music is distinguished by its directness of appeal.

Periods of Music History

Music history is a continuum—an uninterrupted flow of ideas and their expression that evolve through time. Changes in style, content, and form rarely happen suddenly and dramatically. Even though the process of change is gradual, historians like to divide the musical time line from A.D. 600 to the present into distinct segments. Certainly there was music prior to A.D. 600 as evidenced by surviving pictoral representations, ancient instruments, and writings about music. However, historians generally begin their study with the seventh century because the earliest substantial amount of notated music dates from that time.

The time line of music history is divided into six periods: medieval (600–1450), Renaissance (1450–1600), baroque (1600–1750), classic (1750–1828), romantic (1828–1900), and modern (twentieth century). The borders for these divisions are artificially drawn on the basis of broad stylistic trends. These trends mirror the social, cultural, and political movements of the time. Individual musicians have personal style characteristics, but the dominant cultural ideas extracted from all aspects of civilization shape the large identity of that period's music. The overarching philosophical concepts behind the literature, visual arts, drama, dance, and music of a period guide the course of the individual artist's work.

The *medieval* period was distinguished by an emphasis on sacred music of the Christian church and a style characterized by monophonic chant. The *Renaissance* was marked by an emerging emphasis on humanism and sacred music of a polyphonic choral style. The *baroque* period was shaped by a focus on drama and text in both sacred and secular music. The baroque emphasized a more homophonic style and the development of opera. The *classic* era reacted against the excesses of the baroque by stressing a new classicism of form and symmetry. This was particularly reflected in the rise of instrumental music such as the symphony. The *romantic* era was marked by a search for a more personal idiom. The classical restraint of the preceding era was tempered by a more personal and imaginative approach as expressed in the large-scale orchestral works infused with programmatic intent. The *modern* era is characterized by great diversity. The plurality of contemporary approach fuses an eclecticism of past styles with novel techniques that are highly shaped by technological developments, such as electronic music.

Although these time periods encompassing stylistic trends can be useful in examining the music they comprise, one should keep in mind that they are not absolute categories imposed on the composers. The terms were designed in retrospect by scholars who were attempting to describe a large-scale perspective. There is a certain amount of disagreement among historians concerning beginning and ending dates, and some scholars have even proposed alternative perspectives to the six periods. For instance, the musicologist Charles Hamm proposed a system that divides musical history into just three periods: antiquity to 1740 (sacred and aristocratic music), 1740 to 1950 (industrialization and public concerts), and 1950 to the present (music shaped by technology).

For convenience, the study of music may be divided into three types according to function: art, traditional, and popular. These musical types are not mutually exclusive—they nourish and draw inspiration from one another. Because the art music tradition has been documented for well over a thousand years, art music has been divided into chronological periods on the basis of broad stylistic trends. These six periods—medieval, Renaissance, baroque, classic, romantic, and modern—reflect the achievement of individual composers working within a cultural framework of art and ideas.

CHAPTER 11

The Medieval Period

Chronology of Events and Musicians

Middle Ages (600 A.D.–1450)

Gregory the Great becomes pope (590)
Charlemagne crowned king of Franks (768)
    Notker Balbulus (c. 840–912)
Battle of Hastings (1066)
First Crusade (1096)
    Abbess Hildegard von Bingen (1098–1179)
Ars Antiqua (1200–1300)

Léonin (c. 1159–1201)
Pérotin (d. 1238?)
Magna Carta (1215)
        Adam de la Halle (c. 1250–1306)
        Franco of Cologne (fl. 1250–1280)
Ars Nova (1300–1400)
        Philippe de Vitry (1291–1361)
        Petrus de Cruce (fl. c. 1290)
   Guillaume de Machaut (c. 1300–1377)
        Francesco Landini (c. 1325–1397)
Black Death (1350)
Hundred Years' War (1337–1453)

The chronological study of art music usually begins with the medieval period because the earliest notated music dates from this era. As the Roman Empire was disintegrating, the Roman Catholic church grew in importance and became the overarching institution of the time. Every aspect of culture in the Middle Ages was colored by the church, and music's primary function was to serve as an aspect of liturgical worship. The principal form that this music took was Gregorian chant, a monophonic vocal style that was the accompaniment to the central rites of the church. As the period progressed, the church's role waned, and new polyphonic musical structures arose in response to the emerging humanist thought of the Ars Nova period.

Historical Background

In the seventh century, the Roman Empire, stretching from Britain to Saharan Africa and from Spain to the Middle East had, to a great extent, disintegrated. Roman civilization, the thread of unity in the fabric of Western culture, was pulled apart through its own internal weakness and external invasion by barbarians. The Roman Empire was falling as the Roman Catholic church was rising. The emperor's military might was displaced by the pope's sacred authority.

Growth of the Church

Christianity, originally just a small heretical sect within the Jewish religion, swiftly grew to fill the void left by the declining empire. By the time Gregory the Great was installed as pope in 590, the flourishing Roman Catholic church was the supreme political and spiritual power in the Western world. All aspects of civilization were controlled by the church, and the vast number of monastaries, cathedrals, and churches that dotted the countryside served as centers of learning and seats of power. Education was the key to power, and only the clergy were educated. Therefore the ability to write—that magical ability to record and transmit thought—belonged solely to those who received an education within the walls of the church.

Serfdom

Life was a struggle for much of the population. The sharply defined class distinctions of the feudal system kept peasants in a state of servitude to the nobility and clergy. The rich were extremely wealthy while the poor were bound to the land as serfs with little or no hope for advancement. Wars, plague, hard work, poverty, and illiteracy were the lot of peasants in contrast to the nobles who lived a life of relative ease in their fortified castles. Given the despair of daily life, it was only natural that the church's promise of salvation and release from mortal cares appealed to downtrodden serfs. As miserable as this life was, there was still hope for the next world. Thus, the Roman Catholic church colored every aspect of life from the present to the hereafter.

Art and Music

The centrality of the church in medieval life also manifested itself in the artistic achievement of the period. Architects of the late Middle Ages designed glorious cathedrals whose spacious dimensions and high arching ceilings visually transported worshipers beyond daily life. Artists and artisans ornamented the interior with exquisite stained glass windows, monumental statuary, frescoes, mosaics, and paintings. Drama and dance were incorporated into the religious pageantry of miracle plays. Musicians provided an aural environment that bathed listeners in exalted communion with the divine.

Musical life during the medieval period was part of the church. Based on surviving music manuscripts, it appears that almost all contemporary music was designed for liturgical use in sacred worship. Certainly there was some secular music for recreational singing, dancing, and courtly ceremonial use, but most of this music was never written down and preserved. The church had the primary responsibility for training, patronage, and performance of musicians, and as a result, the essential function of music during the Middle Ages was the enhancement of religious observance.

Plainchant

During the fifth and sixth centuries, the church developed a liturgy of prayers used in conjunction with its central rites. These fixed prayers were set to music in a monophonic singing style that fused elements of speech and song. The shape of the melody underscored the important words and, in turn, the rhythm of the words dictated the flow of the melody. Text and tune were married in an articulate expression of sacred purpose. This style, known as plainchant or chant, clarified the meaning of the text and contributed toward the magnificent otherworldly atmosphere of the medieval church. Imagine the effect produced by the combination of the pungent incense, the ethereal illumination of the stained glass and flickering candles, the impressive costumery of the clergy and choir, together with the soaring, flowing chant melody. All aspects of the service were designed to intensify the sense of awe and wonder fostered by the church, and chant was the perfect musical accompaniment to this atmosphere.

Gregorian Chant

During the papacy of Pope Gregory I (r. 590–604) the liturgy of the Roman Catholic church was organized and codified. Prayers were designated for use on specified days and seasons appropriate to the liturgical year. As part of this process, the accumulation of plainchant melodies used in worship was also organized, and certain chants were coupled with specific prayers and rites. This highly structured collection of prayers and chants remained in use for over a thousand years until the reforms of Vatican II in the 1960s displaced Latin as the official language of worship.

Development

Because Gregorian chant was structured during Gregory's papacy, his name was thereafter coupled with it. It is important to realize, however, that Gregorian chant was not actually composed by Gregory himself. It was adapted from centuries of accumulated music drawn from the Hebrew tradition as well as from Greek and Oriental sources. Chant melodies and singing styles reflected a long-standing oral tradition of folk music until they were notated and set down in permanent form while Gregory was pope.

Style Characteristics

Upon listening to chant, one is initially impressed by what is missing rather than by what is present. Harmony, strongly defined rhythmic structure, musical instruments, and dynamic variety are all absent from this music. Medieval musical resources may seem limited and impoverished in comparison with our own modern standards, but it is important to realize that the musical style of the time was perfectly suited to its function. When judged on its own terms Gregorian chant is a beautiful style in which form and function are perfectly matched.

Melody

Chant is sung by male voices in a unison monophonic style. There are no additional harmony lines supporting the melody, and no musical instruments to support the voices. Female voices were missing because women were excluded from the clergy.

Rhythm

The rhythm feels very unstructured and flowing, because the words themselves dictate how long each note should be sustained. Early medieval theory had no system of note values or of meters to structure the rhythm, so the natural pulse and rhythm of spoken language defined the rhythm of singing style.

Range

The range of the melodies was narrow because they were based on the natural limitations of the average male voice. Usually chants hovered within a single octave. The melodic style was conjunct—that is the notes moved stepwise rather than in sudden disjunct intervals.

Dynamic Level

The dynamic level was essentially static with no sudden contrasts or dramatic crescendos. At most there is a slight surge toward the arch of the melodic contour. Some dynamic effect was achieved through responsorial singing in which a solo voice was answered by the choir.

Techniques

The text was set to music in one of four different techniques.

1. *Syllabic* style coupled one note with one syllable in a way that allowed the words to be easily understood.

2. *Melismatic* style, more ornate, matched one syllable with a long series of notes. This produced a jubilant sound, but also obscured the meaning of the text.

3. *Neumatic* technique was somewhere in between those of the first two styles. In neumatic chant several notes were paired with each syllable.

4. *Psalmodic* style employed a single pitch reiterated for several syllables. This style was most often used in recitation, in which the meaning of the text was particularly important.

Modes

Chant melodies are not constructed on the basis of our familiar major and minor scales. Instead they employ a system of modes that presents an unusual sound of antiquity to our modern ears. In construction, these eight-note modes resemble the pattern of whole and half steps found in the major and minor modes. However, each mode has a unique pattern of half steps, which results in its characteristic sound. The following figure illustrates the pitch organization of all the church modes. Note that the Ionian mode is the same as the major scale and the Aeolian mode is identical with the minor scale.

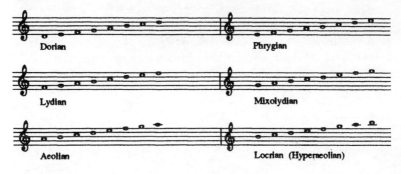

Organization of Church Modes

Uses of Gregorian Chant

The Roman Catholic liturgy was organized into two main divisions: celebration of the mass, and observance of the canonical hours.

The Mass

The mass is the central rite of the church, celebrating a reenactment of the Last Supper of Christ and his disciples. The mass comprises two series of prayers. Those that remain the same week after week are known as the ordinary. Other prayers vary according to the specific day or liturgical season (such as Easter or Christmas), and these are known as the proper.

The Ordinary. Prayers contained in the ordinary include the *Kyrie Eleison* (Lord Have Mercy), *Gloria* (Glory to God in the Highest), *Credo* (I Believe), *Sanctus* (Holy, Holy, Holy), and *Agnus Dei* (Lamb of God).

The Proper. Prayers contained in the proper of the mass include the Introit, Gradual, Alleluia (which is replaced by a Tract during penitential seasons), Offertory, and Communion.

Canonical Hours

In churches and monasteries that were devoted to strict observance, canonical hours were celebrated eight times each day. These worship hours—Matins (presunrise), Lauds (sunrise), Prime (6:00 A.M.), Terce (9:00 A.M.), Sext (12:00 noon), Nones (3:00 P.M.), Vespers (sunset) and Compline (evening)—included the singing of scriptural lessons and psalms designated specifically for use at that day and hour.

Chant Developments

For several hundred years the church maintained the tradition of singing Gregorian chant in strictly monophonic style. However, during the ninth century, a bold new musical texture called *organum* (plural *organa*) changed the direction of Western music forever.

Organum

Instead of simply presenting a single melodic line in unison, the chorus now split into two distinct parts—a melody and a harmony. The harmonic line, called the *duplum*, paralleled the contour of the *tenor* melody, but as it did so it was separated by the interval of a fourth or fifth. Thus, each group sang exactly the same melody, but they began on different notes. Organum was merely a first small step in the direction of independent polyphony, but it pointed the way to the development of harmony, which may be the single greatest contribution of Western art music.

Added Melody

During the years 900–1200 the organum became more complex. Instead of merely shadowing the tenor melody, the duplum acquired independence, becoming a separate melody in its own right. In the style that emerged, the chant was performed in slow drawn-out notes while the duplum melody poured out a rhapsodic stream of shorter notes in a more ornamented style. The original chant melody in the tenor voice (called the *cantus firmus*) was still the foundation of church music, but musicians were now more interested in experimenting with the expressive possibilities of these added melodic lines.

Notre Dame School

These experiments in Gregorian chant came to fruition at the Cathedral of Notre Dame in Paris around the middle of the twelfth century. The grandeur of this massive Gothic cathedral was well matched by the monumental nature of this emerging polyphonic style. Two choir directors, Léonin, and his successor, Pérotin, established a school of composition that was one of the crowning achievements of the medieval world. In their hands, organa became impressive polyphonic works written for three or four distinct voice parts.

Rhythmic Modes

Since the singers were no longer improvising in a simple one-to-one note relationship, a system of rhythm had to be devised that would coordinate all this activity. This system, called rhythmic modes, divided the beat into groups of three (symbolic of the Trinity) or groups of two (called imperfect and used only for secular music) and provided a notation framework that allowed the singers to interpret both the pitch and the rhythm from written score.

The Music of Léonin and Pérotin

We take our present system of musical notation for granted. It seems as though there have always been notes, clef signs, time signatures, sharps and flats, dynamic markings, and rhythmic indications. Contemporary composers indicate their intentions on paper, and performers interpret the composer's wishes with a great deal of accuracy and subtlety.

Such was not always the case, however. During the development of the Notre Dame school (c. 1170–1250) musicians were just coming to grips with the necessity of notation. Music prior to this time was transmitted orally, and even chant notation was merely an aid for memorizing the melodic line. It is an interesting question whether the music developed in response to developments in notation, or the notation evolved to accommodate the demands of the music. Whichever was the case, the complex music of Léonin and Pérotin required a system that could indicate both pitch and rhythm with some degree of accuracy, and with the development of that system, the Western world embarked on a path that led to further development of a harmonic and polyphonic style.

Secular Music

Although the church dominated the musical landscape, some secular music existed as well.

Song

Written and performed by professional entertainers called *jongleurs* or student musicians known as *goliards*, medieval songs concerned such timeless human topics as love, jealousy, and contemporary events. In a time long before newspapers and television, secular song served to transmit and preserve stories of current affairs while entertaining the nobles.

Other songs were composed by the nobility themselves. These aristocratic musicians known as *minnesingers* in Germany, *troubadours* in southern France, and *trouvères* in northern France, wrote artfully crafted music about love and chivalry. However, for the most part, these composers left the performance to lower-class attendants. One of the most important of these musicians was the *trouvère* Adam de la Halle. His play *Le Jeu de Robin et Marion* includes both lovely songs for soloists and chorus and vibrant dances for instrumentalists.

Style

Secular song style resembled monophonic chant, but the texts were in the vernacular rather than in Latin. Also, the settings tended to be syllabic rather than melismatic so that the audience could clearly understand the words. Song rhythms were notated in the same rhythmic modes used for chant, but the clear phrase structure and rhythmic vitality bore more resemblance to dance pieces.

Song Forms

Secular song forms were closely patterned on the text form, matching the phrase lengths, repetitions, and metric structure with corresponding musical ideas. *Refrains,* repeated text coupled with the same musical idea, were especially important in song forms of this period, and they were used to draw attention to the meaning of the text and strengthen musical coherence.

Canso. The most basic song form was a purely strophic canso consisting of six-line stanzas. The first two lines were repeated and then contrasted with a new melody for the final two lines (*AB AB CD*).

Virelai. The virelai generally had a refrain that was interjected between three different stanzas. Within each stanza the text contained a rhymed couplet, which was then followed by a repetition of the refrain. The text form was *AB CC AB AB*. The melodic structure paralleled the text exactly, with the second half of the strophe set to the same music as the refrain. This resulted in an *A b a A* structure.

Lai. Another form used extensively during the Ars Nova was the lai (lay). The poetry of the lai was usually directed toward a woman, and most frequently to the idealization of womankind—the Virgin Mary. Structurally, lais were based on strophes of irregular length from six to sixteen verses, which were musically set as *A A B B C C D D*. Each couplet of text was paired with a different melody.

Instrumental Music

Instruments were seldom used for church music, but they were certainly used to accompany both secular song and dance. String instruments included the *rebec*, a gourdlike bowed instrument with three to five strings imported from the Middle East by the crusades; the *harp*; the *vielle*, an early predecessor of the violin; and the *lute*, an ancestor of the guitar. Wind instruments included the *shawm*, a double-reed instrument similar to an oboe; small *portative* (portable) *organs*; *trumpets*; the *sackbut*, a precursor of the modern trombone; *recorders*; and the *oliphant horn*. There were also a variety of percussion instruments such as bells, tabors (drums), and tambourines.

Although there are very few examples of dance music existing in notated form, that does not mean that musicians of the Middle Ages were not engaged in recreational song and dance. It merely means that they did not bother to write the music down. The music was improvised and passed on orally.

Ars Nova

With the dawning of the fourteenth century, we enter the final chapter of medieval history and set the stage for the coming Renaissance era. The absolute power of the church was declining, and we see an awakening of humanism. This transitional era, known as the Ars Nova (New Art), is the era of Chaucer, Dante, and Boccaccio. The realism depicted in the literature reflected a century that witnessed the horror of the Black Plague and almost constant warfare, but the arts also reflected a concern for the here and now rather than the church's promised hereafter.

New Rhythmic Modes

Music of the Ars Nova was strongly shaped by new approaches to organization. Because the old rhythmic modes were no longer flexible enough to accommodate the rhythmic vitality and syncopation of the new style, a new system evolved to allow musicians to communicate their ideas. This rhythmic framework allowed for both perfect (triple) and duple (double) divisions of the beat in a notational style that began to resemble our present-day system.

New Organizational Techniques

Organization still depended on chant melody as the foundation upon which each additional part was constructed, but new techniques were also employed to provide a greater sense of unity and cohesion. As individual vocal lines acquired more independence, composers searched for ways of imparting a sense of organization to every aspect of their work.

Isorhythm

Patterns of rhythm (*talea*) and melody (*color*) were repeated in the added parts in a style known as isorhythm ("same rhythm"). This short-term repetition imparted an audible sense of organization to the work.

Imitation

Another technique—imitation—provided unity, as ideas were passed from part to part in echo fashion, thus interlocking the separate lines in an embrace of imitative polyphony.

Unified Mass and Guillaume de Machaut

Organizational principles were applied to large formal structures as well. For the first time, the mass itself was conceived as a unified whole rather than as a collection of separate movements. In the hands of the celebrated poet and musician Guillaume de Machaut (c. 1300–1377) the *Notre Dame Mass* became the first unified setting of the mass.

Music in the medieval period centered on its function as an adjunct to the Roman Catholic church. Beginning as a monophonic chant style for use in the mass and canonical hours, Gregorian chant eventually became the basis for a highly developed polyphonic style that reached fruition in the motet and mass structures of the Ars Nova. As the polyphonic style developed, the notational system also evolved, and by the end of the medieval period music had arrived at a pitch and rhythm system that began to resemble that of today.

CHAPTER 12

The Renaissance Period

Chronology of Events and Musicians

Renaissance (1450–1600)

Burgundian Period (transition from Middle Ages) (1400–1450)
John Dunstable (c. 1390–1453)
Guillaume Dufay (c. 1400–1474)
Ascent of the Medici in Florence (1400)
Gilles Binchois (c. 1400–1460)
Joan of Arc burned at Rouen (1431)
End of the Byzantine Empire (1453)

End of Hundred Years' War between England and France (1453)
Gutenberg prints his Bible (1454)
 Johannes Ockeghem (c. 1410–1496)
  Antoine Busnois (c. 1430–1492)
 Josquin des Prez (c. 1440–1521)
  Heinrich Isaac (c. 1450–1517)
  Jacob Obrecht (c. 1452–1505)
  Loyset Compère (c. 1440–1518)
  Jean Mouton (1459–1522)
  Pierre de La Rue (c. 1460–1518)
  Philippe Verdelot (c. 1480–1550)
  Ludwig Senfl (c. 1486–1542)
 Adrian Willaert (c. 1490–1562)
  John Taverner (c. 1490–1545)
  Costanzo Festa (c. 1490–1545)
Columbus lands in America (1492)
  Nicolas Gombert (c. 1495–1556)
  Johann Walter (1496–1570)
William Shakespeare born (1564)
  Christopher Tye (c. 1500–1572)
 Thomas Tallis (c. 1505–1585)
  Jacobus Clemens (1510–1556)
  Andrea Gabrieli (c. 1510–1586)
  Antonio de Cabezón (1510–1566)
  Cipriano de Rore (1516–1565)
Martin Luther posts his ninety-five theses (1517)
  Giovanni da Palestrina (c. 1525–1594)
  Orlando di Lasso (1532–1594)
King Henry VIII marries Jane Seymour, his third wife (1536)
  William Byrd (1543–1623)
Council of Trent (1545–1563)
  Tomás Luis de Victoria (1548–1611)
 Giovanni Gabrieli (c. 1553–1612)
  Thomas Morley (1557–1602)
  Carlo Gesualdo (c. 1561–1613)
  John Dowland (1563–1626)
  John Bull (c. 1562–1628)

Claudio Monteverdi (1567–1643)
Thomas Campion (1567–1620)
Thomas Tomkins (1572–1656)
Thomas Weelkes (c. 1575–1623)
Orlando Gibbons (1583–1625)

The French word renaissance, *meaning "rebirth," is a well-chosen name for the period spanning the years 1450–1600. The Renaissance was a cultural awakening—a time of great intellectual achievement, scientific discovery, and artistic growth. Drawing upon classical Greek and Roman models for inspiration and guidance, Renaissance culture was strongly influenced by humanist philosophy that stressed an awareness of individual potential. Medieval Catholicism, rooted in faith in the hereafter, was replaced by Renaissance interest in mankind during the here and now.*

The Roman Catholic church still exerted considerable influence upon society, but the church's primacy was now tempered by the emerging spirit of humanism, and was further diminished by the challenges of the Protestant Reformation. Science, philosophy, world exploration, and an appreciation of the arts were encouraged by the courts. Creative individuals such as the explorer Christopher Columbus and the artist-inventor Leonardo da Vinci arose. Their vision of humanity and curiosity about the world replaced the mysticism and ignorance of the Middle Ages.

The new balance between church and court, between sacred and secular life, was reflected in the music. Musicians evolved an elaborate polyphonic vocal style composed for the mass and motets, but they also developed new genres of secular music for courtly entertainment, and composed purely instrumental music for dance as well.

In many ways, the Renaissance can be considered the gateway to the modern musical world. Music theory, notation, harmony, instruments, and genres all begin to take on forms that seem familiar to us today, and with the invention of movable type (c. 1450), editions of music published during the fifteenth and sixteenth centuries were widely disseminated and preserved for posterity.

Historical Background

The Ars Nova period of fourteenth-century France initiated a transition that led European musical culture forth from the darkness of the medieval world into the bright new vistas of the Renaissance. The thirteenth century was a relatively stable period, but events of the fourteenth century, such as the Black Plague (1348–1350) and the Hundred Years' War (1337–1453) led to changes in the accepted order. Feudal villages were replaced by cities populated by an emerging middle class. In a church schism the total power of the papacy in Rome was fractured by the counterclaims of popes in Avignon. Humanism, a philosophy that placed mankind at the center of the universe and stressed human potential, began to assert a dominant influence upon all aspects of learning. Writers such as Dante (*Divina Commedia*, begun c. 1307), and Chaucer (*Canterbury Tales* begun 1386), and poet-musicians such as Guillaume de Machaut (c. 1300–1377) and Philippe de Vitry (1291–1361) developed music and poetry within the new humanist aesthetic, and brought the Middle Ages to the threshold of the cultural rebirth that marked the Renaissance.

Burgundy

The artistic development inaugurated during the Ars Nova in France continued in the lowlands areas of Burgundy (present-day Belgium, the Netherlands, and northern France) during the first half of the fifteenth century.

Cosmopolitan Influences

During the enlightened reigns of the powerful dukes Philip the Good (r.1419–1467) and Charles the Bold (r.1467–1477), the arts were strongly encouraged and cultivated for both secular and sacred use. The royal Burgundian court became a magnet, drawing composers and musicians from all over Europe. Here in the lowlands, the Mediterranean temperament intermingled with that of the northern French, resulting in a music marked by the combination of Latin melodic passion and Gallic formal restraint.

For the first time in musical history, a cosmopolitan style emerged in which German, English, Portuguese, Spanish, French, and Italian musicians wrote in a common idiom. Burgundy was the center of the style, but the relative ease of travel and the availability of printed music soon spread it across Europe.

Burgundian Style Characteristics

Four-Part Texture

Burgundian music, as represented by the works of composers such as Gilles Binchois (c. 1400–1460), Guillaume Dufay (c.1400–1474), and Antoine Busnois (d. 1492) was still intended for unaccompanied (a capella) choir, but the characteristic sonority was becoming more modern-sounding. In part, this was due to the addition of a new vocal line, called the *bass*, below the tenor. The new four-part texture (superius, altus, tenor, bassus) had a richer sound than the earlier three-voice texture of the Ars Nova.

Fauxbourdon

Another stylistic contribution that added warmth to the sound was the use of fauxbourdon. Fauxbourdon ("false bass") was the practice of doubling the melody at the interval of a sixth below the melody. This produced a chord in first inversion in which the melody was in the superius (no longer in the tenor), and the resultant harmony was based on the more modern triadic harmony. Composers continued to think in a linear polyphonic mode, but the vertical aspects of harmony became more important as they composed all the parts simultaneously rather than adding one line at a time in relation to the tenor voice.

Landini Cadence

A final distinguishing characteristic of Burgundian music is a special cadential formula known as the Landini cadence. Just as a sentence of prose concludes with a period, so composers indicate their punctuation at the end of a musical section through a cadence idea. The Landini cadence consists of a move from the leading tone (the seventh degree of the scale) down to the sixth, followed by a leap up to the final note of resolution (the tonic).

Vocal Genres

Burgundian composers continued to work in the earlier vocal genres, but they added their own refinements. The mass was invested with more unity because composers now maintained a single melody in the tenor voice for all movements of the mass. This style, referred to as *cantus firmus*, provided a central point of reference for the imitative work in the other three voices. Interestingly, the cantus firmus could now be taken from secular music as well as Gregorian chant. One of the most popular tunes, a song called "L'homme Armé" ("The Armed Man"), was used as the basis for numerous masses.

Chansons. The chanson ("song") was perhaps the most important of the Burgundian genres. Chansons were three-voice secular works in which the music closely mirrored the meaning of the French poetic text. The text, usually an expression of love, was in *rondeau* form with a two-line refrain (*A B a A a b A B*). Although they may have been performed entirely by voices, the usual presentation probably featured a solo voice on the top (superius) line with the bottom two polyphonic lines played by instruments.

Motets. The motet continued its importance during this period, although now it employed a single Latin text for all of the parts rather than the mixture of languages and texts of earlier times. Style characteristics of the mass were also transferred to the motet. There was a cantus firmus running through the tenor line, and the other voices wove about the tenor in imitative polyphony. As with the chanson, the melody in the soprano was emphasized, and instruments might have doubled or even replaced some of the parts.

Flanders

About midway through the fifteenth century, the center of musical culture moved south from Burgundy to what is now northern Belgium and northern France. Flemish composers dominated the musical life of Europe, but they seldom lived at home. In fact, most of these musicians lived and worked in Italy where they were supported by ruling families who acquired their wealth through trade. The Medici in Florence, the Sforza in Milan, the Este in Ferrara, and the Gonzaga in Mantua all maintained large musical ensembles that almost entirely consisted of Flemish musicians and composers.

Italian Influence

The Flemish music—orderly, intricate, and polyphonic—continued to thrive in Italy, where it dominated musical culture until mid-century. Culture is not a one-way street, however, and there was a healthy exchange of musical ideas between Italian and Flemish musicians. The Italian musical style—homophonic, gracefully melodic, and infused with dance rhythms—contributed a warmth of sound and intimacy to the complex northern style. Once again, the Mediterranean mingled with the north, resulting in a new international language that created the "golden age of choral music."

Style Characteristics

Although there was certainly instrumental music designed for courtly dancing or ceremonial use, the dominant musical sound was still the unaccompanied choir. Instruments may have been used to double the vocal lines, but the favored medium was a capella voices equally balanced in four parts: superius, altus, tenor, and bassus.

Imitation

In the past the tenor had held the cantus firmus melody in long sustained notes, but Flemish composers, in the search for unity and balance, bounced the melodic idea back and forth among all the voices so that the listener's attention constantly shifted between successive entries of the melody. This imitation was really the basis of the entire sound. One line of text was set to a melody and then each successive voice imitated the original melody in turn while the original statement continued in overlapping counterpoint. At the end of each section of text, the music cadenced before another series of imitative entries began, rather like a complex version of "Row, Row, Row Your Boat."

Contrapuntal Techniques

In order to structure the work and relate the cantus firmus melody to every vocal line, composers came to rely on a set of contrapuntal techniques to integrate the cantus melody. These compositional tricks for structuring the relationship of each note against the other imparted coherence to the work, but they were not necessarily audible to the listener. In fact, composers sometimes concealed the directions for working them out in riddles and cryptic clues.

Following is a descriptive list of techniques through which Flemish composers developed their contrapuntal style.

Canon. Canon is the use of the same melody in different voices as the voices enter at successive time intervals. The familiar "Row, Row, Row Your Boat" sung as a round is an example of a canon. The canon voices may enter on the same pitch or they may enter on different pitch levels (transposed).

Augmentation. Augmentation increases the duration of each note by a uniform proportion. For instance, if a melody contains eighth notes and quarter notes, an augmented version of the melody might substitute quarter notes for the eighth notes and half notes for quarter notes, thereby doubling the value of each note. This would make the melody seem to move half as quickly, but since the intervals are the same, a listener would perceive it as closely related to the original melody.

Diminution. Diminution is the opposite of augmentation. In diminution, each note value is decreased by a constant proportion. Thus, if we take the same original melody notated in eighth and quarter notes, diminution by one half would replace the eighth notes with sixteenth notes, and the quarter notes with eighth notes. The melody would move twice as quickly, but the listener would still perceive the tune as being essentially the same.

Inversion. Inversion is somewhat like a mirror image of the original melody. Instead of changing time values as augmentation and diminution do, inversion reverses the direction of the melodic intervals. Where the original melody once climbed it would now descend; where it once leaped upward it would now jump down. For instance, if the first interval in the original melody was an ascent of a major third from the note C to E, in the inverted melody it would now descend a major third, from C down to A.

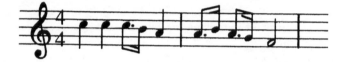

Retrograde. Retrograde turns the melody completely backward. The intervals are all intact, but the first note becomes the last note of the melody as it proceeds through time, backward. Retrograde versions of the melody are not easily perceived as being related to the original melody, but a sense of unity is still imparted because the intervals seem familiar. It is a little like Alice's adventures after she stepped through the looking glass—everything is familiar, but at the same time normal perspective has been slightly altered.

Cancrizans. Cancrizans (a Middle English word meaning "crab") combines the techniques of inversion and retrograde; the term was suggested by the curious walking motion of crabs, which actually walk sideways. Each interval changes direction, and the entire melody starts at the end and, note for note, works toward the beginning of the original melody. This technique can not really be comprehended by the listener, but it does impart an underlying level of organization that can be more easily grasped by looking at the notated manuscript.

Combinations of Techniques. These techniques may be combined to produce intricate structural orders. For instance, a canon on the original melody might be formed by taking a transposed form of the melody, inverting the intervals, putting the melody in retrograde, and finally augmenting the note values. Such complexity and logical order fascinated Flemish composers and reached its zenith in the works of Johannes Ockeghem (c. 1410–1496). It is important to remember, however, that the contrapuntal techniques were simply a means for constructing sublime, expressive music, not an end in themselves. Martin Luther, the theologian, commented concerning Josquin des Prez's use of compositional technique "He is the supreme master of the notes which must express whatever he wants them to. Other composers can only do what the notes want."

Musical Genres

The practice of sacred music is shaped by a conservative tradition. Changes in music designed for liturgical use occur gradually over a long period of time. On the other hand, experimental developments of style and genre are usually immediately incorporated into secular music. The innovations warmly embraced by courtly patrons may be received with suspicion and hostility by the church authorities. Thus, two different

Renaissance styles—sacred and secular—existed at the same time. Composers were compelled to modify their approach to accommodate either the conservative sacred polyphonic choral style or the emerging expressive homophonic secular practice.

Sacred Music

The mass and the motet were still the most important sacred musical genres. Composers' settings of the mass reflected a traditional and conservative approach, while the motet became the forum for innovative techniques.

Imitation Mass

The unvarying structure of the mass, the constancy of the text, and the solemnity of function were not conducive to musical experimentation in mass composition.

Flemish masses still used the cantus firmus techniques of the earlier Burgundian masters. By 1520, however, the new generation of composers went a step further and included various aspects of existing material as the foundation for their works. One common approach was to excerpt all the voice parts of a prior chanson, motet, or mass, rather than simply the melody. Other techniques included the use of various aspects of existing music, such as the texture, certain imitative statements, or characteristic gestures. This genre has also been called a parody mass, but a better term for it is imitation mass.

Composers such as Josquin des Prez (c. 1440–1521), Jacob Obrecht (c. 1452–1505), Johannes Ockeghem (c. 1410–1496), and Pierre de La Rue (c.1460–1518) dedicated a considerable portion of their time and energy to writing imitation masses.

The Counter-Reformation Mass

In the mid-sixteenth century the Roman Catholic church reacted against its clerical excesses and abuses, and matched the reforms of the Protestant Reformation with an internal restructuring known as the Counter Reformation. In an attempt to purge the liturgy of secular influence and musical complexity, The Council of Trent (1545–1563) stressed the importance of the text and the need for the words to be easily comprehended. This led to a more transparent style of counterpoint that was contrasted with large sections of familiar style homophonic texture.

In the hands of exceptional composers such as Giovanni da Palestrina (c. 1525–1594) the mass was a highly devotional and serene expression of the liturgy, perfectly suited to the austerity demanded by the Counter Reformation. Palestrina's flexible arched melodic lines, his studied use of consonance and dissonance, and his beautifully constructed harmonic sonorities became the model for generations of counterpoint teachers.

The Motet

The Early Motet. The early motet (from the French word meaning "word") frequently contained different texts in various languages for each voice part. It was not unusual to have a Latin-texted plainchant in the tenor voice, a Latin hymn in honor of the Virgin Mary in the alto, and a French love song in the top voice. This seems curious and strange to us today, but contemporary listeners found it perfectly normal to relate to the various texts simultaneously. Complexities of word setting and tone painting were simply not an important aspect of the music for early motet composers.

Musica Reservata. As humanism began to exert its influence, composers grew more attentive to text setting. A single Latin text, drawn from scriptural sources, replaced the multiplicity of texts found in the older-style motets. The single text was the motivating force for the motet. Each section of music was presented as a separate musical episode that attempted to highlight the clarity of the text as well as to convey the emotional impact of the words. This style of sensitive text representation came to be known as musica reservata.

Composers developed specific techniques for the musica reservata style. First, the clarity of the words was enhanced through various textures. Second, the natural speech rhythm was matched by melodic rhythm so that the words were correctly accented. Third, syllabic treatment of text and expressive figures were used to portray the message of the text.

Motets of Josquin. This new sensitivity to the text was most perfectly represented in the works of Josquin des Prez. Born near Hainaut in France around 1440, Josquin traveled and worked in Milan, at the papal chapel in Rome, at the court of Louis XII in France, and in Ferrara, and finally returned to his native France where he served as provost of Notre Dame until his death in 1521. Josquin wrote eighteen masses, one hundred motets, seventy chansons, and a number of other secular works as well, but his most striking compositions were his motets. Josquin's motet style is a virtual summary of all the aspects of musica reservata style. His techniques included the following:

1. *Alternating Syllabic and Melismatic Word Setting.* The syllabic style (one syllable per musical tone) was declamatory to strengthen the clarity of text, while the ornamental melismatic style was used primarily at cadence points to increase motion and build excitement.

2. *Use of Contrasting Textures.* To emphasize the text, Josquin used homophonic (familiar) style in which all the voices moved together in the same rhythm. The homophonic sound was now largely triadic in nature, resembling what was to become "hymn style." This homophonic style was surrounded by passages of imitative counterpoint in which a line of text was developed through a series of imitative points of entry.

3. *Use of Varied Choral Resources.* Josquin used various combinations of voices within his choirs that included three to six separate voice parts. The choir was often subdivided into various textures, such as duets and trios. In this way, antiphonal dialogue was produced by contrasting pairs of voices (such as tenor and bass) with other pairs of voices (such as alto and soprano).

4. *Use of Symbolic and Expressive Word-Painting Techniques.* Josquin often attempted to highlight the meaning of the text by coupling the words with a suitable musical gesture. For instance, a word like *descendit* ("descended") would be sung on a descending scale. One of the most famous examples of his expressive text setting is the motet *Absalom fili mi* ("Absalom My Son"). In this motet male voices sing in the lowest part of their range to portray David's sorrow, and the text "but let me

descend to the infernal reaches, weeping" descends both melodically and harmonically.

Other Sacred Genres

As the Renaissance period continued, various reformations of the church took place. Martin Luther began the Protestant Reformation in Germany in 1517, and King Henry VIII of England split from the Catholic church in 1531 (the Act of Uniformity in 1549 legally separated the English church from the Roman Catholic). Reformation of theology led to reformation of the liturgy and its attendant musical practices. In reponse, composers developed new genres that were suitable for the evolving styles of worship.

Chorale. Chorales were hymn tunes in which vernacular German text was set to music suitable for congregational singing. The melodies were adapted from secular folk songs, plainchant, and Latin hymns. Composers such as Johann Walther (1496–1570) arranged the melodies in strophic, four-part homophonic settings with clearly defined phrase and cadence structures. Chorales were designed to be "music for the people" rather than showpieces for professional chapel singers.

Anthem. In the Anglican church, the anthem replaced the motet as the primary genre. Full anthems closely resembled polyphonic motets in all aspects but the text, which was in English. The newer verse anthem style contrasted solo voices with full-chorus sections and instrumental accompaniment. English composers who were important to the development of the early anthem include Orlando Gibbons (1583–1625) and Thomas Tomkins (1572–1656).

Psalm Settings. While the German Reformation led to the chorale, the Protestant movement in France, the Netherlands, and Switzerland, begun by John Calvin (1509–1564), produced music in which rhymed, metrical, vernacular translations of biblical psalms were set to melodies suitable for congregational singing. The earliest psalter, published in 1562, contained text translated by Clement Marot and Thédore de Bèze set to melodies composed by Louis Bourgeois. As with the chorale, four-part choral arrangements in familiar style were eventually added for congregational use. Eventually the French psalter led to the development of English-language psalm settings such as the *Bay Psalm Book*, which was the first music printed in America.

Secular Music

The rise of humanism occasioned an increase in the amount of music composed purely for secular use. The same Italian courts that maintained chapel choirs also required music for ceremonial and entertainment purposes. Sacred music reflected the serenity, devotion, and conservative approach of the Flemish masters; the form grew directly out of the liturgical function. Composers had much more freedom with the form and style of secular genres. Music intended for singing and dancing easily absorbed elements of the progressive Italian style—simple diatonic melodies, homophonic texture, strong rhythmic patterns characteristic of dance, and syllabic text setting.

The Frottola

Frottole ("little mixtures") were Italian songs based on strophic text forms written toward the end of the fifteenth and the beginning of the sixteenth century. They were usually written in four parts in a simple chordal style that featured a melody in the top voice accompanied by the other parts, which were probably intended for performance by instruments. In character, the frottole were light and disarmingly naive, usually dedicated to the subject of love and courtly dalliance. Composition of frottole was generally an Italianate art that flourished particularly in the courts at Mantua and Ferrara, but Flemish composers also wrote frottole that influenced the composition of their more serious motets.

The Chanson

The French chanson was similar in many respects to the frottola. First, the melody was in the top voice with the other lines intended for instruments. Second, the texture was homophonic although some points of imitation were found as well. Third, the text was set syllabically. Finally, the subject matter concerned love. The chanson was distinguished from the Italian form by its French text; its short clearly delineated sections that were usually repeated in a pattern like *aabc*; and its descriptive or programmatic sounds. Janequin (c. 1485–1560) was especially given to imitating the sounds of birds or the noise of battle.

The Madrigal

The madrigal combined in a single genre the most prominent Italian stylistic characteristics—melodic interest in the soprano voice, homophonic texture, and vivid text expression. In the madrigal, all the most progressive and experimental tendencies of the Renaissance converged to form a genre that eventually dominated musical composition and made Italy the center of the musical world. More than any other genre, the madrigal leads us into the next musical era—the baroque.

Composers. The madrigal was originally an Italian form and it was dominated by Italian composers, including Cipriano de Rore (1516–1565); the Prince of Venosa, Carlo Gesualdo (c. 1561–1613), and Claudio Monteverdi (1567–1643). An English school of madrigalists also arose, and musicians such as Thomas Morley (1557–1602) wrote light ballet madrigals with "fa-la-la" style refrains, while Orlando Gibbons composed more austere "spiritual madrigals."

Style Characteristics

1. The form was through-composed, meaning that the music changed throughout the piece. (With strophic text, the music repeats throughout.)

2. The text was based on fine poetry, especially the sonnets of Petrarch (1304–1374).

3. The subject matter was love—but instead of the amatory dalliance of the frottola, this love was usually unrequited, and full of passionate longing.

4. This was chamber music, intended for a single voice per part. There were usually four parts, although later five- and six-voice madrigals became common.

5. The music was filled with "madrigalisms"—musical devices intended to portray the sense of the text. Frequent techniques included chromatic melodies that moved by half steps, sudden pauses, descending "sighing" motives, and word painting.

6. Composers experimented with chromatic harmony and new tonal relationships.

Musical Instruments

The Renaissance was the last great choral era. Works written for voices dominated the period, but musicians became increasingly aware of the power and effect of instrumental music as well. Musical instruments had certainly been used to accompany vocal compositions, doubling or replacing lines in an almost random way. However, except for dance music and keyboard works, there was little music intended purely for instruments. It was only during the Renaissance that musicians began to recognize the idiomatic potential of instruments and consequently began composing in particular genres intended for instrumental rather than choral performance.

Instruments

Keyboard Instruments

Keyboard instruments included both the wind-powered organ and various forms of the plucked or struck keyboard instruments such as the harpsichord. Because keyboards encompassed the range of other instruments and could play a number of notes simultaneously, they were very useful for both accompaniment and solo performance.

Organ

By the sixteenth century, the organ came to resemble today's instrument, complete with one or more keyboards and a pedal board that controlled ranks of flute and reed pipes. The small portative organs faded from use, but they were replaced by portable reed organs called regals.

Harpsichord

The harpsichord created sound by a plectrum that plucked a string. Because of the mechanical action no dynamic variety was possible on the harpsichord. Lightly touching a note had exactly the same effect as striking it with force. In order to remedy this situation, various additional courses of strings were added so that a musician could double or mute some of the strings, thereby altering both the volume and the timbre. There were a number of harpsichordlike instruments that were distinguished by their particular sizes and shapes; these include the virginal, the spinet, and the clavicembalo.

Clavichord

The clavichord was closely related to the harpsichord, but its sound was created by a device that struck rather than plucked the strings. Because the notes were struck, the musician could create some dynamic variety, but the sound was so soft that the clavichord is really suitable only for personal playing.

Wind Instruments

Wind instruments as a group were conceived as a family with a timbre that spanned the entire range from bass to soprano. A family of instruments was often referred to as a "chest," because all the instruments in that family were stored together in a large wooden chest.

Recorder

Recorders remain a familiar instrument today, and are often used in schools to teach music. Recorders are a type of flute played with a whistle attached to a cylindrical pipe. A chest of recorders ranged from the low and rather muted tones of a bass recorder to the bird-like chirping of the tiny sopranino.

Krummhorn

The krummhorn was an early ancestor of the oboe. In shape it looked somewhat like a hook with its J-shaped tube. Its buzzy sound was produced by the vibrations of a double reed set inside a wind cap.

Shawm

The shawm is another early cousin of the oboe. Its characteristic reedy-wood sound was also created by vibrations of a double reed, but the reeds were sounded directly by breath without the cap, and the tube of the shawn was straight, unlike the hooked tube of the krummhorn. Like the recorder, shawms came in many shapes and sizes, from the double bass bombard to the high pitched sopranino.

Sackbut

The sackbut closely resembled its modern relative, the trombone. Its noble, singing tone was achieved by blowing through a cup mouthpiece, and the pitch was controlled by a slide that shortened and lengthened the sounding tube. The bell of the sackbut was narrower than that of the trombone, and therefore its tone was more muted. Thus it was an ideal instrument for use with voices, and it was probably used often to perform the slow, sustained tenor chant melodies.

Cornett

The cornett was a curved hornlike instrument made of either wood or ivory, which produced its sound through breath blown into a cup mute. The cornett had a warm sound that complemented both string instruments and human voices. Although the soprano size was the most common, there were also tenor and bass cornettes that expanded the timbre through additional octaves. A closely related instrument, the *zink*, was straight rather than curved.

String Instruments

Lute

The most popular string instrument during the Renaissance was the lute. At this stage of its development, the lute had five pairs of strings and a single sixth string all of which were stretched over a pear-shaped body. Because the lute was portable and had a wide range comparable to that of keyboard instruments, it was useful for both accompaniment and solo performance. *Tablature*, a special notation based on the strings and fret positions, was devised so that performers could indicate fingerings as well as pitches. A Spanish relative of the lute, the *vihuela da mano*, developed the shape and tradition that would eventually correspond to that of the modern guitar.

Rebec

The rebec was a simple instrument consisting of three or more strings stretched over a slender gourd-shaped body. The rebec, played by drawing a bow across the strings, was especially suited to performing folklike dance compositions.

Viol

The viols closely resembled the modern violin family, but the characteristic viol sound is softer and more subtle. There are also a number of differences in construction and performance practice distinguishing viols from violins. Instead of the characteristic four strings of the violin, viols have six strings (tuned A–D–G–B–E–A) and are often equipped with frets. Viols are positioned between the performer's legs rather than under the chin and the bowing technique is very different. Viols were generally played in *consort*, which means that the entire family—including bass, tenor, and treble—performed as an ensemble.

Instrumental Genres

Ricercar

The ricercar is really little more than a keyboard transcription of a motet. The elaborate polyphonic choral style with imitative points of entry and episodic form was simply arranged for keyboard (usually organ) so that the musical aspects of the motet were reproduced without the text.

Canzona

Like the ricercar, the canzona was an instrumental keyboard form based on a vocal model. In this case, the model was the French chanson. Canzonas were distinguished by their contrasting sections and the imitative fabric of the texture. In general, the canzona was more animated than the ricercar, because it was based on secular rather than sacred works.

Theme and Variations

Theme and variations was a keyboard form and genre that consisted of a stated melody followed by a series of short episodes in which elements of the initial theme were varied. The variations moved the melody from voice to voice, added figuration, altered the mode from major to minor, changed the rhythm and, in general, grew more complex until the melody returned in a grand homophonic statement. A great number of interesting compositions in this genre written by English composers such as William Byrd (1543–1623) and John Bull (c. 1562–1628) were contained in the *Fitzwilliam Virginal Book* (compiled by Francis Tregian during the years 1609–1619).

Dance Pieces

Most of the music composed for instruments during the Renaissance was intended for dance. Social dance was an important aspect of courtly life, and dance music was in great demand by both peasants and nobility. The music was molded according to the function: the rhythm, tempo, and formal structure were based on the particular dance that the works were designed to accompany. Frequently dances were coupled to form a contrast between fast and slow tempi. The most common of these pairings was the *pavane* (a slow dance in duple time) and the *galliard* (a brisk dance in triple time). Other dances that became prominent during the sixteenth century include the *allemande* (a dance in duple time in a moderate tempo) and the *courante* (in a brisk duple meter suited to leaping figures). Eventually these dances became stylized and were collected together in more formal groupings called *suites*.

While the Renaissance period was dominated by the choral polyphonic motets and masses of the Roman Catholic church, the humanist movement was freeing society from the domination of the church. The aristocratic courts also served as patrons of music, and much secular music and poetry was composed and published.

The cosmopolitan union of Burgundian-Flemish structure and order with Italian melody and graceful expression resulted in a period justifiably known as the "golden age of choral music." The Renaissance brings us to the threshold of the modern world. Advances in music notation, the development of musical instruments, printed editions of music, the evolution of a triadic-based harmonic system, the sensitive treatment of text, and the growth of instrumental music lead us to the emerging world of the baroque era.

CHAPTER 13

The Baroque Period

Chronology of Events and Musicians

Baroque Period (1600–1750)

Giulio Caccini (c. 1545–1618)
    Jacopo Peri (1561–1633)
    Jan Sweelinck (1562–1621)
    Michael Praetorius(1571–1621)
    Girolamo Frescobaldi (1583–1643)
Heinrich Schütz (1585–1672)
    Johann Schein (1586–1630)

Samuel Scheidt (1587–1654)

Francesco Cavalli (1602–1676)

Death of Queen Elizabeth (1603)

Giacomo Carissimi (1605–1674)

Johann Froberger (1616–1667)

Antonio Cesti (1623–1669)

Jean-Baptiste Lully (1632–1687)

Marc-Antoine Charpentier (1634–1704)

Dietrich Buxtehude (1637–1707)

Reign of Louis XIV (1643–1715)

John Blow (1649–1708)

The Commonwealth and Protectorate (Cromwell) (1649–1659)

Johann Pachelbel (1653–1706)

Arcangelo Corelli (1653–1713)

Giuseppe Torelli (1658–1709)

Henry Purcell (1659–1695)

Alessandro Scarlatti (1660–1725)

François Couperin (1668–1733)

Tomaso Albinoni (1671–1741)

Antonio Vivaldi (1678–1741)

Johann Mattheson (1681–1764)

Georg Telemann (1681–1767)

Jean-Philippe Rameau (1683–1764)

Johann Sebastian Bach (1685–1750)

George Frideric Handel (1685–1759)

William and Mary on throne (1688)

Gottleib Muffat (1690–1770)

Johann Hasse (1699–1783)

Giovanni Pergolesi (1710–1736)

The period of time spanned by the years 1600–1750 is called the baroque period by music and art historians. The Portuguese word baroque *(meaning an irregularly shaped pearl) was originally a pejorative term that came to mean "heavily ornamented" or "flamboyant." As the music of this time often contained heavily ornamented passages, colorful theatricality, and dramatic effect, the word does seem to em-*

body the essential spirit of the period. The qualities perceived as unattractive stylistic aspects at the time were later recognized as manifestations of an innovative artistic aesthetic.

Baroque music flourished during a time of enlightenment. Scientific inquiry, thriving in an environment of rationality, developed a comprehensive view of the world shaped by such scientists as Newton, Galileo, and Kepler. Philosophy, which had been dominated by Roman Catholic dogma, developed in new analytical directions in the hands of such great thinkers as Descartes, Hobbes, and Spinoza. And the arts, in the hands of writers such as Shakespeare and Milton, artists such as Rubens and Rembrandt, and musicians such as Monteverdi and Bach, produced enduring works that expressed the breadth and depth of human thought and emotion.

Musically, the baroque was distinguished by the rise of secular and instrumental music. The polyphonic choral style of the Renaissance mass and motet was preserved only in the stile antico *("old style") of conservative sacred composition, while the "new" baroque style featured accompanied solo voice, and combinations of instruments in opera, concerti, sonatas, and dance suites. The modal harmonies of the Renaissance were transformed into the more modern triadic major-minor tonality. The complex imitative texture was replaced by a simplified* basso continuo *texture that stressed the relationship of a single melodic voice with a harmonic bass line. Every aspect of baroque music was charged with expression of dramatic contrast.*

Historical Background

The concluding years of the Renaissance were dominated by events of the Reformation and Counter Reformation. The central authority of the Roman Catholic church was challenged by the various emerging Protestant religions, including Calvinism, Anglicanism, and Lutheranism. Some of these religious struggles eventually culminated in bloody warfare, such as the Thirty Years' War (1618–1648) in Germany.

The religious warfare was also a political struggle for control of Europe. Shifting political and religious alliances were reflected in the changing borders that defined both religious beliefs and nationalist states. The Holy Roman Empire was rapidly replaced by large nations governed by powerful monarchs and by smaller areas governed by lesser princes and dukes at regional courts.

During the seventeenth century, Europe continued the transition from an agrarian feudal society, in which all the power was concentrated within the church and nobles, to a mercantile economy with wealth and power increasingly concentrated in the hands of an emerging middle class. The position of the merchant class was especially strengthened by wealth gained from trade with European colonies, such as those in America. While the courts were still the primary patrons of the arts and sciences, and the church supported its sacred music, by the end of the period public performances of opera and oratorio and chamber music written for amateur performance were sponsored by the middle class.

Style Characteristics

Baroque style was based on two guiding principles—the musical codification of emotions, known as affections; and the use of dramatic contrast, called concertato style.

Affections

Composers attempted to portray affections, such as passion, anger, wonder, and majesty, through expressive musical devices. Affections did not represent the personal emotions of the composer, but were stylized representations of idealized states of feeling. Certain musical gestures (such as the "sobbing" descent of a minor third) or the use of particular instruments (such as the oboe as a representation of death, and the trombone of nobility) came to symbolize specific states of mind. These musical affects were formalized through repeated usage, and ultimately became clichés that were easily recognized by audiences of the time.

Concertato

Each work or section of a multisection composition represented only a single affection. Affections could be contrasted with one another in different sections, however, for dramatic effect. Contrast was also the basis for concertato style, which pitted ideas against one another. In concertato style, groups of instruments, choruses, or solo voices in duet alternated with one another in animated call-and-response fashion.

Texture

Stile Antico

The elaborate polyphony of the Renaissance remained only in the liturgical works written in a more conservative style known as *stile antico* ("antique style") or *prima prattica* ("first practice"). In the old style, music was considered more important than the text, and the subtle working out of the imitation and counterpoint was stressed at the expense of textual clarity. Specific rules for writing in this style were codified by the theorist Zarlino based on the music of composer Adrian Willaert (c.1490–1562), who wrote polychoral (employing more than one chorus) compositions for the Cathedral of San Marco in Venice. Baroque composers were still expected to write in the stile antico in addition to mastering the more advanced techniques of the stile moderno.

Stile Moderno

The *stile moderno* ("modern style") or *seconda prattica* ("second practice") was characterized by a more homophonic texture, known as basso continuo, that highlighted the clarity of the text.

Basso Continuo. Basso continuo featured a dominant soprano melodic line that was paired with a strong fundamental bass voice. Between the soprano and bass, an unobtrusive supporting harmony part was performed on a continuo instrument such as a harpsichord. The treble and bass lines were the featured voices while the harmony served merely as the glue that bound these two lines together.

Figured Bass Realization. The basso continuo, or thoroughbass texture, called for a special performance technique known as figured bass realization. In figured bass, one of the continuo instruments (harpsichord, clavichord, lute, or organ) played the bass line, which was strengthened by a bass instrument such as a cello or a bassoon. In addition to playing the bass voice, the continuo improvised chords to provide an accompanying harmony.

These chords were dictated by the direction of the bass line, but special directions were also provided for more colorful chords or specific chord voicings through numbers written under the bass notes. These numbers represented intervals figured in relation to the bass note. The continuo performer had to interpret or *realize* these figured bass symbols while playing, but within the specified chords the performer had considerable freedom to improvise.

Counterpoint. While the homophony of basso continuo texture dominated the baroque musical landscape, there was also a move toward a new polyphony. This polyphonic texture, usually called counterpoint (meaning "note against note") was different from the Renaissance version. There was still an emphasis on the rhythmic and melodic independence of the individual lines, but the new counterpoint also had to conform with the functional harmony expressed in the continuo. A horizontal sense of line was preserved, but it had to fit in with the vertical chordal sonority. During the final years of the baroque, contrapuntal practice reached its zenith in the works of Johann Sebastian Bach.

Harmony

During the baroque period the concept of harmony completed its transition from an older modal sound to the more modern major-minor tonality.

Triadic Chords

Triadic chords (two intervals of a third superimposed over a root tone) were formed over each note of a scale. The chords formed on the first, fourth, and fifth scale degrees (the notes C, F, and G in the key of C major) were major; those chords formed on the second, third, and sixth degrees (the notes D, F, and A) were minor, and the chord built on the seventh step was diminished.

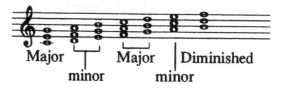

Key Centers

Each major and minor scale has major and minor chords that occur in exactly the same position—so, although the notes that constitute the chord change according to the specific key, the chord quality itself (major, minor, diminished) and the harmonic function remain the same. For instance, a triad, such as C–E–G, might serve as a major tonic chord built on the first degree of a C major scale, but that same chord would *function* differently in the key of G major, where it would be based on the fourth degree of the scale. In the key of C, the C major triad feels stable and secure. In the key of G major, that very same C major chord creates a sensation of motion and demands a return to repose.

Modulation

Because the same chord might belong to different keys, composers found that they could modulate, or change keys, merely by making the chord that was common to both keys change functions. Through this modulation, the tonal feeling of being at rest in one key was simultaneous with a sensation of movement followed by a return to "home" in another area.

Harmonic Progression

This interrelationship of keys provided the basis for functional harmony, in which chords expressed relative amounts of stability or motion. Certain harmonic progressions (patterns of chord sequences) became commonplace because they provided both motion and resolution in predictable and satisfying ways.

Common Practice

The harmonic system that consists of major and minor scales, triadic chords that assume functional meaning, key centers, and modulation between key centers is usually referred to as "common practice." Common-practice harmony is the basis for tonal music written from the sixteenth century to the present. Almost all the music performed today in concert settings by symphony orchestras, chamber groups, and solo recitalists is based on repertoire written in common-practice harmony.

Equal Temperament System

An important development that made common-practice harmony possible was the adaptation of a new method of tuning known as the equal temperament system. In this system, octaves were tuned exactly and all the other intervals were slightly adjusted. Thus, enharmonic equivalent notes (notes that represent the same degree of the chromatic scale but are notated differently) sounded the same. For instance, if you played the note C♯ a half step above C, it would sound the same as D♭, the note a half step below D. Through the subtle compromises made in the equally tempered system, composers were able to modulate freely from one key to any other while the instrument remained in tune.

Dynamics

Baroque dynamics represented yet another aspect of dramatic contrast. Whereas Renaissance music generally maintained a constant level of intensity throughout a composition, baroque style contrasted loud passages for the entire ensemble with quieter sections performed by a smaller group. Instead of the gradual dynamic transitions between soft and loud that we hear today, baroque musicians desired the sudden contrasts produced through different textures and orchestrations. This concertato style of dynamics is usually referred to as *terrace dynamics* because the intensity changes in sudden jumps rather than in gradual increments.

Rhythm

The rhythmic structures of the baroque can best be characterized as dance-influenced and strongly propulsive.

Contrast

Based on the notion of baroque affections, there is usually a single underlying rhythmic pattern stated at the outset which unifies the composition or movement. As with the use of dynamics, there is little gradual shading, little use of gradual tempo changes such as *ritardando* (gradual slowing) or *accelerando* (gradual speeding up); instead, the element of contrast is manifested in sudden tempo changes from one movement to the next.

Senza Battuta

Although most baroque rhythm had an insistent dancelike drive, there was also a style of music that was performed *senza battuta* ("without beat"). This free rhythmic style was used for instrumental works with an improvised character or vocal narrative–style singing. An entire movement maintained its own particular rhythmic shape but, once again, dramatic contrast could be achieved by coupling a senza battuta movement with a section with a strong metric drive. Examples of this use of contrasting rhythm include the pairing of the keyboard free fantasia with the metric fugue, or of the operatic recitative with the more rhythmic aria.

Rhythmic Notation

The baroque rhythmic concept is largely *metric*. Composers determined an orderly, or metric, pattern of weak and strong beats, and divided these patterns into separate groupings indicated by bar lines. The meter was then subdivided into rhythmic patterns that contained the same note divisions (whole notes, half notes, etc.) that we employ today. Thus, the system of rhythmic notation that developed by about 1650 is essentially the same as that of today. If Johann Sebastian Bach were brought to life again, he would have little difficulty in performing from a modern score.

Melody

During the baroque, musicians began to develop *idiomatic melodic writing*—that is they made distinctions between melodies written specifically for instruments and those intended for vocal performance. The voice was still the model for melodic expression, but composers became more attentive to the special techniques, range, and capabilities available on each instrument. Vocal music could be performed on instruments, but it was more difficult to sing instrumental music.

Instrumental Melodies

Instrumental melodies exhibit the following general characteristics: (1) even phrase structures of four or eight measures; (2) melodic contours that outline triads; (3) heavy ornamentation; (4) motivic ideas that can be excerpted from the melody for sequential treatment; (5) greater range and more disjunct motion than earlier vocal-based melody; and (6) a driving, dynamic melody whose constant development infused a work with a single unifying rhythm and affection. Instrumental melodies seem more structural than lyrical.

Vocal Melodies

Vocal melodies can be divided into two main styles: the lyrical and ornamented *bel canto* ("beautiful singing") style of the aria, and the more chantlike free rhythmic style of the recitative.

Bel Canto. Bel canto style is heavily ornamented, possesses a melismatic text, a strongly rhythmic character, and employs the full range of the voice including disjunct as well as conjunct motion.

Recitative. Recitative, or monody, is declamatory in character, with many repeated notes, a sense of free, unmetered rhythm, and a syllabic text setting. The general impression is rather "tuneless," because the melody is less important than the clarity of the text.

Vocal Genres

Opera

Opera, a dramatic production in which the actors sing a libretto (text) rather than deliver spoken lines, was the single most influential genre of the baroque period. From its birth in Italy, opera soon spread throughout Europe, where it quickly became the most popular form of musical entertainment. Italian became the dominant language for interpretive indications (interpretive indications in music are usually still given in Italian today), and operatic style influenced all aspects of sacred and secular composition throughout the period.

Origins

Opera arose in Florence, Italy, at the end of the sixteenth century when a small group of musicians, poets, and philosophers known as the *Camerata* ("society") set out to replace polyphonic style with a more simple, direct, and dramatic medium based on ancient Greek models. The singing style for this earliest form of opera was a declamatory speech-song known as *monody*. Eventually this monody evolved into the more musical recitative, which was capable of portraying action with dramatic clarity.

Monteverdi's Opera

Claudio Monteverdi (1567–1643) developed the genre further beyond its limited scope and recitative style with the production of his opera *La Favola d'Orfeo*, which was produced in Mantua in 1607. Monteverdi included instrumental dances such as *overtures* and *ritornellos* (an instrumental introduction to an aria that is repeated after the aria), madrigallike choruses, and various vocal arias and duets that provided relief from the constant recitative and greatly expanded the potential for contrast and dramatic expression. Whereas the earliest operatic recitative was accompanied only by a continuo instrument such as a lute, Monteverdi wrote for an orchestra of forty musicians, which included strings, sackbuts, flutes, and cornettos, in addition to continuo instruments such as the harpsichord, lute, and organetto.

Singing Styles

As opera developed, two separate singing styles emerged—the narrative recitative and the lyrical aria.

Recitative. Recitative told the story in as direct and speechlike a way as possible. Accompaniment could be *secco* ("dry"), with just a continuo instrument, or in more dramatic passages, it might include orchestral forces. There was no set form for the recitative because the libretto dictated the form of the music.

Aria. Arias commented on the action. The singing style, the virtuosity of the performer, and the grace of the ornamentation were all more important than the clarity of the text. One interesting performance practice involved the use of *castrati* for principal heroic roles. Castrati were male singers who were neutered in childhood to preserve the purity and range of their voices. As a result of this peculiar artificial condition, their voices possessed a unique timbre and they had a mature lung capacity that enabled them to sing particularly long phrases.

Eventually three forms evolved for the aria: *strophic* form in which music was repeated over changing stanzas of text; *ostinato-bass* in which a melody was imposed on top of a fixed repeating bass line; and *da capo*, which stated a melody, interposed a contrasting section, and then returned to the initial melody in highly ornamented form (*A B A'*).

Italian Opera

As opera spread across Italy and into other European countries it began to assume different stylistic characteristics.

Comic Opera. Roman opera, arising in the 1620s, placed less emphasis on the drama of the libretto while stressing the singing style, and clearly separated the recitatives from the arias in a style that became known as comic opera.

Opera Seria. Italian opera seria developed later in the baroque and was based on mythology. It stressed the drama of the libretto through a particularly melodic style.

French Opera

Tragédie Lyrique. In France, the *tragédie lyrique* ("lyrical tragedy") developed a recitative style based on the French rather than the Italian language, and expanded the pageantry of large choruses and ballet interludes to reflect the opulence of the court of Louis XIV. Instead of the developed arias of Italian opera, *tragédie lyrique* favored simpler dance-style airs.

Opéra Comique. French *opéra comique*, arising about 1715, was not really more comic, but it did employ spoken dialogue rather than sung recitative.

Oratorio

The dramatic content and vocal style found in opera pervaded other aspects of baroque music as well. Oratorio preserved the sacred content of scriptural text, but in form, the oratorio most closely resembled an unstaged opera. The dramatic arias, recitatives, instrumental interludes, and choruses of opera were retained. All that was lacking were the costumery, sets, and stage action of the fully mounted production.

The oratorio's kinship with opera is revealed in its origins. Oratorio was originally a substitute for opera during Lent (the religious penitential period preceding Easter), when opera was prohibited. The oratorio was acceptable to the church because of the sacred nature of the plot, while its drama and entertainment elements were appreciated by lay audiences. The oratorio is perhaps best known today through Christmas-season presentations of Handel's *Messiah*.

Passion

The passion is an opera-influenced multimovement genre similar to the oratorio, but its story always concerned the events leading to the crucifixion of Christ as told by one of the biblical gospels (Matthew, Mark, Luke, or John). As with oratorio, there was no actual stage production with sets and costumes, but the music itself was intensely dramatic. Orchestral effects, impassioned arias, choruses portraying crowd scenes, and the recitative of the evangelists told the story in a convincing way that needed little additional support. One of the most outstanding examples of this genre, the *St. Matthew Passion* (1727) of J. S. Bach, interposes Lutheran chorales for chorus as a commentary on the action.

Cantata

The cantata is yet another multimovement genre that bears a strong resemblance to opera. However, cantatas are on a smaller scale than the oratorio or passion. They contain only four or five separate numbers as compared with the expanded dimensions of an oratorio, which may include thirty or forty distinct sections. Cantatas are generally based on sacred themes and are intended for liturgical use, but there are also secular cantatas intended simply for entertainment. J. S. Bach wrote many cantatas based on chorale tunes for use in the Lutheran church.

Verse Anthem

During the late Renaissance, English musicians began writing anthems that contained solo passages as well as motet-style choral polyphony. By the baroque period, opera had influenced Anglican service music and, as a result, the verse anthem was expanded into a sectional form containing an overture, arias, and dramatic choral sections, all of which were now accompanied by an instrumental ensemble. While English composers such as John Blow composed for this genre, the most striking examples of the idiom are the *Chandos Anthems* (1717 and 1718) written by George Frideric Handel, a German composer who spent many years in England.

Instrumental Music

The Baroque period witnessed the rise of purely instrumental performance. For the first time, music was composed specifically for instruments and designed for the distinctive capabilities and sonorities of instruments. Using the voice as a model, Renaissance composers freely doubled or replaced voice parts with instruments. Aside from some keyboard and viol consort works, almost all music was conceived for some combination of voices.

Keyboard Genres

Toccata

Toccata, meaning "touch," is a keyboard work with a freely rhythmic improvisational character. Although there is no set form to a toccata, it usually involves virtuosic passages contrasted with wide arpeggiated chords. Toccatas were often used as a prelude to a fugue, with the rhapsodic nature of the toccata contrasted with the structured procedure of the fugue. The most famous example of this genre is the Toccata in D Minor by J. S. Bach.

Fugue

Fugue, meaning "flight," is an imitative genre that best represents the baroque art of tonal counterpoint. A fugue usually contains three to five voices or melodic lines.

Exposition. The principal idea, called the *subject*, is introduced in one of the voices. Subsequently, one of the other voices presents this same idea in imitation, but this time the idea is stated in the dominant key area. The fugue then proceeds with statements and answers, alternating between tonic and dominant keys until the final voice has completed its first entrance; this concludes the first section, the exposition.

Development. Following the exposition, the composer takes both previously stated material from the exposition and new ideas called *episodes*, and weaves an elaborate web of polyphony in a development section using contrapuntal devices such as fragmentation, augmentation, inversion, and sequence.

Conclusion. After the development, the composer usually recalls the theme in a majestic homophonic restatement of the exposition.

Bach's Fugues. The fugue was primarily a keyboard genre but it was also applied to other media, being especially well suited to an ensemble of balanced voices such as a chorus. The twenty fugues based on a single subject contained in J. S. Bach's *Art of Fugue* (completed in 1749) present a summary of all of the possible ways in which an idea could receive harmonic contrapuntal treatment during the baroque period.

The Suite

The suite satisfied both the aesthetic of affection and the concept of concertato. A suite generally contained a sequence of four dances structured in the order of *allemande, courante, sarabande,* and *gigue,* but other dance forms could be either substituted for one of the four standard dances or inserted as an additional work. The dances did not contain common thematic material, but were unified only by being cast in the same key.

Because each movement of a suite was based on a separate dance, the unity of affection was preserved within that movement. The element of concertato was also provided, because the tempo, meter, and character of each dance contrasted with one another.

Allemande. The allemande was in $\frac{4}{4}$ meter and moved at a moderate tempo. Allemandes were characterized by a running figure in short note values that moved from one voice to another in a contrapuntal texture.

Courante. The moderate tempo of the allemande was usually followed by the livelier courante. The Italian-style courante (spelled *corrente*) is in a quick $\frac{3}{4}$ or $\frac{3}{8}$ meter and was characterized by running melodic figures against an accompaniment texture. The French courante was a more elegant version, marked by a $\frac{3}{2}$ or $\frac{6}{6}$ meter that changed accents through *hemiola*. Hemiola is simply the alternation of accented beats in groups of twos with those in groups of threes (*1* 2 3 *1* 2 3 to *1* 2 *3* 1 *2* 3). The texture was generally melodic against accompaniment, although the melodic figuration sometimes passed into another voice.

Sarabande. The second pairing of a slow and fast dance in the suite began with the dignified sarabande. Although the sarabande started as a wild and passionate Spanish dance, by the time it became stylized in the baroque suite it was performed in a grave triple meter (usually $\frac{3}{2}$) with an accent on the second beat. The texture was generally very homophonic.

Gigue. The gigue, related to the Irish jig, provided a bright and spritely conclusion to the suite. This dance moved at a brisk tempo in $\frac{6}{8}$ meter, and was charged with a characteristic dotted rhythmic gesture (♩ ♪ ♫). Melodically, the gigue was marked by wide intervallic jumps and a very contrapuntal texture in which the theme bounced between voices in imitation.

Trio Sonata

The trio sonata was the perfect medium for exploration of the basso continuo style. It revealed the clarity of the thorough-bass texture while providing the excitement of tonal counterpoint.

Instruments

Two instruments (usually violin, flute, or oboe) intertwined in melodic counterpoint, challenging and imitating each other. Below the duet, a cello provided a supportive bass line, but also engaged in some interplay with the soprano voices. The continuo instrument bound the top and bottom together, providing a harmonic glue and doubling the bass line.

Movements

Like the suite, the trio sonata combined movements in a slow-fast contrast that fulfilled the baroque notion of concertato. Though there was no fixed number of movements or specific dance forms to which the movements had to conform, a typical pattern included four movements in slow-fast-slow-fast order. The movements were usually all set in a common key, but some trio sonatas contained movements in a contrasting key such as the relative minor. The trio sonatas for violin by the Italian composer Arcangelo Corelli (1653–1713) are particularly representative of this genre.

Concerto Grosso

The baroque concertato aesthetic is best represented by the concerto grosso. This genre pitted two groups of instruments against each other: a smaller ensemble or soloist, called the *concertino*, versus the full ensemble, called the *tutti* or *ripieno*.

Dynamic Contrast

Because the concertino might contain three musicians, and the ripieno an entire string section plus assorted flutes, oboes, trumpets, and horns, there was quite a bit of dynamic contrast. Statements made by the large group could be softly echoed by the concertino, and ideas stated by the small ensemble could be boldly seconded or loudly disputed by the ripieno. The baroque concept of terrace dynamics was most evident in this genre.

As with the suite and trio sonata, concertato effect was also produced by the contrast of separate movements. There was no rigid formula dictating the tempo or number of movements in a concerto. The general tendency was toward a three-movement form (fast-slow-fast), but there are numerous examples of four- and five-movement concerti.

Ritornello

If the concerto was in three-movement form, the beginning and concluding movements were often structured in a form based on the contrast of the two ensembles. This form, called ritornello, began with a theme stated by the ripieno, which reappeared throughout the movement in varied form and in different keys. The concertino sections alternated with the ritornello and consisted of new thematic material or development of ideas drawn from the ritornello. The work concluded with a final statement of the full ritornello in the tonic key.

Bach's Concerti

The six *Brandenburg Concerti* (1721) of J. S. Bach represent the essence of concertato style as evidenced by their novel combinations of instruments, dramatic contrast, and elaborate counterpoint.

Solo Concerto

The solo concerto was similar in form to the concerto grosso, but instead of the concertino ensemble, the ripieno was contrasted with a solo performer. Ritornello form was used often for the allegro movement, in which the soloist was given virtuosic passagework to develop in the episodes between tutti ritornelli. Italian composers such as Giuseppe Torelli (1658–1709) and Antonio Vivaldi (1678–1741) were particularly important to the development of the solo concerto, which was an excellent medium for showcasing the potential of their common instrument, the violin.

Music Instruments

Because of the increased demand for instrumental music during the baroque period, instrument-builders developed the technology to improve current models and invented entirely new instruments to accommodate the new orchestral needs. While the sheer number of performers in a baroque orchestra was much smaller than that of the modern orchestra, the modern instruments themselves were almost all represented in the baroque orchestra by the mid-eighteenth century.

Violin

Because of the brilliance of sound and the ease of performance, the violin family, including violas, cellos, and double basses, gradually replaced their earlier ancestor, the viol. Because the violin was an Italian instrument, and Italian music dominated the baroque, the violin spread throughout Europe, and the string section rapidly became the foundation for an emerging concept of orchestra. The baroque was the golden age of violin building, and the craftsmen of the Stradivarius, Guaneri, and Amati studios produced magnificent instruments whose value continues to escalate today.

Woodwinds

Flute

The flute of the baroque included both the earlier recorder and the transverse flute, which was first used in the orchestra by the French composer Jean Baptiste Lully. This early transverse flute was made of wood and was assembled in three sections so that it could be tuned by extending or shortening the tube. Other technical innovations included changing the bore from cylindrical to conical, and adding a key at the end, which facilitated performance.

Oboe and Bassoon

The oboe developed as a replacement for the Renaissance shawm, whose penetrating timbre and difficulty of performance made it ill-suited to baroque melody. In the same way, the bassoon developed as the bass voice of the double-reed family. The baroque oboe and bassoon closely resemble the modern instruments, except for their less-mechanical action keys.

Clarinet

The clarinet developed from an instrument called the *chalumeau* (today the lower register of the clarinet is still called "chalumeau") toward the end of the baroque, so it was not really incorporated into the orchestra until the next historical era.

Brass

Trumpets and Horns

Trumpets and horns were used extensively for brilliant color and contrast during the baroque. At this time, however, valves had not been invented, so builders were experimenting with different sizes and shapes for the instruments to accommodate different keys and timbres. One way of solving the problem was to insert a length of tubing called a crook into the instrument (much like the slide of a trombone) so that the harmonic fundamental pitch could be raised or lowered as the tube was extended or contracted.

Trombone

The evolution from the Renaissance sackbut to the trombone involved very little change. The size of the instrument was expanded and the bell was enlarged to produce more sound, but the slide mechanism functioned well enough to meet the demands of baroque music. The trombone's use was mostly confined to martial music, although it also appeared in opera orchestras for military and heroic color.

Keyboard

The keyboard instruments were very important during the baroque. They served as the continuo that held the music together. The harpsichord and clavichord closely resembled the Renaissance instruments, but they became larger and featured extra courses of strings and keyboards (and even a pedal board) to correspond with the expansion of the orchestra.

Organ

The organ also resembled earlier instruments, but it increased in size and featured expanded ranks (sets of pipes) that included both flute and reed stops of various timbres. The typical French or German organ of Bach's day had two manuals (keyboards) and a pedal board that could control a number of stops, including flutes, reeds, and mixtures (combinations of stops that produced intervals such as fifths and thirds).

Pianoforte

In 1708 Bartolomeo Cristofori invented the prototype of the piano, the pianoforte. This instrument had a hammer action rather than a plucked mechanism so that different dynamic shadings could be controlled by the performer. Cristofori's instrument did not gain much recognition at the time. It was only later in the classical period that the pianoforte acquired importance. Perhaps the piano was not widely used during the baroque because it was unfamiliar to performers and audiences, and its mechanism was not yet perfected. Another explanation may be that the piano simply did not correspond to the baroque aesthetic. The concept of drama and contrast was well suited to the terrace dynamics of the harpsichord, but the piano was designed to express subtle shadings of dynamics that stressed development rather than contrast.

Baroque music forms the bridge between the ancient world and the modern. During the 150 years of this period, the old-fashioned stile antico of the Renaissance world was swept aside and replaced by the innovative dramatic expression of the baroque stile moderno. Modern audiences find many baroque works easily accessible because the harmonies, textures, instrumentation, and forms of the baroque lay the groundwork for the "common practice" of the last several hundred years.

The sacred choral polyphony of the Renaissance was replaced by secular homophony and tonal counterpoint, which emphasized the dramatic potential of music. Instrumental music emerged as an equal partner with vocal music, and the string orchestra augmented by wind instruments became an important ensemble. The tonal concept of theory, functional harmony, and well-tempered tuning became established in common usage. Both the concept of affections, which maintained emotional unity within a movement, and the idea of concertato, which provided contrast, dictated the form, dynamics, and basso continuo texture of the period. New genres, such as the suite, opera, and the fugue, embodied aspects of baroque style.

CHAPTER 14

The Classic Period

Chronology of Events and Musicians

Classic Period (1750–1828)

Domenico Scarlatti (1685–1757)
Johann Quantz (1697–1773)
Giuseppe Sammartini (1695–1750)
Franz Richter (1709–1789)
Wilhelm Friedmann Bach (1710–1784)
Jean-Jacques Rousseau (1712–1778)
Frederic the Great of Prussia born (1713)

Carl Philipp Emanuel Bach (1714–1788)
Christoph Gluck (1714–1787)
Johann Stamitz (1717–1757)
    Georg Wagenseil (1715–1777)
    Georg Monn (1717–1750)
Franz Joseph Haydn (1732–1809)
Johann Christian Bach (1735–1782)
    Michael Haydn (1737–1806)
    Karl Ditters von Dittersdorf (1739–1799)
    John Antes (1740–1811)
    Luigi Boccherini (1743–1805)
Thomas Jefferson (1743–1826)
    William Billings (1746–1800)
    Domenico Cimarosa (1749–1801)
The Seven Years' War (1756–1763)
    Wolfgang Amadeus Mozart (1756–1791)
Reign of King George III of England (1760–1820)
    Luigi Cherubini (1760–1842)
    Jan Dussek (1760–1812)
Reign of Catherine the Great of Russia (1762–1796)
Napoleon born (1769)
    Ludwig van Beethoven (1770–1827)
American Revolution (1776)

The use of the terms "classic" and "classical" to refer to the musical period spanning the dates 1750–1828 has caused confusion because these words can also refer to the history of art music, or describe any work of art of lasting value. In attaching the label "classic" to the period between the death of J. S. Bach and that of Beethoven, music historians have drawn attention to the symmetry, balance, formal clarity, and emotional restraint that distinguish musical compositions written during this time. It is most accurate to refer to the period as "classic" and to use the term "classical" to describe specific characteristics of the "classic" period.

The classic era witnessed the development of almost all the essential genres, forms, instruments, and instrumental combinations that have since become the foundation for the modern concert repertoire. The symphony, string quartets, woodwind quintets, sonatas, opera, and concerti all emerged as distinct genres with their own particular formal structures and instrumentation. A clear sense of musical architecture, based on such forms as the sonata allegro, theme with variations, minuet and trio, ternary, rounded binary, and rondo evolved in response to the classical ideal of logic and clarity. Finally, composers wrote for specific combinations of instruments that were readily available rather than the somewhat haphazard groupings of the baroque period. Ensembles, such as the orchestra and string quartet, became standardized, so that published compositions could be played at the courtly centers of arts. The classic period transmitted a legacy of genres, forms, and repertoire that has left an indelible mark on the history of composition and performance during the last two centuries.

Historical Background

Although the term "classic" is used to describe the music of this period, the musical aesthetic is only a single aspect of a much broader cultural and philosophical movement known variously as "the age of reason," or, simply, "the Enlightenment."

Arts and Sciences

Philosophers such as Rousseau and Kant stressed the potential of reason as a means of understanding the universe and creating a more effective social order. Artists such as Hogarth, Fragonard, David, and Goya not only captured the balance and order of nature, but also exposed the problems of society through satire and stark realism. Writers such as Voltaire, Johnson, and Swift employed elegant prose and biting satire to present revealing portraits of contemporary culture. And scientists such as Franklin, Linnaeus, and Lavoisier used scientific method as a powerful tool in the search for universal laws and practical applications. Instead of looking outward to seek meaning in supernatural forces, philosophers, artists, and scientists of the eighteenth century looked inward to humanity and the human ability to think critically.

Social Changes

Even by contemporary accounts, the classic era was viewed as a watershed in history—a historic epoch in which the power of human reason had the potential to transform the world. The creative thought initiated early in the century resulted in the sweeping reforms that arose out of such events as the American and French Revolutions and the Napoleonic Wars. By the end of the century humanity had turned the corner into the modern world. At the conclusion of the Enlightenment, political and social domination by the aristocracy was replaced by a strong middle class of merchants, professionals, and artisans. The industrial revolution was initiated, resulting in a population shift from an agrarian to an urban society. The dignity of man and the worth of the individual were affirmed in social reform and fostered through enlightened despots such as Catherine the Great of Russia and through experimental democratic governments such as that of the United States.

The Profession of Music

The changes effected by the Enlightenment also strongly affected music. At the beginning of the century composers were still dependent upon wealthy aristocrats for their living. Music was produced on demand for a patron in response to a specific request. That music was then either performed for the court by professional musicians or played for personal entertainment by aristocrats who were often very talented amateurs. Composers had a certain social standing because they were intimately associated with the court, but they were still essentially indentured servants, dependent upon the aristocracy for their livelihood. In time, the middle class became wealthy enough to support public concerts available to lawyers, doctors, and merchants. Finally, composers were able to earn a living as independent professional musicians. By the end of the period composers had their precious freedom to write whatever they wanted but, in the process, they became dependent on public will and public taste for their support.

Major Composers

A glance at the three most important composers of the classic period reveals the changes that occured in the patronage system. Franz Josef Haydn (1732–1809) remained an employee of the Esterházy family from 1762 to 1790, at which point he finally began composing and conducting in public concerts. Wolfgang Amadeus Mozart (1756–1791) was nominally employed during his early years by the bishop of Salzburg, but his fiercely independent nature made him hardly a model employee. In 1781 he was angrily dismissed by the bishop and forced to compose on a free-lance basis. He died in poverty ten years later. Ludwig Van Beethoven (1770–1827), who never held an official position, made his living by teaching piano and selling his compositions. However, he also had wealthy patrons who provided a yearly stipend on the condition that he remain in Vienna.

Style Characteristics

Style characteristics were all shaped by the classical aesthetic that stressed symmetry, balance, moderation, and clarity. Artistic expression has always been based upon the relationship between form and content. All artistic decisions are shaped by the balance of these two elements. Content is the idea or thought being expressed, and form is the process or structure that brings that expression to life. Throughout history certain periods have stressed one at the expense of the other. Periods in which the content is emphasized are said to be "romantic" while those that focus on the form are called "classic." Thus, as we might expect, the classic period exhibits a certain focus on the form or shape of the music.

Dynamics

The baroque period featured the sudden contrasts of "terrace dynamics" and "concertato style" to achieve the desired dramatic effect. Classic style stressed gradations of change, gradual dynamic movement through crescendo (increasing volume) and diminuendo (decreasing volume).

At the beginning of the period composers seldom notated the dynamic level they desired, assuming that performers would interpret the character of the music and perform it at an appropriate volume level. As the period progressed, however, technical improvements in the construction of musical instruments made them more responsive to dynamic nuances. At the same time, solo and ensemble performance technique acquired more polish. As a result, musicians were capable of performing with more dynamic subtlety and composers, in turn, began indicating subtle shadings of dynamic contrast with more care.

Rhythm

Whereas the baroque period stressed insistent dance-influenced rhythms that permeated an entire movement or work, classical rhythms acquired more freedom of expression. Flexibility of tempo, dramatic pauses, and syncopation allowed musicians to express changes of mood or character within a single movement. Changes in momentum were frequently achieved by altering note values so that the music sounded proportionally faster or slower although the basic metronomic tempo remained the same.

Melody

Classical melodic shape was very clearly defined. The melodic idea usually outlined a harmonic progression with the key notes of the melody highlighting notes of a triad.

Construction

Melodic construction usually contained a pattern consisting of a pair of phrases linked by an antecedent consequent relationship in which the second phrase provided a tonal "answer" to the "question" posed by the initial phrase. In keeping with the general symmetry of the time, these phrases were almost always four measures long.

Components

The concept of melodic shape was closely linked with a hierarchy or pyramid of structure on which the form for the entire movement or work was built. A *motive* was the generating spark around which a melodic *phrase* was constructed. This four-bar phrase was then paired with another four-measure phrase to complete the thought. This pair of phrases was coupled with a contrasting antecedent-consequent pair of phrases to form a *period* of sixteen measures. Periods became the larger "building blocks" around which the large *sections* of a work were fashioned.

Harmony

Harmonic System

Classical composers inherited essentially the same harmonic system left behind by the baroque. Major and minor scales, triadic construction, and functional movement of harmonic progressions as codified by the theorist Jean-Philippe Rameau (1683–1764) dictated the relationship of consonant and dissonant sounds. Harmonic motion defined the speed at which the music moved, and highlighted the formal architecture. Harmonic cadences separated phrases, periods, and sections; and musical ideas were distinguished by the keys in which they were stated.

Alberti Bass

Classical texture was more homophonic than that of preceding periods, so the relationship between melody and accompaniment was founded on harmonic progression. One specific musical gesture, the Alberti bass, highlighted the harmony by breaking up the chords in the bass by presenting the notes individually in a linear fashion.

Timbre

Timbre during the baroque period was guided by dramatic contrast and sheer practicality. Baroque composers desired the contrast of concertato and ripieno, or the contrast of woodwind against string instruments, so timbres reflected the separation of instrumental colors rather than the concept of ensemble families. Musicians also were compelled to adjust to the practical demands of a situation in which there were no "standard" ensembles. Parts were written for whatever ensemble might be available. For instance, a treble part had to be adaptable to either violin, flute, or oboe.

Classical timbre, on the other hand, reflected the aesthetic of balance and symmetry. Ensembles tended to be grouped in terms of "families" of instruments. Strings, winds, woodwinds, and percussion were balanced with one another in the most important ensemble of the period—the orchestra.

Orchestra

The "standard" orchestra, developed in Italy and Germany by composers such as Giovanni Sammartini (1701–1775) and Johann Stamitz (1717–1757), ranged in size from small chamber groups of approximately twenty performers at the beginning of the period to large ensembles of sixty players by century's end.

Types of Instrument. The orchestra usually included first and second violins, violas, cellos, and basses in the string section; paired flutes, oboes, clarinets, and bassoons in the woodwinds; paired trumpets and French horns in the brass; and two timpani in the percussion section. With a few additions, such as trombones, this same orchestra is still in use today.

Functions of Instruments. The strings were the backbone of the orchestra. The lower instruments provided the harmonic accompaniment while the first violins performed the principal melodic lines. The woodwinds provided a colorful voice that was often used both for contrast with the strings and to state counterthemes. The brass instruments were limited by their technical construction. Because they could not easily change keys or play difficult figuration, their role was limited to fanfarelike passages in the original key. The timpani accented the tonic and dominant at climactic moments.

Other Ensembles

Other ensembles became standardized as well. The *string quartet*, consisting of two violins, viola, and cello, was a unified ensemble that carried the string sound through a range of seven octaves. Other chamber groups included the *piano trio* (violin, cello, and piano), the *woodwind quintet* (flute, oboe, clarinet, bassoon, and French horn) and the *brass quintet* (two trumpets, French horn, trombone, and tuba).

Piano

The major timbral innovation of the classic period was the introduction of the piano as the dominant keyboard instrument. Although the harpsichord was well suited to the continuo style of the baroque, it was rendered obsolete by the elimination of continuo texture and the introduction of new dynamic shading characteristic of classical compositions. In contrast, the piano, with its touch-sensitve dynamic capabilities and louder volume, was perfectly adapted to the new style. Consequently, the piano was widely used in solo sonatas, chamber ensembles, and as a solo instrument contrasted with the orchestra in concerti.

Forms

In response to the expression of formal clarity that was so important to the classic aesthetic, composers of this period developed a significant number of formal structures. These were applied especially to multi-movement genres such as symphonies, sonatas, and concerti, in which specific movements distinguished by a particular character were coupled with complementary forms.

Sonata Form

Sonata form is the most important and pervasive form developed during the classic period. The basic concept of sonata form is deceptively simple: First, ideas are presented. Then they are varied. Finally they return again. The concept is simple, but so is the premise of human life—birth, life, and death. The infinite variations on sonata form, the rich diversity of life, are what make the simple premise consistently interesting. Sonata form is also called "first-movement form" or "sonata-allegro form" in order to distinguish it from the multimovement genre called sonata. Frequently sonata form is the first movement of a sonata (or a concerto or symphony), but not every movement of a sonata is in sonata form. A complete discussion of sonata form is found in chapter 8.

Theme and Variations

The question of balancing unity with variety is embodied in theme-and-variations form. A theme is first presented in an unadorned version. Then, during a series of clearly articulated sections, the theme is subjected to various transformations. This form was often used as the slow second movement of a multimovement work such as a symphony, sonata, or string quartet, or as the basis for an independent composition. One particularly brilliant example of the independent genre is Beethoven's *Diabelli Variations* for solo piano. A more thorough discussion of this form is found in chapter 8.

Minuet and Trio

Minuet and trio is a compound ternary dance form that introduced a minuet dance theme in an initial tonality, modulated to a new tonality for a contrasting theme in the trio, and then returned to the initial theme and tonality in a repeat of the minuet. This form was generally reserved for the third movement of symphonies and string quartets because its graceful character provided an effective contrast with the other movements. Concertos do not usually include a minuet movement because it does not lend itself well to the virtuosic development of concerto style. Later, Beethoven infused the character (but not the form) of the minuet with a faster, more diabolical nature, and called the movement a *scherzo* ("joke"). A more complete description of minuet and trio is found in chapter 8.

Rondo

Because the rondo features a bright, lively tempo coupled with periodic climactical restatements of the main theme, the form is often used by composers to conclude a symphony or concerto. The typical *A*

B A C A rondo form opens with a theme with a lively and strong character. Then the composer proceeds to state that theme against contrasting episodes that alternate with reappearances of the initial theme. The contrast of themes is further heightened by the choice of keys. The principal theme (*A*) is usually stated in the tonic, and the episodes (*B*, *C*, etc.) modulate to other tonal areas. This produces the sensation of a series of events that always conclude with a triumphant return home. A more complete description of rondo form may be found in chapter 8.

Instrumental Genres

Symphony

The rise of the orchestra as an established ensemble and the cultivation of the symphonic genre were perhaps the most significant developments of the classic period. Prior to this time instrumental music was generally considered less important than vocal music. A baroque composer typically focused much of his energy on extended vocal works such as operas, passions, and oratorios. Instrumental compositions such as suites and sonatas were intended primarily for the gracious entertainment of court and amateur. During the classic era, however, composers seized upon the symphony as the principal medium for extended, exalted thought. As a result, symphonies constitute a large percentage of classical compositions, and today much of the art music performed by orchestra consists of symphonies.

Early Symphonies

Symphonies were originally written on demand for courtly entertainment. These early compositions were relatively short works (lasting about fifteen minutes), which featured an extended first movement followed by three short movements that were almost inconsequential in their brevity. The balance of the compositions was strongly tilted toward the first movement. Because the early symphonies were short, commissioned for entertainment, and governed by conventional patterns, composers were capable of producing vast numbers of works in this genre. Haydn, for instance, wrote 102 symphonies.

Classic Development

As the classic period progressed, composers began to regard the symphony as a serious forum for emotional and intellectual expression rather than simply as an entertaining diversion. Composers increasingly wrote for themselves rather than for their patrons, so they acquired the freedom to extend the parameters of the symphony to reflect their personal vision. The development section of the first movement was charged with added significance and, consequently, both the importance and the length of the sonata allegro were increased. Realizing that the symphony would be overbalanced by the first movement, composers began to focus attention on the succeeding movements. As a result, the total length of the symphony grew to still greater proportions.

Beethoven's Symphonies

By the end of the classic period, Beethoven had expanded the symphony to vast dimensions. Instead of limiting development to the development section of sonata form, Beethoven subjected the entire symphony to a process of continual organic development. This increased the scale of the genre to unprecedented length. In addition, Beethoven increased the instrumentation and size of the orchestra, added voices to the instrumental forces (in the famous Ninth Symphony), juxtaposed literal or philosophical *programs* (nonmusical ideas or stories) with the abstract symphonic form, and altered the character of the minuet to a more aggressive scherzo. As some indication of the new proportions, consider that Haydn wrote over a hundred symphonies while Beethoven, a prolific composer, completed only nine.

Symphonic Movements

Individual Characteristics. Symphonies of the classic period are divided into four distinct movements, with each movement possessing its own special character. The first movement is generally charged with excitement and drama, pitting a strongly rhythmic primary idea against a more lyrical secondary theme. The second movement has a gentle songlike character that offers a slow contrast to the fireworks of the preceding movement. The third movement picks up the tempo again in a courtly dance, and the final movement provides a lively conclusion to the work.

Unity. Although each movement is a separate entity, invested with its own particular character, melody, and form, the individual movements are not really effective if performed as independent works. Each movement supports the unity of the whole work by providing contrasting moods, ideas, and perspectives. The symphony as a whole may be unified by a common tonal framework (the relationship of keys) or a high philosophical program, but at this point in history movements did not usually share common melodies or motives.

Concerto

Philosophers and artists of the Enlightenment gave much thought to societal relationships. The concerto is an exploration of the contrast between the soloist and the orchestra, which might well have been a metaphor for the role of the individual in society. The soloist and orchestra exchange thematic material, confront each other, and intertwine in mutual expression. Sometimes the soloist is heard as a solitary voice; at other times, fully integrated within the texture of the orchestra.

Development

The concerto evolved from the earlier concertato style contrasts between the concertino and the ripieno of the baroque concerto grosso. During the mid- to- late baroque, composers such as Vivaldi and C. P. E. Bach (one of J. S. Bach's sons) replaced the concertino with a solo instrument, thereby setting the stage for the classical concerto. In the hands of classical composers, the concerto became an extended multi-movement form that featured the virtuosic display of solo instruments such as piano, violin, trumpet, and cello.

Form

In form, the concerto closely resembled the design and scope of the symphony, although there were a few important differences.

Number of Movements. The concerto eliminated the third minuet movement, so that the typical structure consisted of three movements: a sonata form with a fast tempo, a lyrical song form at a slow tempo, and a brisk concluding rondo or theme with variations.

Double Exposition. The opening sonata-allegro movement included a double exposition, in which the orchestra's statement of thematic material was followed by the soloist's exposition before the development section began.

Cadenzas. The opening and closing movements usually contained a cadenza that allowed the soloist to display his or her technical facility in a brilliant unaccompanied passage toward the end of the movement. Originally these cadenzas were improvised by the performer of the concerto, but eventually cadenzas, were notated by either the composer or a virtuoso soloist and published along with the score.

Chamber Music

Chamber music is considered "music for musicians." Genres such as divertimenti and serenades were light suitelike compositions designed for courtly entertainment. However, other chamber music genres such as sonatas and string quartets were designed to challenge and engage the performers themselves.

The Sonata

The sonata was a three-movement work constructed according to the formal scheme of the concerto. Because the piano was one of the most exciting developments associated with the classic era, musicians naturally focused much of their attention to works featuring this instrument. Composers particularly favored the medium of the solo piano sonata as a means of exploring novel techniques and sonorities. Beethoven's thirty-two piano sonatas are a striking record of classical piano technique and style. In addition to the solo piano compositions, sonatas were composed for other instruments such as violin, flute, or trumpet. These works were provided with a piano accompaniment that complemented the melodic lines with harmonies and supportive counterpoint.

String Quartet

The string quartet was both an ensemble (consisting of two violins, viola, and cello) and a specific genre (a four-movement work based on the symphonic model). Classical composers found the balanced timbre and the expressive nature of the string family well suited to an intimate, conversational chamber style. Haydn, the "father of the string quartet," best described the genre as "an engaging discussion amongst four witty conversationalists." In this "discussion" the first violin is "first among equals," being entrusted with most of the principal melodies. However, the other three instruments actively participate by trading thematic material, interjecting countermelodies, and supplying accompanimental figuration.

Vocal Genres

Interest in instrumental music increased during the classic period and the position of vocal music as the dominant medium rapidly diminished. Traditionally, much vocal music had been written for sacred use. The Enlightenment philosophy's secular emphasis relegated sacred music composition to a position of less importance. Composers still wrote masses, oratorios, and passions, but fewer of them. Church music tended to be conservative in style, but composers did incorporate new classical features such as orchestral accompaniment, formal clarity, and new harmonic vocabulary.

Opera

Opera Seria

The most important vocal medium was opera. Italian opera, called opera seria, developed the aria at the expense of earlier recitative and choruses. The plot situations became increasingly complex. Intrigues, false identities, and bizarre situations were artificially resolved through a series of beautiful songs, with the heroic male roles performed by castrati.

Opera Buffa

Another form of opera gradually emerged from subplots of opera seria. This new genre, opera buffa, moved toward plots that were more straightforward and humorous, and characters who were drawn from middle and lower classes. To correspond to this new style, composers developed a new form of recitative called *parlando*, in which the dialogue is sung with a quasi-spoken delivery. Opera buffa characters engage in spirited conversational song that is frequently written for trios or quartets.

Composers

Of the three most important instrumental composers of this period, Haydn and Beethoven almost completely avoided opera. Mozart, on the other hand, wrote some of the most beautiful and enduring works in the operatic repertoire. His *Don Giovanni* elevated the art of opera far beyond mere entertainment.

The classic period is generally characterized by an emphasis on form rather than on content. To highlight this form, classical music developed various genres and structures based on an aesthetic of symmetry and order. The most important of these forms was the sonata allegro, which was used as the opening movement of symphonies, concertos, sonatas, and string quartets.

This was an instrumental era, marked by the evolution of the orchestra, orchestral genres such as the symphony and concerto, and chamber music such as the string quartet. The period was also strongly affected by the rise of the piano. Composers continued to write sacred vocal works in the older genres of oratorio and mass, but most of the innovative vocal developments are to be found in the two styles of opera—opera seria and opera buffa. The classic period was responsible not only for most of the genres and forms, but also for many of the compositions that are still current in the Euro-American art music repertoire.

CHAPTER 15

The Romantic Period

Chronology of Events and Musicians

Romantic Period (1828–1900)

Johann Hummel (1778–1837)
Anthony Philip Heinrich (1781–1861)
John Field (1782–1837)
Niccolò Paganini (1782–1840)
Carl Maria von Weber (1786–1826)
French Revolution (1789)
Gioacchino Rossini (1792–1868)
Lowell Mason (1792–1872)
Franz Schubert (1797–1828)
Gaetano Donizetti (1797–1848)
Vincenzo Bellini 1801–1835
Louisiana Purchase (1803)

Hector Berlioz (1803–1869)
Mikhail Glinka (1804–1857)
Fulton's first steamboat (1807)
Fanny Mendelssohn (1805–1847)
Felix Mendelssohn (1809–1847)
Frederic Chopin (1810–1849)
Robert Schumann (1810–1856)
Franz Liszt (1811–1886)
Napoleon retreats from Russia (1812)
Giuseppe Verdi (1813–1901)
Richard Wagner (1813–1883)
William Fry (1813–1864)
Battle of Waterloo (1815)
Charles Gounod (1818–1893)
Clara Schumann (1819–1896)
Cesar Franck (1822–1890)
Bedřich Smetana (1824–1884)
Anton Bruckner (1824–1896)
George Bristow (1825–1898)
Stephen Foster (1826–1864)
Louis Moreau Gottschalk (1829–1869)
Alexander Borodin (1833–1897)
Johannes Brahms (1833–1897)
Telegraph invented (1836)
Georges Bizet (1838–1875)
Modest Mussorgsky (1839–1881)
John Paine (1839–1906)
Pyotr Il'yich Tchaikovsky (1840–1893)
Antonin Dvořák (1841–1904)
Edvard Grieg (1843–1907)
Nikolai Rimsky-Korsakov (1844–1908)
Gabriel Fauré (1845–1924)
Communist Manifesto (1848)
Vincent d'Indy (1851–1931)
Crimean War (1853–1856)
Arthur Foote (1853–1937)
George Chadwick (1854–1931)

Leoš Jánáček (1854–1928)
John Philip Sousa (1854–1932)
Edward Elgar (1857–1934)
Giacomo Puccini (1858–1924)
Edward MacDowell (1860–1908)
Late Romantic-Postromantic
Gustav Mahler (1860–1911)
Hugo Wolf (1860–1903)
Isaac Albéniz (1860–1909)
American Civil War begins (1861)
Bismarck becomes Premier of Prussia (1862)
Claude Debussy (1862–1918)
Horatio Parker (1863–1919)
Richard Strauss (1864–1949)
End of American Civil War (1865)
Jean Sibelius (1865–1957)
Paul Dukas (1865–1935)
Amy Beach (1867–1944)
Henry Gilbert (1868–1928)
Arthur Farwell (1877–1952)
Alexander Scriabin (1872–1915)
Sergei Rachmaninov (1873–1943)
Impressionists hold first exhibition in Paris (1874)
Maurice Ravel (1875–1937)
Invention of telephone (1876)

The label "romantic" is generally attached to the period of time bounded by the death of Beethoven (1827), and the conclusion of the ninteenth century. While eighteenth-century classicism was identified with symmetrical formal expression, the nineteenth century was marked by romantic tendencies that placed an emphasis on content rather than form.

Romanticism was, at the same time, both an evolution and a revolution. Artists, writers, and philosophers inherited traditional thought and formal expression from the preceding century. Romantic composers reserved forms such as the symphony, concerto, string quar-

tet, and opera, but they adapted, developed, and expanded these forms in order to express contemporary romantic thought. Romanticists also rebelled against aspects of the past. Turning their back on conventional approaches, romantic thinkers pursued innovative personal idioms that allowed them freedom of expression. Forms were stretched to the breaking point by the emotional, subjective, and programmatic content. As a result, radical new formal approaches were created to replace obsolete classical structures. The content demanded new forms for its expression.

Romantic music strongly reflected the turbulent spirit of the times. Just as writers and philosophers challenged traditional solutions to political and cultural problems, so composers challenged the rules and constraints of conventional musical expression. The pursuit of life, liberty, and happiness was mirrored in the search for musical freedom.

Historical Background

The romantic movement was etched against a background of sweeping social, political, and cultural change that left the world ready for modern times. Napoleon (1769–1821) succeeded in totally rearranging the political structure of Europe. In the preceding century, the French (1789) and American (1776) revolutions had set the stage for democracy. America's bold experiment in government and society was not widely imitated in Europe, but the ideals of freedom and equality certainly altered the relation between government and the individual, and undermined traditional class structure.

Rise of the Middle Class

The church had long since ceased to exert influence in temporal matters. During the nineteenth century the rule of monarchs and courts declined as well. The balance of power shifted from a privileged few to the consensus of a large and prosperous middle class. The polar extremes of society appeared to be progressing toward a common ground on which the middle class expanded, the aristocracy dwindled, and the lower class aspired to the middle class.

Effects of Industrialization

As the industrial revolution took hold in Europe and America, cities grew at an enormous rate. Rural peasant existence, tied to a life of perpetual serfdom, was abandoned for the promise associated with an urban industrial environment. For the most part, however, the poor merely traded in their backbreaking agricultural work for backbreaking, poorly paid labor in the mills and sweatshops. In response, German philosopher Karl Marx (1818–1883) developed his philosophy in the *Communist Manifesto* and other treatises. Marx claimed that rule was based on the productivity of a class; the contribution of the worker in industrial society thus necessitated the rule of the working class.

Problems of the Era

The romantic spirit had to reconcile the dichotomies—the paradoxes of the era. How much freedom could each individual possess without dissolving the fabric of society? How did one realize the glorious potential of humanity in light of the wretched realities of poverty, war, and disease? How was one to tap into the world of visions and ideas while still grappling with earthbound daily life? How was the mystery of faith, of the supernatural, and of God to be reconciled with the logical belief in the truth of science? How was the model of nature to be applied to an increasingly urban and industrial environment?

The romantic approach was not unified according to its approach to these questions but rather was defined by common problems. Individual responses were widely varied, but all romantics reacted to the same set of problems. Romanticism was not simply a style but, rather, a state of mind, an artistic and philosophic movement.

Writers

Romantic composers were highly influenced by literature of the romantic period. Composers employed romantic poetry as text for art song and modeled orchestral tone poems after romantic prose. Writers included social realists such as Dickens; idealists and dreamers such as Coleridge, Poe, and Scott; German romantics such as E.T.A. Hoffman, and Arnim and Brentano, whose collection of folk tales *Das Knaben*

Wunderhorn was tremendously influential. French romanticism flowered somewhat later in the emotion-charged works of authors such as Hugo and Dumas.

Artists

Although the visual arts drew much of their imagery from aspects of nature, history, and literature, the real focus was on inner, personal vision. Artists such as Goya portrayed the turbulence of life in fantastic scenes. The English painters Turner and Constable represented nature, while William Blake portrayed visionary scenes many of which were inspired by the Bible. Other painters, such as the French artist Delacroix, represented imaginary and historical scenes from exotic places.

Scientists

Science was in a state of ferment. Pure theoretical science was giving way to practical application as the industrial revolution encouraged activity. This resulted in inventions such as Fulton's steamboat, McCormick's reaper, Ampère's experiments with electricity, and Morse's telegraph. More speculative work was completed by scientists such as Charles Darwin, who rewrote biological thought in his book *On the Origin of Species*, and Pasteur, who explored the relation of bacteria to disease.

Philosophers

Philosophy was particularly concerned with the role of the individual in society. Schopenhauer stressed irrational human will at the expense of intellect in his rather bleak perspective. Kierkegaard reacted against the depersonalization of society and founded a school of existentialism. Marx and Engels were concerned with class struggle, and Nietzsche postulated a rational/passionate dichotomy in human nature.

The Role of Music and the Musician

The changes that occurred during the nineteenth century forced musicians to redefine their function and find a new means for earning their living. Obviously, the role of musician as servant of the court was altered by the decline of the aristocracy. Because the middle class was becoming the source of wealth and power, the musician was now dependent upon this public for support.

The Business of Music

At this point the composer theoretically had absolute freedom to write whatever he wanted—but, in reality, his freedom was limited by the degree of support fostered by a large, diverse public that was nowhere near as cultivated as the old nobility. For the first time, music actually became a business. In order to survive, the musician had to make the transition from artisan to businessman, from artist to entertainer. The success of a composer was dependent upon the sales or commission of published "popular" works, and upon his personality and showmanship as a performer.

Virtuoso

This emphasis on personality and showmanship was reflected in the concept of the virtuoso, a highly skilled performer. Audiences were not so much concerned with the music being performed but with the performer himself. Virtuosi such as Paganini and Liszt dazzled listeners with fast, colorful passages, delivered with theatrical flourish. Composers such as Dussek intentionally pandered to popular taste by writing pieces based on sensational subjects such as Marie Antoinette's encounter with the guillotine.

Conductor

The romantic period also witnessed the rise of another virtuoso musician—the conductor. Formerly, orchestras usually had been led either by the composer directing the ensemble from the keyboard, or by the *concertmaster* (first violinist) from his chair in the violin section. As the size of the orchestra grew, as the music became more complex, and as the cult of personality increased, a single musician—the conductor—was entrusted with order in the orchestra.

The conductor's instrument was the entire orchestra. In rehearsal and performance he maintained the tempo by beating time with his hand. Through expressive gestures he also controlled the volume level, shaped phrases, and imposed correct balance among sections. Eventually the conductor became the most important member of the orchestra, somewhat like a quarterback on a football team. The conductor's success was dependent on his ability both to interpret the composer's original intent and to transmit that interpretation to the performers.

The Literature of Music

Much of the impetus behind romantic thought was provided by literature. More than any other period, the nineteenth century was shaped and molded by the printed word. Romantic music exhibited this influence. Many composers were avid and cultured readers, and they often constructed programs for instrumental works based on novels and plays. Vocal music adapted to song poetry by writers such as Heine and Mörike. In addition, musicians themselves wrote about music through criticism published in journals, such as Schumann's important *Neue Zeitschrift für Musik* (New Musical Journal), or in books such as *Evenings with the Orchestra* by Berlioz.

Style Characteristics

Earlier historical periods possess a common characteristic style, a unified backdrop against which differences of individual expression are contrasted only subtly. While most listeners can identify the distinctive sound of an entire period, it is more difficult for the general audience to distinguish stylistic traits of individual composers.

In contrast, the romantic period possesses no single, universal style. The only unity is the diversity of approach. Since there are so many different and often contradictory approaches, it is difficult and misleading to generalize about romantic style. Instead, we must note a number of strongly individual styles matched with the temperament, nationality, and personal convictions of each composer.

Stylistic Concepts

Composers were generally divided over broad concepts of musical style: absolute versus programmatic, universal versus national, and grand versus miniature.

Absolute versus Programmatic

Traditionalists such as Brahms favored an absolute style that allowed the music to express itself. Other composers, such as Liszt and Wagner, used music to express extramusical programmatic ideas. Smetana explicitly depicted the long and twisting course of a river in his tone poem *The Moldau*, while Tchaikovsky presented more subtle autobiographical content in his Sixth Symphony. Some composers provided a written program to describe the intention of a work, while others used the program only as a personal compositional device.

Absolute. Absolute music tended to embrace accepted formal structures that were largely adapted from procedures developed during the classic period. Composers utilized symphony, concerto, sonata, and string quartet genres; and sonata allegro, rondo, and variation forms, but all these were altered in the romantic period by more liberal application. Works acquired greater length and proportion through continuous development, and elements of one form were combined with aspects of another to create hybrid forms such as sonata rondo.

Programmatic. Programmatic composers often felt compelled to create new forms to represent the ideas, stories, or emotions being portrayed. These works were based on the composer's ability to represent nonmusical content through music. Some composers employed leitmotifs, which could be transformed to represent the development of a person or idea. Other composers simulated natural sounds, such as water, the pounding of horses' hooves, or birdsong through similar musical representation.

Universal versus National

Universal. The classical-influenced style of absolute composers was based on a universally accepted language. The expression of the composer transcended national borders and crossed over the boundaries of time as well (there was a revival of interest in earlier music sparked by Mendelssohn's performance of Bach's *St. Matthew Passion*). Music was considered an eternal art that transcended human limitations of time and space.

National. On the other hand, the musical expression of some midcentury composers was linked with a conscious effort to cultivate nationalistic elements in their music. Musicians, such as the Russian group known as "the Five" (Cui, Borodin, Mussorgsky, Rimsky-Korsakov, and Balakirev), intentionally incorporated modal, melodic, and rhythmic features of their folk music and also simulated sounds of native instruments such as the balalaika and bagpipe. Another trend, exoticism, was related to nationalism. In this style, instead of turning inward to native music, musicians turned outward to draw upon exotic sounds as inspiration for their music. Rimsky-Korsakov's symphonic suite *Scheherazade* (1888) conjures the exotic atmosphere of the Orient through brilliant orchestration and sensuous melody.

Grand versus Miniature

Grand. Much romantic statement was grand and monumental. The symphony became a vast arena for the confrontation and development of elemental themes. Wagner's opera was the stage for the enactment of massive creation myths. The complex piano works of Liszt posed challenging philosophical constructs. While a classical symphony could be measured in minutes, a comparable romantic work might be calibrated in hours.

Music was viewed by some as a means for striving beyond small earthly concerns—a way of answering transcendent questions about God and man. The broad scope of some of this music is reflected in the technical virtuosity and large gestures of performers. The conflict of individuals within society was symbolized by the solitary piano soloist challenging the entire orchestra. The virtuosic violin performance of Paganini seemed to transcend the limits of human capability, so that some people claimed he was the devil incarnate.

Miniature. On the other hand, some romantic statement was small in scale, intimate in nature. The weighty symphonic and operatic literature was contrasted with miniature jewels for solo and chamber performance, which revealed the personal side of a composer's art. The delicate preludes of Chopin and the lieder of Schubert are every bit as beautiful and fully as romantic as the large orchestral works from the period.

Dynamics

Romantic musicians expanded dynamics at both ends of the spectrum. Soft sounds became more whispery; loud sounds grew more forceful. The usual range of dynamic indications during the classical period ranged from *ff* to *pp*. But, by Tchaikovsky's time we see markings as extreme as *ffffff* and *pppppp*.

Sudden Contrasts

Composers often used this expanded range to convey turbulent and dramatic contrast. Instead of the restrained classical balance, romantic music could suddenly explode into climaxes or dissolve into near silence. Frequently composers indicated dynamic attacks such as *sfz* (sforzando; a sharp attack followed by soft dynamic level) or *fp* (forte-piano; loud followed by soft) to articulate subtle shadings of dynamic meaning.

Gradual Changes

In addition to the subito (sudden) dynamic shifts, composers employed subtle and gradual diminuendos and crescendos that increased or diminished the intensity in small increments. This technique was used especially to underscore a gradual build to a climax, or slowly to diffuse the energy released after a climax was reached.

Intensity

Because of the technical improvements made in instrument construction, and because of the increased size and instrumentation of the orchestra, music could be performed at increasingly high levels of intensity. The forte of the classical orchestra of Haydn resembled the mezzo piano of the huge Wagnerian orchestra.

Rhythm

The element of time was treated more flexibly by romantic composers. The same tempi and proportional rhythms inherited from classical practice were employed, but the regularity of symmetrical patterns was destroyed through the pronounced use of syncopation, cross rhythms, and odd meters such as $\frac{5}{4}$. Some composers, such as Brahms, explored the interesting relationship between duple and triple time in *hemiola* passages.

$$\quad\text{♩ ♩ ♩} = \text{♩. ♩.}$$

3:2

Hemiola Rhythm

While dramatic contrast was achieved by sudden changes of tempo, subtle freedom could be attained through gradual accelerando (speeding up) or ritardando (slowing down). Important rhythmic flexibility was imparted by musicians, such as Chopin, through *rubato* techniques, which subtly increased or decreased the melody in relation to the beat. The total effect resembled the fluid ebb and flow of water rather than the machinelike regularity associated with dance.

Melody

Romantic musical expression was dependent on melody to create its magic. The freedom and emotional intensity of the period were mirrored in the passionate singing melodies that refused to be constrained by symmetrical phrases or bounded by conventions of harmonic cadences. Melodic material was still largely based on major and minor scales but, as the period progressed, composers began to explore more chromatic possibilities. This chromaticism, culminating in Wagner's operas, invested the melodic line with subtle shifts of tension and release, and pointed the way to expanded harmonies and novel modulations.

Harmony

Because homophony was the dominant musical texture, the emphasis was on melody and the supporting harmonic framework. This harmonic fabric was based on the classical major-minor tonality, but romantic composers expanded traditional practice by exploring chromatic possibilities.

Chromatic Chords

The basic sonority of the simple triadic chord was charged with more color and dissonance by augmenting the triad with additional thirds. With each additional third a new chord was created, known as a seventh, ninth, eleventh, or thirteenth chord. Each of these new chromatic chords possessed a characteristic sound and required special harmonic resolution of tension.

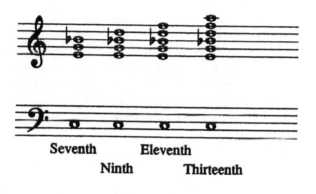

Seventh   Eleventh
      Ninth   Thirteenth

Expanded Chords

Modulation

Chromaticism also created new possibilities for modulation. Classical composers usually employed the closely related keys of the subdominant (IV) and dominant (V) for their modulations. Romantic composers expanded the system by modulating to remote keys such as the submediant (VI) and mediant (III). Much of the excitement in a romantic developmental section was derived from the bold harmonic twists and turns that took the listener far away from the security of the tonic key. Instead of purely a structural underpinning, romantic harmony became a vivid means for coloristic and dramatic expression.

Timbre

Romantic music depended heavily upon the effect of tone color to express moods, ideas, and programmatic content. Timbre is perhaps the most important and easily identifiable element of romantic musical style. In earlier periods it was possible to isolate the notes and rhythm from the timbre. The same work might easily be adapted for various combinations of instruments. Romantic musical expression, however, fuses the music and the medium in an indivisible unity. Compared to the rainbow-hued spectrum of romantic timbre, the tone color of preceding musical periods appears rather prosaic.

Improved Instruments

The romantic concept of timbre strongly paralleled technical developments in the field of instrument construction.

Woodwind, Brass, and Percussion. Woodwind instruments acquired more versatility through the introduction of a system of fingering invented around 1830 by flutist Theobald Boehm. About 1815 trumpets and French horns became capable of more fluid performance in various keys through the addition of valves. During the classic period timpani were relegated to simple tonic and dominant support at climactic moments. In the romantic period, though, the addition of pedals that facilitated rapid tuning enabled timpani to be used in every possible key.

Keyboard. Important technical improvements also increased the versatility and performance potential of keyboard instruments. The harp had been used since ancient times, but it was little more than a folk instrument until the romantic period. In 1810 Sebastien Erard introduced a system of seven double-action pedals that allowed the harp easily to play six and one-half octaves in all keys. Through his invention of the double escapement system in 1821, Erard also increased the velocity with which the piano could be played. In addition, the piano sound was made louder and brighter through the addition of a cast-iron frame invented by Alpheus Babcock in 1825.

New Instruments

Orchestral and chamber tone color was enriched through the creation and addition of new instruments. The piccolo extended the flute range upward, and the contrabassoon stretched the bassoon range downward; the bass clarinet increased the range of the clarinet, and the English horn provided a piquant extension of the oboe sound. The percussion section was expanded through the introduction of cymbals, triangles, snare drums, celesta, marimba, and xylophone. The brass family now regularly included trumpets, French horns, trombones, and tubas. Around 1815, valves were simultaneously invented by Bluhmel and Stölzel, making all the chromatic pitches available to brass instruments.

Orchestration

With such a wealth of sound to draw from, orchestration—the combination of these instruments, became an art in itself. Berlioz and Rimsky-Korsakov both published orchestration treatises that described the ranges and timbres of the various instruments, and outlined ways of combining them to achieve various effects.

Instrumental Genres

Symphony

Romantic composers generally adapted the four-movement form of the classical genre, but in their hands every aspect of the idiom was greatly developed and expanded.

Changes in Orchestra

The orchestra increased in size from approximately fifty performers to an ensemble of one hundred. In addition, the string-dominated makeup was now augmented by many brass, woodwind, and percussion instruments, which provided great contrasts of tonal color. Following the precedent of Beethoven, some composers even added choral voices to the total sound.

Changes in Form

The length of the symphony was increased in response to a changing concept of its nature. Rather than a commissioned work produced for the entertainment of aristocracy, the symphony became the favored genre for a personal, philosophical exploration or statement. Instead of the segmented introduction, development, and recapitulation of ideas that characterized classical sonata form, composers now treated their material as a continuous process of development or thematic transformation. Instead of limiting development to an isolated development section, composers fostered a sense of organic growth that permeated every aspect of the work.

This continuous development often intentionally obscured the clear-cut architecture of the classical form. Cadences were delayed or evaded; phrase lengths were asymmetrical; sections were no longer delineated by key; and movements sometimes merged without any pause. In this way romanticism evoked the continuous flow of life rather than an artifically frozen moment.

Program Symphony

The symphonic genre was also deeply affected by the romantic interest in program music. Composers were compelled to reconcile abstract form with programmatic content. As a result, new symphonic genres were created. A program symphony, such as Berlioz's *Symphonie Fantastique*, contained aspects of traditional form, but the work also presented each of the five movements as a chapter in a fanciful autobiographical narrative.

Tone Poem

The orchestral genre of the tone poem, or symphonic poem, was created by Liszt to enable the content to dictate the form. Tone poems closely resemble the idea of a program symphony, but they usually consist of only a single extended movement in which the music tells a story or describes a scene. Interesting examples of this genre include works by Liszt (*Prometheus*), Smetana (*Die Moldau*), and Richard Strauss (*Also Sprach Zarathustra*).

Symphonic Suite

Symphonic suites are multimovement works for orchestra that are based around a program. Most frequently they are adaptations of a ballet put into concert form; but some symphonic suites, such as Mussorgsky's

Pictures at an Exhibition, are written specifically in the genre. The movements of a suite are shorter than symphonic movements, and they do not usually display the thematic development and unity that are characteristic of a symphony.

Overture

Concert overtures are single movement works that resemble tone poems. Although they may be either programmatic or absolute, the form is usually rather free. They are most often performed as the first work on a concert program.

Concerto

The three-movement form of the classical concerto was adapted by romantic composers. However, the balance between soloist and orchestra, as represented by the double exposition, was transformed into a conflict or struggle between the individual and society—soloist and ensemble. As the technical prowess of the virtuoso became more important, the concerto grew to showcase the performer's skills in long and elaborate cadenzas. Most of the romantic concertos featured the piano, but some works were also written for other instruments, including the violin and cello.

Piano Genres

Since the piano was such an important instrument during the romantic period, it was natural for composers to create new genres that explored various aspects of the solo piano. These piano genres included the following short compositions.

> *Nocturnes:* "night sketches" that featured a singing melody over an arpeggiated accompaniment

> *Ballades:* lyrical narrative pieces in a free extended ternary form

> *Etudes:* studies that explored a specific sonority or technical problem

Preludes: short studies that sometimes subjected a motive or figure to various key modulations

Fantasies: improvisatory-sounding character pieces that simulated a dream state

Chopin also created a repertoire of short piano works that were loosely based on the character of certain national dances. These included:

Waltzes in $\frac{3}{4}$ time

Mazurkas based on Polish dances in triple meter

Polonaises modeled on stately Polish marches in triple meter

Vocal Genres

Solo Song

Romantic composers were fascinated by the potential for synthesis between literature and music. The solo art song provided the ideal medium for the fusion of texted poetry and the wordless expression of song. Solo songs, known as *lieder* in Germany and *chansons* in France, were intimate and personal works whose form was suggested by the shape of the poetry. Some were strophic or modified-strophic in which each stanza was subtly transformed. Other texts dictated a through-composed treatment to capture the progressive quality of the poetry.

Balance Between Voice and Piano

Romantic sensitivity to text was reflected in the beautiful balance between melody and accompaniment, between voice and piano. Supportive piano figuration in the works of Schubert or Schumann provided commentary, evoked a mood or atmosphere, and completed thoughts left unsaid by the voice. Neither overshadows the other; piano and voice are equal partners united in lyrical expression.

Song Cycles

These songs could also be gathered into a larger unity known as a song cycle. In the cycle, each song was a separate and distinct work, but they might all be related through a common subject, or by the fact that all the texts were written by a single poet. Examples of song cycles include Schubert's *Winterreise* (Winter Journey) or Schumann's *Dichterliebe* (Poet's Love).

Opera

At the beginning of the century, opera was closely based on the classical model with an emphasis on bel canto singing of arias. The chorus and orchestra were merely background support for the vocal pyrotechnics of the virtuosic soloists. Opera flourished most strongly in Italy, where composers such as Rossini, Bellini, and Donizetti maintained a traditional and conservative style.

Opera Verissimo

By mid-century, opera began to develop in some exciting new ways. The *opera verismo* of Puccini and Verdi presented plots of greater realism. To portray these dramatic subjects, composers constructed a more unified and seamless style in which arias, recitatives, choruses, and orchestra were treated as a continuum rather than as a series of separate unrelated pieces.

Wagner's Operas

Music Drama. In Germany, the trend toward organic unity culminated in the massive music dramas of Richard Wagner. These huge works based on Germanic legend fused every aspect of artistic presentation—staging, sets, costumes, lighting, orchestra, and vocalists—in a highly unified dramatic production. The music was a continuous ebb and flow of voice and orchestra in which there was no artificial separation of aria and recitative.

Leitmotifs. Unity was strikingly imparted through a system of leitmotifs, in which a musical theme was associated with a person, mood, or idea. Transformations of the leitmotif were interpreted by the listener as developments of the person or idea.

Continuous Flow. Through his opera, Wagner stretched the parameters of the romantic period. His harmony became so chromatic that the listener could scarcely discern a tonal center. In the continuous flow of music, all feeling of sectional form was eliminated. Cadences were constantly evaded and tension was never completely resolved. Modulations and dynamic surges led the listener through dizzying waves of climaxes.

Culmination of Romantic Style. In Wagner many romantic tendencies converge and culminate. The use of musical program, the synthesis of literature and music, nationalism, chromatic expansion of the harmonic system, grand and monumental expression of great length, wide spectrum of timbre and dynamics, free extension and adaptation of form, and the cult of the individual—all are elements of Wagner's personal style and are representative of the musical style of the entire period.

The romantic period is marked by highly individualized solutions to a common set of problems. There is no single romantic style. The period is shaped by the personal adaptation and extension of forms and genres inherited from the classical period. Romantic works tended to focus upon content as the generating force of the music. New genres were developed, including orchestral works based on extramusical programs such as the tone poem, and solo piano works such as ballades and nocturnes. Little music was written for chorus, but composers did explore the unity of text and music in solo art songs such as lieder.

CHAPTER 16

Music of the Twentieth Century

Chronology of Events and Musicians

Twentieth Century (1900–)

Gustav Mahler (1860–1911)
Hugo Wolf (1860–1903)
Isaac Albéniz (1860–1909)
American Civil War begins (1861)
Claude Debussy (1862–1918)
Horatio Parker (1863–1919)
Richard Strauss (1864–1949)

Jean Sibelius (1865–1957)
Paul Dukas (1865–1935)
Erik Satie (1866–1925)
Ferruccio Busoni (1866–1924)
Amy Beach (1867–1944)
Henry Gilbert (1868–1928)
Scott Joplin (1868–1917)
Suez Canal opened (1869)
Arthur Farwell (1877–1952)
Ralph Vaughan-Williams (1872–1958)
Alexander Scriabin (1872–1915)
Sergei Rachmaninov (1873–1943)
Charles Ives (1874–1954)
Maurice Ravel (1875–1937)
Arnold Schoenberg (1874–1951)
Manuel de Falla (1876–1946)
Carl Ruggles (1876–1971)
Ernest Bloch (1880–1959)
Béla Bartók (1881–1945)
Igor Stravinsky (1882–1971)
Zoltán Kodály (1882–1967)
Anton Webern (1883–1945)
Edgard Varèse (1883–1965)
Alban Berg (1885–1935)
Heitor Villa-Lobos (1887–1959)
Nadia Boulanger (1887–1979)
Paris International Exposition (1889)
Sergei Prokofiev (1891–1953)
Arthur Honneger (1892–1955)
Darius Milhaud (1892–1974)
Walter Piston (1894–1976)
Paul Hindemith (1895–1963)
Carl Orff (1895–1982)
William Grant Still (1895–1978)
Roger Sessions (1896–1985)
Virgil Thomson (1896–1989)
Henry Cowell (1897–1965)

George Gershwin (1898–1937)
Roy Harris (1898–1979)
Boxer Rebellion in China (1898–1900)
Edward "Duke" Ellington (1899–1974)
Francis Poulenc (1899–1963)
Carlos Chavez (1899–1978)
Aaron Copland (1900–1990)
Ernst Krenek (1900-)
Kurt Weill (1900–1950)
George Antheil(1900–1959)
Ruth Crawford Seeger (1901–1953)
Harry Partch (1901–1974)
William Walton (1902–1983)
Stefan Wolpe (1902–1972)
Wright Brothers' first flight (1903)
Luigi Dallapiccola (1904–1975)
Einstein's Theory of Relativity (1905)
Dmitri Shostakovitch (1906–1975)
Paul Creston (1906–1985)
Ford's Model-T car is mass-produced (1908)
Olivier Messiaen (1908-)
Elliott Carter (1908–)
Samuel Barber (1910–1981)
William Schuman (1910–)
Gian Carlo Menotti (1911–)
John Cage (1912–)
Conlon Nancarrow (1912–)
Benjamin Britten (1913–1976)
Witold Lutoslawski (1913–)
World War I begins (1914)
Milton Babbitt (1916–)
Alberto Ginastera (1916–1983)
Russian Revolution (1917)
Leonard Bernstein (1918–1990)
George Rochberg (1918–)
Leon Kirchner (1919–)
World War I concluded (1918)

Bruno Maderna (1920–1973)
Ralph Shapey (1921–)
Iannis Xenakis (1922–)
Lukas Foss (1922–)
György Ligeti (1923–)
Luciano Berio (1925–)
Pierre Boulez (1925–)
Gunther Schuller (1925–)
Hans Werner Henze (1926–)
Earle Brown (1926–)
Karlheinz Stockhausen (1928–)
Thea Musgrave (1928–)
Great Depression in America begins (1929)
George Crumb (1929–)
Pauline Oliveros (1932–)
Krzysztof Penderecki (1933–)
Morton Subotnik (1933–)
Peter Maxwell Davies (1934–)
Terry Riley (1935–)
La Monte Young (1935–)
Steve Reich (1936–)
Philip Glass (1937–)
David Del Tredici (1937–)
Charles Wuorinen (1938–)
World War II begins (1939)
John Adams (1947–)

The twentieth century has been a time of rapid scientific, technological, artistic, and cultural development that has reshaped human civilization. Because these changes have come at such a swift pace, it is difficult to make accurate generalizations about the twentieth century. How do you view the forest when you are among all the fast-growing trees?

Scholars generally concur in their assessment of previous historical periods. Each period, medieval through romantic, seems unified by a common approach to a distinct set of questions posed by the times. It is possible to speak of basic philosophic attitudes, general scientific directions, and universal aesthetic principles and styles. However, the twentieth century is marked by a plurality of styles and approaches that, within a brief span of time, are disseminated, assimilated, and then abandoned. Any discussion of twentieth-century artistic trends must deal with a series of distinct "isms," including impressionism, symbolism, neoclassicism, surrealism, expressionism, serialism, minimalism, and modernism.

Whatever the rate of change and the diversity of styles and developments, it is always difficult to maintain an objective perspective on one's own century. Incidents that seem trivial at a particular time may grow in significance when judged against future developments. Composers or artists who experienced contemporary popularity may be neglected by successive generations, while creative artists who labored in anonymity during their lifetimes may be acclaimed after their death. However, as the end of the twentieth century nears, it is becoming easier to gain some perspective on these times. Musical works that were once denounced as mere noise have been fully absorbed within the standard concert repertoire. With the clarity of historical hindsight, we can now render some objective assessment of the composers, compositions, and performers that have left their mark on the twentieth century. The "sieve of time" generally insures the survival of superior artistic achievements while sifting out lesser works.

Historical Background

The Technological Revolution

When the sun rises on January 1 in the year 2000, historians may well dub this century the era of technology. The rapidly expanding technology of the twentieth century has revolutionized the way we view ourselves and our planet, and how we carry on our daily activities. As the nineteenth century and its industrial revolution was powered by steam, so the twentieth century and its rapid technological growth was shaped by the harnessing of electricity. Electrical advances were most closely identified with the work of Thomas Edison (1847–1931), whose inventions such as the incandescent light bulb and electric power plants changed society by channeling inexpensive and efficient energy into our daily lives. By the end of the Second World War, humanity was poised on the threshold of another age—this one ushered in by the discovery and proliferation of nuclear energy. Albert Einstein (1879 –1955) was more of a speculative scientist than Edison. His theories concerning relativity and quantum mechanics completely altered our perception of the universe and led to such monumental achievements as atomic fission and manned space flights to the moon.

During previous centuries people scarcely sensed the impact of events beyond their confined regional boundaries. For the most part, countries produced their own goods and fed their own inhabitants. Conflicts were resolved by civil wars involving factions within the same country, or by territorial wars pitting neighboring countries against one another. Geographical boundaries such as mountains, rivers, and deserts insulated countries from one another; and cultural divisions such as language and religion defined the societal borders. Travel, trade, and artistic and scientific advances crossed over these borders, but they moved at a pace limited by foot, horse, boat, and steam-powered transportation.

During the twentieth century, the tempo of communication and travel accelerated wildly. People across the world became progressively linked together through an elaborate web of printed words, radio, recorded sound, telephone, television, satellite communication, computer networks, and facsimile transmission. Communication became instantaneous and, as a result, isolationist geographical and cultural barriers are beginning to disappear. These technological developments have altered every aspect of our political, social, and cultural way of life. Instead of isolated villages, regions, or countries, humanity has become one extended global community.

Global Interdependence

In a global community, autonomy of regional isolation is largely dissolved. Wars, especially World War I (1914–1918) and World War II (1939–1945), involved countries across the globe. The threat of nuclear holocaust has imperiled the entire earth. Economies are no longer contained within borders. The Great Depression of the 1930s affected the world; today stock markets and currency values across the earth are interdependent. Trade and travel quickly and freely span borders. All of Europe will soon be united in a common market with unified currency. Even previously "closed" societies such as the Soviet bloc and China are being assimilated into the world market.

International Artistic Exchange

As might be expected in an era of international exchange, the world's leading intellectual leaders are no longer content to remain isolated in the country of their birth. Increasing travel, communication, and displacement brought about through two world wars have taken the careers of these key figures throughout the world. As a result, it has become increasingly difficult to characterize artistic schools in terms of nationality. Developments that originate in one country may soon spread and become absorbed into an international language of the arts.

Cultural Developments

The social sciences (psychology, sociology, anthropology, and political science) emerged as disciplines that provided new insight into ourselves and the world. Psychology, in particular, presented a novel vision of humanity that strongly influenced directions in arts and literature. The psychologist Sigmund Freud (1856–1939) explored our inner motivations through books such as *The Interpretation of Dreams*, and Carl Jung (1875–1961) established the practice of analytical psychology based on the conflict and resolution of extroversion (outward to people) versus introversion (inward to symbols and myths).

Literature

Writers such as James Joyce (1882–1941) initiated a prose style that proceeds via a "stream of consciousness" technique and makes the author a personal participant in the action of a novel. Joyce's novel *Ulysses* (1922) abandoned traditional chronological structure in presenting two days of Dublin life as an interlocking series of shifting perspectives. Poets such as T. S. Eliot (1888–1965) and Ezra Pound (1885–1972) also strongly challenged traditional form. Eliot's *The Waste Land* (1922) painted a bleak view of the world through a type of literary collage that fused obscure images and references with collo-quial popular expression.

Architecture

Other art forms made just as revolutionary a break with inherited traditional forms and structures. Architects such as Frank Lloyd Wright (1867–1959) stressed an "organic" style in which form and function are based on nature, in an environmental context. Architects such as Walter Gropius (1883–1969), Le Corbusier (1887–1965) and Mies van der Rohe (1886–1969) developed the modernist Bauhaus style which was based on clean, abstract lines and nonsupporting walls constructed from glass, concrete, and steel.

Visual Arts

The visual arts broke radically with realistic treatment of subject matter. Pablo Picasso (1881–1973) distorted reality, presenting more than one perspective simultaneously through the cubist style. Some artists, including Salvador Dali (1904–1988) developed a surrealist style based on Freudian psychology, in which everyday objects were presented in unusual, dreamlike contexts. Another group of artists, including Wassily Kandinsky (1866–1944), Piet Mondrian (1872–1944), and Paul Klee (1879–1940) completely abandoned representa-tional art, abstracting the concepts of color, light, and form from concrete images. Photography developed from documentary into art through the work of such people as Alfred Stieglitz (1864–1946) and Edward Weston (1886–1958).

The Effects of Technology on Music

All the technology of the twentieth century had a direct and pro-found bearing on music. From Edison's invention of the phonograph in 1877 to the laser-read compact disk and digital-audio tape technology of today, the capability of recording sound has forever altered our perception of music. Electronic reproduction preserved and dissemin-ated sound so that for the first time, a single performance could be heard out of context, separated from the original event by both time and space.

Diminished Participation

Today, audiences can hear any sort of music—be it opera, rock, Balinese gamelan, or Gregorian chant- whenever and wherever they desire. This has put a world of music, past and present, literally at our fingertips. At the same time, this easy access has diminished our inclination to participate actively in music. It is simpler to turn on a machine and listen passively than to attend a live performance or take part in the performance ourselves.

Preference for Older, Familiar Music

Recorded sound has strongly affected our concert repertoire, that corpus of popular works that are regularly performed and recorded. For the first time, contemporary composers and performers have been forced to compete with music and performances of the past. Most listeners seem to prefer hearing more familiar music composed during the last two centuries than the more adventurous contemporary works. The Schwann catalog of recordings lists over seventy recordings of Beethoven's Fifth Symphony, whereas most compositions written during this century have but a single listing.

Taking Music for Granted

The easy availability of music, referred to as "sound inflation," has also affected our ability to concentrate intently on the music. Although we are accustomed to hearing a constant stream of music from sources such as Muzak, television, and portable cassette players, we seldom listen with our full attention. As never before, music has become a background activity—a soundtrack for our lives. Audiences of the past listened to music with different ears; the sounds they heard constituted a unique and magical experience. It was possible that the work would never be performed again, and certain that that particular performance would vanish forever. Audiences today take music for granted, knowing that they can listen to the same work over and over again.

Higher Performance Standards

Advances in recording technology and sound reproduction have greatly altered our listening expectations. Currently it is possible to engineer "perfect" performances in which every human flaw and imperfection of intonation, balance, or articulation is corrected. Through digital recording processes, the sound can be shaped and engineered to suit the most discriminating ear. As a result, audiences critically measure live performances against artificially high standards set by synthetically perfect recorded performances. This has elevated the level of performance, but it has also created some unrealistic expectations in which spontaneity is sacrificed to technical polish.

Synthesizer-Assisted Performance and Composition

Through digital sampling and sequencing, the sounds of acoustic instruments can be reproduced and assembled slowly, layer by layer. With the assistance of a relatively inexpensive synthesizer, it is possible for a person possessing very limited keyboard skills to simulate the full orchestral sound of a Beethoven symphony. This technology has been successfully applied to commercial and pop music, and it is now strongly affecting the performance and composition of art music as well. Some musicians are successfully using synthesizers and sequencers to provide their orchestral or chamber group accompaniment while they perform live.

Style Characteristics

Twentieth-century musical style is defined by its eclecticism and diversity of approach. There is no single set of distinguishing characteristics that can be broadly applied to the wealth of innovative personal compositional techniques invented during this century. Faced with the breakdown of traditional tonality and the emergence of new technology, composers were forced to consider experimental ways of framing their musical ideas.

Personal Idioms

Some composers broke radically with tradition and established new "contextual" systems of tonality that rejected the common-practice rules of triadic harmony. Others took a more conservative approach and merely "bent" the rules of traditional tonality by stretching the paarameters of the old system through extreme chromaticism, expanded chords, and unusual key relationships. Some composers incorporated influences from outside the Euro-American tradition, while others drew upon aspects of the distant past to shape their musical language. In all these approaches, evolutionary or revolutionary, the only constant was the emphasis upon experimentation and the desire for a distinctly personal idiom.

Tonality

The most striking aspect of change in the transition from nineteenth- to twentieth-century style is found in the area of tonality. Romantic musicians inherited a tonal system of triadic functional harmony. Nineteenth century composers weakened the functional aspect of harmony through deceptive and evaded cadences, large ambiguous chords, and modulations to distant keys through chromatic movement. This approach obscured traditional resolutions of tension and created the impression that any note could lead to any other note.

While these innovations stretched the tonal system to its limit, romantic composers never completely abandoned the tonal system. In fact, their new style was still dependent upon the traditional system, succeeding only because it provided a fresh perspective on traditional audience expectations. You cannot be surprised unless you expect something. Although some twentieth-century composers continued to write in a postromantic style that still clung to traditional harmony, others·broke with the past and invented new ways of ordering their material. These new approaches were largely shaped by changing views on the definitions of consonance and dissonance.

Enriched Harmony: Dissonance

During the baroque and classic periods harmony was based on the triad, which was formed by placing two successive thirds above a root tone. These highly consonant triads provided a systematic framework for expressing tension and relaxation. Composers of the late nineteenth and the twentieth centuries increased the complexity of harmony by making chords more dissonant. This was achieved by adding one or more thirds to the original triad, thereby creating seventh, ninth, eleventh, and thirteenth chords (so called according to the interval separating the root tone from the last added pitch).

Seventh chords create a clear sense of harmonic movement and melodic direction. The dissonant interval of a seventh is compelled to resolve, and this resolution creates a clearly defined sense of direction. On the other hand, ninth, eleventh, and thirteenth chords contain several dissonant intervals whose dissonance creates a static or ambiguous sound. These complex chords present no distinct sense of harmonic force or direction, and without that force and direction, harmony becomes more colorful, yet less functional. This coloristic sense of harmony is best represented by Claude Debussy (1862–1918) and other composers of the impressionist school.

Polytonality

An eleventh chord may also be perceived as two different triads sounded simultaneously. This possibility suggested a new harmonic approach in which layers of chords could be placed against one another. Depending upon the instrumentation and spacing of the chords, this bitonality or polytonality (more than one tonal center sounded simultaneously) could be perceived as either several distinct layers of sound or a single complex chord. Extended passages of this polytonality can be found in the compositions of Charles Ives and Igor Stravinsky.

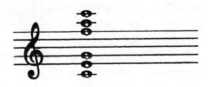

Polychord (C major and F Major)

Quartal Harmony

Another approach to harmony involved avoiding the use of triads altogether. One such technique was a quartal harmony in which chords were formed by stacking fourths instead of thirds over a root tone. This created an "open" sound that combined modern dissonance with the sound of medieval parallel organum.

A Quartal Chord

Clusters

Chords were also built of successive major or minor seconds. This created a highly dissonant cluster of sounds in which specific pitches could not be distinguished. Instead, the cluster was perceived as an indefinite and percussive sound mass.

A Cluster

Alternative Scales

As an alternative to the traditional tonal system, some composers based their melodic and harmonic material on various scales and modes belonging to music of different cultures. Through increased artistic interchange, composers acquired some appreciation and understanding of foreign music, which they then applied to their own compositional style.

Alternative Scale

Pentatonic Scales

Pentatonic scales are five-note scales that are found in traditional music throughout the world. The most common pentatonic scale is constructed by playing only the black notes on a piano. The French composer Debussy (1862–1918) was excited by the different pentatonic scales he heard performed by a Javanese gamelan orchestra at the 1889 Paris International Exposition. Thereafter, he incorporated various five-tone scales within his own music.

Pentatonic Scale

Whole-Tone Scale

The whole-tone scale begins like the standard major scale, but because it is built on a series of whole steps without intervening half steps, it contains only six notes. This is a scale that was widely used by Debussy and the jazz pianist Thelonious Monk.

Whole-Tone Scale

Microtones

Western musical tradition has established the half step as the smallest building block of scales. Some cultures in Africa and the Orient regularly divide their scales into smaller increments known as microtones. Microtones seem "out of tune" to Western listeners, whose hearing has over the course of centuries grown accustomed to the half step. However, some composers, such as Charles Ives, have expanded Western musical vocabulary by introducing microtones and quarter tones (halfway between a half step). Interestingly, the "blues" note (flatted third, or seventh) probably appeared as a result of a musical "compromise" effected between African and European traditions.

Atonality

Tonality is a sense of "gravity" imparted by the arrangement of notes bound to a central tone through the relationships of scale and key. This is a little like our solar system, in which the planets revolve in their established order around the sun. Atonality is based on the deliberate removal of that sense of tonal center. All twelve notes have an equal relationship to one another. There is no single star to exert gravitational force upon the orbits of other heavenly bodies.

Schoenberg's Early Experiments

The first atonal music was written early in the twentieth century by the German composer Arnold Schoenberg (1874–1951). In works such as *Pierrot Lunaire* (1912), Schoenberg explored a new musical vocabulary that completely avoided triadic chords, scales, and keys. Instead, he developed motives and melodic fragments within a framework of dissonances that did not necessarily resolve. The most challenging and disturbing aspect of the sound was the new definition of dissonance implied by the music.

Schoenberg's early atonal works were ordered according to individual *contexts*. The "tonality" and procedure for each composition were structured by the musical material that was presented initially. Somewhat like a scientific hypothesis and proof, each piece had its own specific construction that was developed in a unique way.

Twelve-Tone Serial Composition

By the early 1920s Schoenberg had formalized his experiments with atonality in a new system referred to as the "serial" or "twelve-tone" system. In this approach, the composer took all twelve tones of the chromatic scale (C, C♯, D, D♯, E, F, F♯, G, G♯, A, A♯, B, C) and put them into a specific order, which was maintained throughout the work. To ensure that each tone received equal emphasis, so that no single tone became a central focus, Schoenberg indicated that all twelve tones should be played in sequence before returning to the original tone. Since notes cannot be repeated, according to a strict interpretation of this system, no tonal center is emphasized. When you establish your original sequence of tones, known as the *tone row* or *set*, you dictate the order of intervals and the characteristic sound of the entire work.

A Tone Row from *Symphony*, Op. 21, by Webern

Tone Row Manipulations

The series of intervals implied by the tone row limited the choices a composer could make, but the system also provided various means for manipulating the row so that the composer was not completely bound to the original sequence of tones. These methods include transposition, retrograde, inversion, retrograde inversion, and chord structures.

Transposition. A row may be transformed by raising or lowering each tone by the same degree. This is comparable to changing key within traditional tonal harmony.

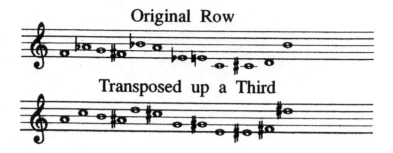

Original Row

Transposed up a Third

Retrograde. The row may be reversed so that the first note becomes the last note sounded. In this way the intervals are maintained, but the sequence occurs backward.

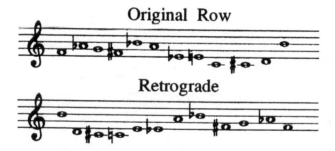

Original Row

Retrograde

Inversion. The inverted form of the row changes the basic direction of the row. The intervals that ascended in the original row are now placed upside-down so that they descend. This inversion resembles a mirror-image of the original.

Original Row

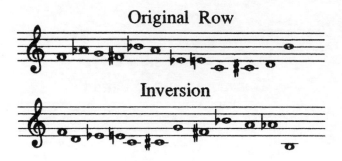

Inversion

Retrograde Inversion. The retrograde inversion form of the row combines the retrograde (backward) process with the inversion (upsidedown) process, so that the row is now not only heard in reverse order but the direction of each interval is exactly the opposite of the original.

Original Row

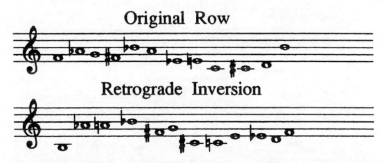

Retrograde Inversion

Chords. Chords can be formed from any version of the row (transposition, retrograde, inversion, retrograde inversion) by sounding several intervals at once. These chords will not display the simple triadic or quartal qualities of traditional harmony, but may well consist of a mixture of consonant and dissonant tones. Chords will consist of three or more tones.

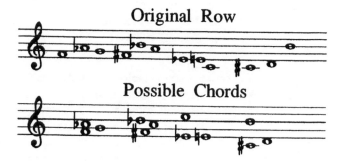

Total Serialization

Based on the model of a sequentially ordered tone row, composers such as Milton Babbitt extended the system to include other aspects of the sound including dynamics, rhythm, and timbre. Thus, eventually every aspect of the musical material might be constructed according to the highly mathematical process of serial composition.

Choice of Tone Row

The choice of tone row is important because it generates all the harmonic and melodic material that will be developed during the composition. However, it is also important to remember that the composer is responsible for every musical choice; the twelve-tone system is merely an artistic tool. Tone rows may imply certain directions, but they never completely dictate the direction a work will take. The process is not really very different from the strict contrapuntal structures explored in a fugue by J. S. Bach. Each composer who chooses to employ the twelve tone system must adapt the technique to suit his or her own personal expression.

Combined Tonality

The orthodoxy of twelve-tone composition strongly shaped the tonal material of many compositions written from the 1920s through the 1960s. Recently, however, compositions have reflected a more eclectic tonality that equally embraces elements of early church modes, traditional harmony, chromatically extended harmony, exotic tunings and modes, and atonalism. Rather than be governed by a single tonal system, composers now feel free to incorporate tonal characteristics from a multitude of different systems into their work.

Melody

A discussion of twentieth-century melody cannot be separated from the previous discussion of harmony. Melodic shape was largely determined by the musician's choice of tonality. Composers writing in a postromantic or impressionist style continued to shape their tonal melodies in long conjunct lines. Melodic interest was enhanced through unexpected chromatic movement that evaded cadence points.

On the other hand, composers who wrote in an atonal or twelve-tone style generally constructed brief, motivic melodies that implied more than they actually stated. The melodic contour more closely resembled a connect the-dot picture than a completed flowing line. The phrasing was short, the intervals were disjunct, and the contour was fragmentary. The melody was no longer the focus of the music; instead it became a building block in the work's architecture. Because of the disjunct quality, these melodies are technically challenging to perform and initially difficult to comprehend.

Rhythm

While the importance of "catchy" and singable melody decreased during the twentieth century, the role of rhythm grew ever more prominent. Composers expanded the entire range of temporal expression to produce a sense of rhythmic tension, motion, and surprise. It was almost as though composers had gone as far as they could with tonality, and now it was time to explore another parameter—rhythm.

Rhythmic structures during much of the romantic era were based on predictable patterns, constant tempi, and regular meters that were maintained throughout a work. Twentieth-century composers developed a more flexible rhythmic vocabulary that included asymmetrical phrasing, odd meters, changing meters, polyrhythms, changing tempi, and syncopation.

Asymmetrical Phrasing and Odd Meters

The ideal "classical" phrase occupied four measures in $\frac{4}{4}$ meter (sixteen beats altogether). Both the meter and the phrase length remained constant throughout the work in order to highlight the clarity of the musical architecture. Twentieth-century works sought to conceal or obscure that rigid formal sense by presenting phrases of unequal length. Frequently these ideas were based on odd meters, such as $\frac{5}{4}$ and $\frac{7}{4}$, in which there were uneven groupings of notes. For instance, $\frac{5}{4}$ might unexpectedly contrast a group of notes in triple meter with a group of notes in duple meter. The surprise occurred as the listener expected the first beat of the second measure to sound as though it were an unaccented last beat of the previous measure.

$\frac{3}{4}$ meter   *1* 2 3 *1* 2 3 *1* 2 3 *1* 2 3

$\frac{5}{4}$ meter   *1* 2 3 *1* 2 *1* 2 3 *1* 2

Changing Meters

The idea of surprise created by odd meters could be extended to changing meters. Rather than retain the same meter throughout a work, composers started changing meters, sometimes as often as every bar, in order to shift the accented beat. The basic pulse of the tempo remained constant, but the listener was kept in a state of anticipation because there was no predictable rhythmic regularity.

Polyrhythms

The concept of asymmetric rhythms was also applied to the simultaneous use of more than one layer of sound. Polyrhythms result when more than one rhythmic pattern or meter is heard on different lines that are sounded simultaneously. For instance, a trumpet might play in three (*1* 2 3 *1* 2 3) while an accompanying piano played a duple pattern (*1* 2 3 4 *1* 2 3 4). This produced an exciting conflict of accents and syncopation as each performer's constant metric pattern intertwines and contrasts with the other part.

1 2 3 *1* 2 3 *1* 2 3 *1* 2 3 *1* 2 3 *1* 2 3

1 2 3 4 *1* 2 3 4 *1* 2 3 4 *1* 2 3 4 *1* 2 3 4

Duple and Triple Polyrhythms

Tempo Changes

Changes in tempo, the basic pulse of the beat, can be simulated through proportional augmentation or subdivision of the beat. These changes sound rather sudden and rigid because they are always bound by some proportion to the original beat.

Proportional Tempo Acceleration

More flexible tempo changes can be produced by altering the frequency of the beat itself. Twentieth-century composers often used gradual changes (*ritardandos* and *accelerandos*) as well as sudden tempo shifts. In an effort to achieve exactly the desired effect, composers indicated specific metronomic markings. The traditional terms, such as allegro or largo, gave the performer considerable freedom of interpretation, but adherence to metronomic markings ensured the "correct" tempo intended by the composer.

Syncopation

Syncopation is the use of an accent in an unexpected place. Through the influence of jazz, it became a key element in musical expression. Asymmetrical rhythms, irregular phrases, and unpredictable rhythms all create surprises through various syncopation techniques. To achieve this syncopation, the expectation of regular meter must first be established so that irregular accents take place within a frame of reference. Syncopation can be effected by the following techniques:

    (a) Accents (more attack and volume)

    (b) Polyrhythms (more than one meter sounding at a time)

    (c) Rests placed on the normally accented beat

    (d) Tones held across the bar line

    (e) Meter changes

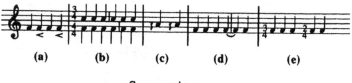

(a)   (b)   (c)   (d)   (e)

Syncopation

Timbre

The universe of sounds practically exploded with new possibilities during the twentieth century. Musicians developed new techniques for extending the potential of traditional acoustic instruments. They also explored the exciting sonic possibilities created by the emerging electronic technology. Instead of a supporting character in the service of pitch and rhythm, tone color was often thrust into the spotlight as the central focus of musical expression. Some compositions, written in a style called *klangfarbenmelodie* ("tone-color melody"), actually focus exclusively on timbre, repeating but a single pitch throughout the work.

String Timbre

String timbre innovations included the use of *col legno*, a new and more percussive technique of producing sound that called for the performer to tap on the strings with the wooden part of the bow. Other effects, such as *pizzicato* (plucking the string with fingers) and *spiccato* (detached strokes), were more widely used for long passages, including entire movements. String tone was often modified by playing either *sul tasto* (over the fingerboard), which produced a darker sound, or *sul ponticello* (over the bridge), which produced a bright, thin color. The use of various *harmonics* (produced by lightly touching the string at specific places) yielded clear ringing tones.

Pitch and timbre were both affected by different tunings, known as *scordatura*, which were sometimes called for to exploit certain sounds or facilitate fingering patterns. Composers also made greater use of various *glissandi* (sliding along the string) and called for a wide range of *vibrato* (slight fluctuation of pitch). Finally, the entire range of the instruments was explored, compelling the performer to skate along the very top of the fingerboard.

Woodwind and Brass Timbre

Woodwind and brass timbres were extended through more pronounced use of the saxophone family. Although Adolphe Sax invented the instrument in 1840, it was not until the twentieth century that it was widely embraced in both jazz and art music repertoire. New techniques were applied to the more traditional wind instruments as well. Musicians were required to click keys, hum or sing into the bell, and use a variety of different mutes. New fingerings and breathing techniques allowed for extended ranges, the use of *multiphonics* (chords), and coloristic effects such as *flutter-tonguing* (produced by rolling the tongue).

Percussion Timbre

The exploration of percussion timbre was one of the most important aspects of twentieth-century music. Previously percusssion had been relegated to a supporting role. Typically in the past a cymbal player might wait for well over an hour before delivering the final crash at the end of a piece. During the twentieth century, however, percussion instruments participated more fully in a work, and greater numbers of percussion instruments were called for in chamber and orchestral literature. Eventually the percussion ensemble itself became recognized as an independent section, and specific compositions were written for groups of percussion without any additional string or wind instruments.

Keyboard Timbre

The Harpsichord. After centuries of neglect, the harpsichord returned in the twentieth century because its delicate percussive sound enhanced various chamber music ensembles. In addition, the harpsichord could now be amplified so that it could serve as an equal partner with other instruments in the full orchestra.

The Piano. Musicians explored the full range (over seven octaves) of the piano and made additional use of the three special pedals. Some composers also "prepared" the instrument by inserting chains, bits of felt, or other objects inside the case to alter the timbre. Other novel effects were achieved by having performers strum, scrape, or pluck strings inside the piano without using the keyboard.

Vocal Timbre

Twentieth-century music placed unusual demands on vocal technique. Singers were called upon to span widely disjunct leaps, to produce various vibratos and coloration, and to achieve intonations that sometimes required microtones. One approach known as *sprechstimme* is a mixture of speech and song in which ascending or descending motion is indicated, but not specific pitches. Modern composers, such as Luciano Berio, require a vast arsenal of sounds including whispers, gurgles, moans, and screams, previously not considered "musical."

Ensemble Timbre

Twentieth-century composers continued to write for the traditional orchestral and chamber ensembles, but they were also more inventive in assembling chamber groups. Instead of maintaining the homogeneous string quartet or woodwind quintet, composers mixed instruments from various families to produce a timbre marked by strong contrast. The romantic-scale orchestra containing approximately one hundred members was still widely used, but orchestra performances were usually devoted to repertoire drawn from the classical and romantic periods, and composers focused more of their attention on chamber music.

Electronic Timbre

Nothing had a greater impact on the world of timbral possibility than the advent of electronic technology. From the early tape manipulations of the sound known as *musique concrète* to the sophisticated synthesizer technology of today, electronics has opened a world of sound in which any noise imaginable can become music. The roar of a jet, the gentle patter of rain, an oboe playing the note E♮, can all be incorporated into a musical composition. Armed with a synthesizer, the composer's use of timbre is limited only by his imagination.

Dynamics

Dynamics in the twentieth century utilizes the full spectrum of intensity from the barest whisper of a *pppppp* to a thunderous *ffffff*. Composers have become increasingly specific in their dynamic indications, sometimes indicating a certain dynamic level for each note. The use of electronic amplification has allowed subtle nuances of balance between performers, and increased the total scale of dynamics to include sound at the threshold of pain.

Form

Composers of the twentieth century have used every available form developed during the preceding centuries. Song forms, binary and ternary forms, return forms, arch forms, sonata form, imitative forms, and dance forms have all been employed and invested with new meaning and relationships. Much contemporary music derives its architecture contextually, developing formally on the basis of the specific material rather than according to a preestablished model.

The twentieth century also witnessed a marked resurgence of interest in variation forms. However, variation became a guiding principle; no longer was it simply a discrete form encompassing a stated idea followed by a series of distinct sections. Instead of presenting musical ideas through exact repetition, composers preferred to subject their material to continuous variation.

Instrumental Genres

Twentieth-century composers continued to write in the same established genres. In general, musicians favored smaller-scale works that were shorter and called for fewer performers. Thus, multimovement compositions such as symphonies, operas, and concerti were often written for chamber-size groupings and were designed on a smaller scale.

Film and Television Music

Most of the new musical genres were composed as functional music to accompany dance, cinema, television, and video. As film and television became the dominant media, many musicians found studio work both lucrative and interesting. Although the primary function of television and film scoring was supportive, composers had quite a bit of creative freedom in the way they chose to highlight the action.

Electronic Music

The development of electronic technology led to the genre of electronic music. Some composers used synthesizers merely to simulate traditional instruments or provide new timbral effects within traditional genres; others created electronic compositions that explored the unique capabilities of electronic media. Electronic music could be quite different from other genres in its presentation. For instance, a piece might well be performed on tape with no living performers whatsoever on stage. Since this type of performance lacked a human dimension, other pieces coupled live performers with tape playback, added slides and video to a taped performance, or featured "live" performance on synthesizers. Exciting new possibilities occasioned by this expanding technology are still being explored.

Some Stylistic Trends

Impressionism

Impressionism was a French-dominated style that bridged the transition from the nineteenth to the twentieth century. Influenced by French symbolist poets such as Rimbaud, and painters such as Monet and Renoir, musicians developed a style that captured the fleeting impression of an object. Impressionist art implied more than it actually stated. Claude Debussy (1862–1918), the foremost composer in this style, developed a personal idiom that featured flexible rhythms, splashes of brightly colored timbre, and harmonies that appeared as free as water or wind.

Neoclassicism

In an attempt to recollect the balance and symmetry of the classical period, musicians such as Igor Stravinsky (1882–1971) returned to a formally ordered style known as neoclassicism. While the harmony, rhythm, and timbre were clearly modern, the adherence to earlier formal principles informed neoclassic works with grace and clarity of expression.

Expressionism

In reaction to French impressionism, German writers, painters, and musicians developed a subjective and emotion-charged style known as expressionism. If impressionism was a glimpse of nature, then expressionism was a penetrating vision of the inner psyche. The music, by composers such as Arnold Schoenberg (1874–1951) and Alban Berg (1885–1935), is marked by extreme dissonance, wide ranges, disjunct melodies, and passionate expression.

Nationalism

While musical style became an international language in the twentieth century, some composers looked to their own tradition of folk music to assert their particular ethnic heritage. The Hungarian composer Béla Bartók (1881–1945) collected vast amounts of traditional music, which he assimilated into his personal musical style. Similarly, American composers such as Charles Ives (1874–1954) and Aaron Copland (1900–1990) incorporated fragments of jazz, band marches, and hymns into a peculiarly American style.

Experimentalism

Much of the music composed during the twentieth century has been experimental. Centuries of accumulated musical culture have left the twentieth-century composer little room for originality. As a result, musicians struggled for new and creative approaches that would not just echo musical traditions of the past. These experimental styles include aleatoric, serialist, and minimalist music.

Aleatoric (Chance) Music

Conceived by John Cage (1912–), aleatoric music allows for some musical choices to be made randomly so that the composer and the performer are only partially responsible for the performance. *Klavierstück* ("Piano Piece"), written in 1956 by the German composer Karlheinz Stockhausen, is a good example of the application of aleatoric principles to music composition. The nineteen short sections of the piece may be shuffled around and performed in any order.

Serialism

In serialist music, the twelve-tone system for ordering pitches developed by Schoenberg was applied to every aspect of the music so that timbre, rhythm, and dynamics were ordered according to numerical systems. Composers such as Milton Babbitt (1916–) sought to marry the related disciplines of music and mathematics.

Minimalism

Minimalism is a style developed in the 1960s by La Monte Young (1935–), Philip Glass (1937–), Steve Reich (1936–), and others. In rejecting the complexity of modern music, minimalism developed as a compositional style inspired by the rhythmic and melodic cycles of northern Indian and West African music. Minimalism is marked by repetitive melodic ostinatos, consonant and static harmonies, and very gradual development of ideas. Composers such as John Adams have extended the minimalist aesthetic in works such as *The Chairman Dances*.

Mixed Media

The interrelationship between the various artistic disciplines has been explored in the past through the genres of opera, ballet, and theater. Twentieth-century composers have continued to work in these genres, but they have also explored new ways to combine the arts. Some have coupled slide shows with live or electronic performance; others require the musicians to create a dramatic presence through costumes and speech. Works in the genre known as "performance art" fuse elements of visual arts, acting, and music in a new medium that challenges the static relationship between audience and performer.

Neoromanticism

In reaction to the extremely dissonant sound and abstract intellectual character identified with much modern music, a number of composers have returned to a more subjective and tonal style known as neoromanticism. Composers such as David del Tredici (1937–) and Krzysztof Penderecki (1933–) employ a wide arsenal of contemporary sounds, but the expressive core reflects the passion and idealism of nineteenth-century romanticism.

Musically, the twentieth century is a culmination of all the styles and techniques that have come before. There is no single unified style; rather, the era is dominated by many highly personal approaches that result in a number of trends or "isms." Technology, especially electronic sound production, has radically changed the ways in which music is produced and consumed. In general, art music of this century can be characterized as dissonant, brief in duration, composed for mixed-instrument chamber ensembles, and based on the development of short motivic ideas. As we approach the end of the twentieth century, some critics believe that we have come to the end of the "modern" era. The new period we are now entering has been termed "postmodern." It is characterized by eclecticism, reintegration of the past, and a blurring of the borders between folk, popular, and high art.

CHAPTER 17

Music and the World

The previous six chapters have been devoted to the chronological development of Euro-American art music. This perspective reflects the history of art music as seen from the vantage point of Western civilization; it is by no means an all-inclusive portait of human musical achievement. To complete the picture, we need to consider other worlds of music—from art music conceived outside the Euro-American tradition to popular and traditional music performed throughout the world.

Since the study of world music is such a vast topic, all we can do in this chapter is draw attention to the way in which non-Western musical approaches differ from those of the Euro-American tradition. Music throughout the world contains the same basic sound elements: timbre, duration, pitch, and dynamics. It is the way in which these elements are shaped and molded into music that defines a particular style.

Historical Perspective

While the history of Euro-American art music is central to our understanding of Western thought, it is ultimately no more or less important than the venerable traditions of Asiatic, Oceanic, and African culture. These civilizations all possess extensive musical traditions that are in many cases older or more sophisticated than the Western ones.

Cultural Differences and Similarities

Music is not really "the international language" that some people have claimed it to be. The aesthetic, style, function, form, and context as well as tonal, rhythmic, and timbral vocabulary vary—sometimes radically—from country to country. Nonetheless, music is an aspect of our common humanity. Every culture in the world has a need for musical expression and employs the same basic musical elements.

Cultural Interchange

Throughout history, music has functioned as a bridge between nations, and musicians have served as some of the most successful ambassadors. The twentieth-century explosion of technological advances in transportation and communication served to intensify cross-cultural awareness. Indeed, all the world is now a stage. Contemporary performers crisscross the globe, disseminating their musical culture. It is no longer unusual to hear Beethoven symphonies performed in Japan by highly skilled Japanese orchestras. By the same token, it is possible to attend Japanese Noh drama performances produced in the United States. Recordings, radio, and television routinely disseminate music of every culture throughout the world.

Timbre

When listening to a non-Western musical work, perhaps the first thing that strikes a listener is the difference in timbre. The West African percussion ensemble, the Indonesian gamelan orchestra, and the Andean panpipe and charango groups possess completely different tone colors from those of the Western symphony orchestras.

The "facts" of sound production are the same regardless of culture. However, each culture, hearing the basic physical properties of sound produced by strings, wind, reeds, and percussion, develops its own characteristic timbres based on aesthetic choices. Indigenous instruments are created, instrumental techniques are developed, and particular combinations of instruments are chosen. The droning timbre of an Indian tamboura may sound peculiar or boring in a Western context, but in northern Indian music the tamboura's resonant sound is a vital complement to the sitar and tabla.

Although each culture possesses its own timbral aesthetic, a certain amount of cultural interchange also takes place. While the performing technique may vary considerably, virtually the same instrument may often be found dispersed across geographically diverse areas. In basic construction, the American hammer dulcimer is remarkably similar to the Persian santir, the Hungarian cymbalom, the Chinese yang ch'in, and the German hackbrett. However, while the instrument may look the same, the aesthetic, technique, and repertoire are completely different. A listener would have little difficulty distinguishing the "Temperance Reel" played on the hammer dulcimer from "Tao Yi Ch'u" performed on the cheng.

Even that most universal instrument—the human voice—assumes various timbres according to the technique and combinations of voices adopted by a particular culture. The penetrating color of a Bulgarian women's chorus is vastly different from the rich vibrato of an Italian operatic tenor. In Western culture the voice is almost always used to express words, but people in other cultures, such as the Native American Indian, often simply sing vocables (sounds that are not words) to express their music.

Texture

Harmony in Western Music

The history of Western music can be viewed as an exploration of harmonic practice. Since the ninth century, when medieval composers first added melodic lines to the original monophonic melody, theorists have tried to establish a system that would govern the use of consonance and dissonance. By the baroque period, a coherent system of tonality had been established that determined pitch relationships within scales and keys. Subsequent periods can be viewed as a perfection of that system (classic era), an extension of that system (romantic era), and a reaction to that system (twentieth century). Composers might write in a polyphonic style that stresses the interrelationship of melodic lines, but those lines are always structured in accordance with harmonic practice as well. The chordal texture of homophony has been the dominant texture of the Euro-American tradition, and tonal harmony has provided the "rules" for textural usage.

Other cultures have not been similarly obsessed with harmony. In fact, the concept of harmony is conspicuously absent from most of the world's music. Non-Western cultures may have intricate systems that determine melodic structure, but the simultaneous sounding of tones seems to be largely a matter of coincidence, except for styles that exhibit a drone accompaniment.

Other Textural Approaches

Rhythmic Polyphony

Although the rhythmic polyphony of the West African percussion ensemble bears little similarity to Western homophony, its texture has been a major influence in the development of jazz. In this texture, layers of drums, rattles, and gongs are organized in relation to a continuous beat pattern sometimes called a "time line." Other West African styles include melodic instruments or voices in a "hocket" sort of texture, in which a single melodic line is composed of interlocking parts performed by various musicians.

Diaphony (Melody with Drone)

The most basic form of accompaniment is the coupling of melody with a continuously resonating "drone" sound. This texture is found worldwide, from the Scottish bagpipes to Bulgarian women's choruses. A variant is found in northern Indian raga music. In this style, the traditional ensemble comprises a sitar (a string instrument with seven melody strings and approximately twelve sympathetic resonating strings), tabla (two tuned drums), and tamboura (a four-stringed accompanying instrument). Its texture is best described as melodic improvisation over harmonic pedal point, which is supported by rhythmic counterpoint. The tamboura provides harmonic support for the rhapsodic sitar, and the tabla maintains rhythmic unity.

Heterophony

Heterophony is a commonly used texture that is especially prominent in folk music throughout the world and in Oriental musical styles. Heterophonic texture results when performers play similar but different versions of the melody simultaneously. There is a basic underlying concept of the melodic shape shared by the ensemble, but each performer personalizes the melody through various ornamentations. Heterophony may have the freedom of Appalachian Old Regular Baptist Church lined-out style, or the highly ordered layers of melodic invention characteristic of Balinesian gamelan music. (Gamelan is an orchestra largely composed of mallet-struck percussion instruments and gongs.)

Monophony

Monophony is a single line of sound. It is, of course, the most basic and elemental texture. Wherever a mother sings a lullaby to her child, wherever a folksinger recounts a ballad for family, wherever an instrumentalist plays alone for personal enjoyment, monophony is found. Although monophony is universal to every culture and time, some cultures make exclusive use of this texture. Traditional Native American Indian music is almost always sung monophonically, either by a soloist or by a chorus singing in unison. Frequently this singing is also accompanied by the steady rhythm of bells, rattles, and drums. On first hearing, monophony may seem simple, but in actuality this is music of great subtlety and complexity.

Call and Response

Call and response, or responsorial texture, is most often found in vocal music belonging to cultures that are preliterate or that possess a strong oral tradition. In responsorial music a leader sings a melodic phrase that is then repeated, often in elaborated form, by a chorus. There is a strong tradition of responsorial work song in West Africa that greatly influenced the development of such African-American musical styles as spirituals, blues, and jazz.

Duration

Some very basic differences between Eastern and Western philosophies are evident in the respective approaches to time of these two traditions. In general, the Euro-American tradition conceives of time as a continuous, linear unfolding of events as represented by the time line of history. Eastern philosophies generally stress a cyclical view of nature, which is represented in such concepts as reincarnation. Because Eastern and Western views of time are so different, it is only natural that music, which is based on the measure of time, should reflect the basic philosophical differences.

Divisive Time

Euro-American music is generally based on a divisive time system that is constructed around equal fractional divisions of basic rhythmic values. For instance, in this system, $\frac{4}{4}$ meter can be expressed as a whole note, or it can be subdivided into two half notes, four quarter notes, eight eighth notes, and so on. By maintaining a constant meter, rhythmic patterns can be established by subdivisions of the beat. The sensation of tempo or speed changes can be effected either by changing the fractional note values or by accelerating or retarding the basic pulse.

Additive Time

Many world cultures conceive of musical time as an additive rather than a divisive process. Instead of the regular metrical divisions of accented and weak beats, they construct their rhythms by adding beats in regular recurring cycles of accented and unaccented values. The basic regularity of the Euro-American metrical approach is very different from the repeated patterns of asymmetric rhythms produced by African and Asian techniques.

West African Time

West African drum ensembles, such as those of the Ashanti ethnic group in Ghana, organize their sense of time around layers of twelve-beat rhythmic ostinatos (short repeated melodic patterns) that are all performed continuously in relation to a specific pattern. These patterns, or "time lines," as they are sometimes called, are not restricted to duple or triple meter, but are usually an asymmetrical mix of meters. Western notation does not accurately reflect this music, but a typical twelve-beat pattern could be represented as

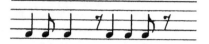   or   3+2+3+3+1.

Oriental Time

Oriental music also reflects the additive approach. Indonesian and Balinesian gamelan music layers percussive rhythm patterns that are often built on cycles of sixteen beats. The clarity of these cycles is punctuated by loud splashes by a gong (called a *kempur*) every sixteen beats. Similar to Ashanti drumming, each layer is based on a central melodic pattern sometimes referred to as the "nuclear" melody.

Indian Time

Rhythmic organization in northern Indian music is provided by repeated patterns or cycles known as *tala*. These tala contain varying numbers of beats that are then arranged according to strong and weak beats. The tala called *ektal* has the twelve-beat 4+4+2+2 pattern, while the ten-beat tala *jhaptal* has a 2+3+2+3 pattern that alternates duple and triple meter.

Free Time

Throughout the world there are musical forms that are not strictly measured by beats, and are organized by either a divisive or an additive system. They are performed in free time. Free time is generally found in solo performance, because simultaneously sounding parts require distinct points of correspondence to keep the parts in time with one another.

Music of northern India contrasts free time with additive time. In the *alap* section, the sitar initially presents the raga (scale) in free rhythm. Since the only accompaniment is the drone of the tamboura, the rhythmic irregularity poses no problems in coordinating the two instruments. Following this exposition of melodic material, the *gat* (developmental) section begins. At this point the music becomes metrically organized as the tabla adds a specific tala (metric pattern).

Pitch

Euro-American System

Music of the Euro-American tradition has gradually established a system of scales and keys based on a well-tempered system of tuning. Seven-step major and minor scales built on successive intervals of half and whole steps are the foundation of the system. The intervals in this system are partially based on the acoustical property of sound, but certain aspects of tuning have been decided according to cultural aesthetic.

Pentatonic Scales

Non-Western cultures have started with the same acoustical foundation, but they have made different choices regarding tuning, scales, and degrees of consonance and dissonance. Many cultures divide the octave into five portions rather than seven, forming various pentatonic scales. An example is the *akadinda* (a xylophonelike instrument) music of Uganda.

African-American Music

Some scholars think that the discrepancy between Euro-American and African tuning systems is the basis of the "blues" notes of Afro-American music. Slaves brought to America from West Africa attempted to accommodate their tuning practices to the European tonal system. In the process of acculturation, they evolved a scale that was neither European nor African, but uniquely American. These blue notes (such as the major-minor third) create an interesting sense of tension that adds spice to African-American influenced musical styles.

Asian Music

Pentatonic scales are also found in Asiatic music such as the gamelan music of Bali and Indonesia. In gamelan, the *slendro* (five-note scale) divides an octave into five equal tones. This means that each step is slightly larger than the whole step of the Western system. In addition, there is no uniformly agreed-upon standard pitch. Thus, while an A (440 vibrations per second) would be the same in any Euro-American music, in gamelan, each orchestra is tuned to a different basic pitch. No two gamelan orchestras can play together.

Microtones

Use in World Culture

The half step is the smallest interval generally recognized in Euro-American tonality. There are certainly tones "between the cracks" in the piano keyboard, but these *quarter tones* or *microtones* between the half steps are perceived only as being "out of tune." Twentieth-century composers, including Charles Ives and Ben Johnson, have experimented with the use of microtones, but their use requires special training on the part of the performers, modifications of the instruments, and alterations in the listening sensitivity of the audience. Other world cultures, however, routinely make use of microtones as a natural form of expression.

Ragas

Northern Indian music is built upon ragas, which are scalelike collections of pitches. Unlike Western scales, however, ragas have different ascending and descending forms, and they may contain various steps such as quarter and eighth tones. While Euro-American music is generally built on just two scales—major and minor—there are literally hundreds of raga. A raga is not simply a series of pitches. Each raga implies certain subtleties of tuning and indicates the types of ornaments and musical emphasis appropriate to each pitch.

Euro-American scales are abstract and functional—their purpose is to provide hierarchical tone organization. They can create expression, but they are not expressive in and of themselves. On the other hand, raga, described as "that which colors the mind," contains both structural and emotional content. Ragas very specifically concern mood, time of day, and season. While the Western generic C major scale can be used for any type of music, at any time of day, one would never consider playing a composition based on *Bauli* (early-morning raga) in the evening. Ragas are not simply scales, they are an expressive force with their own personality.

Dynamics

Of all the musical elements, dynamics is perhaps the most universal in its application. Sound can only remain at a static volume, or increase or decrease in intensity. Throughout the world, an increase in volume is usually perceived as an increase in excitement or tension. To generalize broadly, music of world cultures other than Western tend to perform at a relatively static dynamic level. Expressive variations in volume occur but are more subtly distinguished, and the overall range is more limited. Few non-Western cultures have sounds that would rival the thunder of heavily amplified heavy-metal rock, or the fortissimo of a full symphony orchestra, or match even the sound of a single expansive pipe organ. Whereas many cultures distinguish various shades of softness, Western culture broadly contrasts various levels of volume.

The phenomenon of music is universal, but the practice of music is specific to the cultural context. While all cultures share the same basic elements of sound—timbre, duration, pitch, and dynamics—they shape them to conform to particular cultural aesthetics. The texture, the melodic shape, the form, the rhythmic sense, and the basic function of music vary according to the culture. It is important to evaluate a culture's music according to its own aesthetic rather than compare it to the Euro-American approach. In gaining an understanding of a culture's music one gains insight into the culture itself.

CHAPTER 18

Popular Music

Popular music and traditional music are similar in that they appeal to a broad spectrum of people. In contrast to art music, no special understanding or study is needed to appreciate these types of music. Folk music fulfilled the function of popular music early in American history, but with the commercial dissemination of music in the nineteenth century, the lines separating the two forms became more sharply etched. Whereas folk music is spread gradually from person to person, popular music is rapidly disseminated through mass media. The life of a popular song is tied directly to its appeal, reflected by its rise and fall on sales charts such as those published by Billboard Magazine. *Popular music is intentionally created to be popular, and is consciously marketed to appeal to the majority of the public.*

The Rise of Popular Music

During the eighteenth and nineteenth centuries popular music, showcased in light opera and musical productions, was disseminated by sheet music for amateur players at home. Later, toward the end of the nineteenth century, the popularity of ragtime was encouraged by sheet music sales as well as through the new medium of player-piano rolls. The rise of popular music accelerated with Thomas Edison's invention of the phonograph in 1877, and by the early 1920s both phonograph recordings and radio broadcasts were spreading popular music—Tin Pan Alley tunes, jazz, and country music—with unprecedented success. By the end of World War II popular music had become a major industry that included songwriters, performers, producers, agents, recording engineers, studios, and radio stations that churned out the "hits." Today popular music is a global phenomenon that is largely based around various rock styles spread throughout the world by live performance, radio, recordings, and television.

The Emergence of African-American Styles

The story of popular music in America is directly tied to the confrontation and compromise arising from the clash of two cultures—European and African. American popular music is the audible history of integration. As generations of African-Americans adapted their musical practices to a dominant Euro-American culture, certain purely American forms of popular expression developed. Styles such as ragtime, blues, jazz, rock, and country were neither African nor European, but a fusion of the two.

At the close of the nineteenth century three important African-American musical styles emerged—ragtime, blues, and jazz. These three styles all sprang from a common ancestry of spirituals, minstrel songs, and work hollers, but they flowered in distinct and unique ways. Ragtime was a composed and notated syncopated piano style. Rural, or delta, blues was a narrative vocal style that combined the sound of a male vocalist with guitar accompaniment. And jazz was an improvised instrumental style that featured a small ensemble of wind and rhythm instruments. While each of these styles possessed a distinct identity, aspects of each strongly influenced the others. Blues vocal timbre contributed to jazz instrumental techniques, and many jazz pieces maintained the form and feeling of blues. Jazz was also marked by the syncopated rhythms and sectional form of ragtime. Similarly the improvised nature and combo instrumentation of jazz affected both blues and ragtime performance.

Ragtime

Emerging as a distinct style about 1895 in the area around St. Louis and along the Mississippi River basin, ragtime was a piano style built on the contrast between a syncopated right-hand melody against the regular accents of a solid "oom-pah" bass played with the left hand. In the early 1900s ragtime underwent a brief period of phenomenal popularity in which live performance, published sheet music, and player-piano rolls spread the style across America and Europe. However, with the onset of World War I, the novelty wore off, and ragtime declined as an important genre.

European Influence

Formally and harmonically, rags reflected European musical practice in that they were structured along the lines of a marching-band composition, with sectional form. There were usually four different themes with a returning *A* section and a contrasting trio section set in a different key. This common formal procedure, heard in Scott Joplin's "Maple Leaf Rag," is best illustrated as

A A	*B B*	*A*	*C C D D*
1st Theme	2nd Theme	Return	"Trio" Sections
			Contrasting Key

African Influence

The African influence is felt in the rhythmic tension created by layering the $\frac{2}{4}$ metric regularity of the left hand against the cakewalk-styled syncopations (♩ ♫ ♫ ♩ | ♩) heard in the right hand.

Ragtime Composers

Rags differ from jazz in that rags were usually not improvised, but carefully composed and notated. In this respect, ragtime more closely resembled the American art-music tradition of parlor songs. Scott Joplin (1869–1917), whose 1897 publication of the "Maple Leaf Rag" sparked interest in the style, even wrote a full length ragtime opera called *Treemonisha*. Other important ragtime composers include Thomas Turpin, James Scott, and Louis Chauvin.

Blues

Although there is no single identifiable time at which blues appeared, most scholars agree that it was at the turn of the century, and that it took place in the Mississippi Delta. The delta, or rural, blues is a song form in which a male singer recounts a narrative accompanied only by his guitar. The essence of the blues is truth, and the song reflects an earthy view of life shaped by the black experience in America—pain, sorrow, and enduring humor.

Blues Form

Blues started as a cathartic expression, drawn out of the soul by basic human need. The form and style was quite irregular, and musicians half-sang, half-wailed the lyrics in a highly personal style that was not bound by dictates of harmony or metrical barlines. Gradually, a more formulaic "blues form" became codified as musicians began to play together. A blues soloist could play as idiosyncratically as he wanted, but a group of musicians playing together required ground rules.

Traditional blues form couples a regular text structure with a harmonic pattern that is repeated over the course of each stanza. Blues lyrics are assembled in stanzas of rhymed couplets with the first line repeated. This is an interesting innovation. Blues were originally improvised; perhaps the repetition of the line gave the singer more time to construct a contrasting line. In any event, the repetition creates more drama by building anticipation for the final rhymed "punch line."

Example of a Blues Lyric

The sun's setting low and the day's almost done,
The sun's setting low—my day's just about done,
Oh, the day means hard work, but the night means fun.

The text form is complemented by the simple and direct twelve-bar harmonic formula. Each text phrase is matched by a different tonal area, and the relationship between the contrasting phrases is mirrored in the relationship between the tonic and dominant chords. The blues form is best represented as follows:

Text Phrase:	A		A^1			B			
Harmonic Area:	I		IV	I		V	IV	I	V^7
Measures:	1–4		5–6	7–8		9	10	11	12

Blue Notes

Another feature of blues is the use of "blue notes"—tones whose intonation does not strictly match the third, fifth, and seventh degrees of the Euro-American system tuning. Blue notes reflect the compromise between African and European tuning practices. The result is an achingly expressive sound that cannot be defined as either major or minor.

Classic Blues

Although the delta blues style can still be heard today, African-Americans continued to develop the blues idiom, and new blues styles emerged. The first new style, usually referred to as "classic blues," developed in response to the relationship with jazz. Classic blues (from approximately 1920–1940) featured a vocalist (often female) whose singing was accompanied by a jazz style combo. Musicians of this period include Bessie Smith (1894–1937), whose performance in songs such as "Empty Bed Blues" reveals the intimate relationship between the singer and the instrumental accompaniment.

Urban Blues

As African-Americans migrated from the south in search of jobs in the industrial north, large pockets of black culture formed in cities such as Memphis, Detroit, and Chicago. In these cities, especially Chicago's south side, a more driving urban blues style evolved that featured the sound of a small combo consisting of a rhythm section with electric guitars and saxophones. Musicians such as Muddy Waters (1914–) and B. B. King (1925–) may have been born in the rural south, but the electric sound of the city was captured in their hard-edged electric playing.

Rhythm and Blues; Rock and Roll

The sound of urban blues was further transformed by an emphasis on backbeat, faster tempos, and the choice of more youth-oriented subject matter to produce a style identified as rhythm and blues. With a small injection of country sound provided by musicians such as Elvis Presley (1935–1977), the rhythm and blues sound was again transformed—this time into the rock and roll of musicians such as Chuck Berry (1926–).

Jazz

There is no clear starting point in the history of jazz. Some claim it to be when Buddy Bolden (1868–1931) first extemporized a melody on his trumpet with a marching band in New Orleans. Others point to Jelly Roll Morton's (1885–1941) piano improvisations on rags as the source of the style. As with blues, the evolution of jazz was a gradual process that flowered some time around the dawning of the twentieth century.

New Orleans Style

Most historians agree that although the earliest concentration of jazz activities was in New Orleans, quite a bit of jazzlike music was associated with other cities at about the same time. Still, the New Orleans musicians soon became the dominant force in the spread of jazz from its cradle in New Orleans to northern cities such as Chicago, St. Louis, and New York.

New Orleans certainly provided a nurturing environment for this new art form. The cosmopolitan mix of French, Spanish, Anglos, and African-Americans coupled with the ample performance opportunities afforded by life in the "big easy," as New Orleans was known, certainly encouraged jazz. The active parade and dance-hall life provided work for instrumentalists, and the brothels of Storyville kept the pianists busy. While the early history of New Orleans jazz was never recorded, we can get an idea of the sound through the early recordings of Joe "King" Oliver (1885–1938) and Louis "Satchmo" Armstrong (1900–1971), made with New Orleans sidemen in Chicago studios during the 1920s.

Improvisation

Whereas ragtime was piano-oriented and blues was vocally oriented, jazz was an instrumentally dominated music. The essence of early New Orleans–style jazz was the collective improvisation between the lead line of the trumpet, the countermelody line of the clarinet, and the low brass voice of the trombone. The interplay of the melody instruments was supported by a rhythm section that included banjo, piano, or guitar, a string bass or tuba, and a trap set of drums.

Form

The harmonic and formal basis of the improvisation was provided by either sectional ragtime-style pieces or strophic blues compositions. A typical piece would begin with a short two- to four-measure introduction. The entire ensemble would then introduce the theme or themes in an opening chorus or two. Thereafter, each soloist took one or more choruses to improvise over the harmonic framework. Then the entire ensemble would engage in a climactic final chorus (called a *shout chorus*), which was completed by a little two- to four-bar tag or ending.

Chicago Style and Swing

As the focus of jazz activity moved north to Chicago and New York, the style continued to evolve. In general, the sound featured more solo improvisation and less of the counterpoint of the New Orleans sound. Soloists, influenced by Armstrong's work, began improvising new melodies over the harmony instead of simply embroidering the theme in a type of improvisation known as *chorus improvisation*.

The Big Band Sound

The overall sound became larger and more modern through the substitution of the trumpet for the cornet, the guitar for the banjo, and the introduction of the tenor saxophone instead of the clarinet. Because this music was now intended for use in dance halls rather than for marching, the string bass usually replaced the tuba. As the success of jazz brought in more customers, the halls grew larger, and more musicians were needed to fill the hall. Thus, we see the beginnings of the big band sound in which additional musicians were added to the trumpet, reed (saxophone and clarinet), and trombone parts. Singers were often added to the bands, and Louis Armstrong popularized a style of singing called *scat* in which the voice imitated an instrument, singing nonsense syllables instead of words.

Arrangements

As the bands grew in size, it became difficult to improvise with the same amount of freedom afforded by the small combos. Thus musicians became more dependent on charts, or arrangements that indicated the notes that each of the accompaniment parts were to play. Only the soloist generally improvised. Don Redman, Fletcher Henderson's arranger, developed the characteristic big band sound that featured antiphonal chatter between reeds and brass, and solos accompanied by members of the other section (reed solos accompanied by brass and brass solos accompanied by reeds).

Form

Formally, the arrangements avoided the earlier ragtime style sectional form that had two or more themes, and began to use charts based on popular songs. As the typical pop song consisted of a thirty-two-bar chorus in *AABA* form, this harmonic scheme became the foundation of the style. Musicians continued to use the blues as the foundation for much of their repertoire.

Band Leaders

In New Orleans jazz the musicians are the focus of the listener's attention; in swing the arranger or bandleader demands our interest. The arrangement became the key to a band's success, and the great bandleaders succeeded in imparting their own personal stamp to the group style. Important musicians include Edward Kennedy "Duke" Ellington (1899–1974) whose band had a dramatic orchestrated style, and William "Count" Basie (1904–1984), whose band featured a light, swinging rhythm section.

Bebop

Swing became America's popular music during the 1930s. However, the advent of World War II and the economic difficulties of keeping a twenty-piece band on the road brought big bands into a period of decline during the mid-1940s. Musicians who felt constrained by reading charts began to explore a new style that was based on a return to combo-sized groups and more adventurous rhythmic and harmonic improvisation. This style, called "bebop," or simply "bop," originated in New York City and was largely based around the performance of saxophonist Charlie "Bird" Parker (1920–1955) and trumpeter John Birks "Dizzy" Gillespie (1917–).

Form

The general format consists of a short introduction, followed by the *head*. The head is a theme stated by the saxophone and trumpet in unison over a harmonic progression that is repeated over and over during the piece. After the head, the saxophone and trumpet take turns engaging in improvisations that are sometimes followed by piano, drum, and bass solos. After the last solo, the work concludes with a final return to the head.

Improvisation

Bop musicians based their improvisations around the same blues and popular songs favored by swing musicians, but they used these songs in a different way. Bop musicians explored the harmonic progression of a song and scarcely ever played the original melody line. They inserted substitute chords and added entirely new chords to the progression. Because the original song melody was not played (at most, quoted fragments of it were woven into an improvisation), the public had difficulty in finding a melody and trouble appreciating the style. Jazz, which had been America's popular music during the swing period, became a more rarified art form marked by impeccable virtuosity and musical experimentation during the bop era. Instead of popular music intended for dance, it became an art music intended primarily for listening.

In bebop style *the melody is the improvisation*. To comprehend the essence of a bop tune, the listener must follow the rapid melodic twists and turns of the improvisation as it relates to the foundation of the rhythm section. The bass outlines the harmony, the piano highlights the chords in a concise rhythmic style called *comping*, and the drummer lightly keeps time on the cymbals and accents with the drums. The solo improvisations always relate to this foundation, but the fast tempo and the complexity of the harmonic invention sometimes make this relationship difficult to discern.

Later Jazz Styles

Although New Orleans (now usually called *Dixieland*), swing, and bop styles continued, new directions in jazz evolved as well. Styles such as "hard bop," "cool jazz," "free jazz," "third stream," "funk," and "fusion" developed as musicians looked for new sounds and new ways of improvising, and sought new sources for their music.

Free Jazz

Improvisation can be equated with freedom. In music as in society, complete personal freedom leads to anarchy. In jazz, personal freedom of improvisation was always tied to a tune or harmony. During the 1960s, however, some musicians, such as Ornette Coleman, attempted a completely free form of jazz unfettered by predetermined harmonies. The result was "free jazz," a style marked by spontaneous interchange and "sheets of sound." Free jazz succeeded in stretching the boundaries of the art, but found audiences generally unresponsive.

Cool Jazz

Cool jazz evolved directly from bop, but instead of bop's frantic pace and intense improvisations, cool jazz musicians favored a more "laid-back" feel. Cool jazz, often identified with the innovations of trumpet player Miles Davis and West Coast musicians such as Dave Brubeck, affected a more subtle and intellectual approach. Played with an emphasis on the intellect rather than the heart, cool jazz incorporated procedures and instruments "borrowed" from art music.

Third-Stream Jazz

Third-stream jazz explored the fine line dividing the "popular" genre of jazz from the "serious" genre of art music. Composers such as Stravinsky (1882–1971), Gershwin (1898–1937), and Milhaud (1894–1974) had incorporated jazz elements in "classical" works for some time, but third stream was a conscious effort to create a fusion of both styles. Within third stream, the orchestra, and formal procedures such as concerto or fugue, became the arena for jazz-styled improvisation. One of the foremost proponents of this style was composer-conductor-writer Gunther Schuller (1925–).

Fusion (Jazz Rock)

Jazz has been fusion music during its entire history. It has continually fused musical ideas from African and European cultures, and adapted elements of folk, pop, and art music in its eclectic evolution. The style called fusion (or jazz rock) combines electric rock instrumentation and the more simple and direct approach of rock style. The improvisation and rhythmic complexity are pure jazz, but the harmonic simplicity, amplification, and the direct beat are characteristic of rock. Instead of being structured around harmonic progressions, fusion frequently superimposes the improvisation over layers of repeated ostinato patterns.

Current Jazz

Jazz is no longer purely an American art form. Performers throughout the world have adapted the medium to their own particular cultures, and enriched jazz through the fusion of additional cultural influences. Jazz is a vital art, always in the process of growth and change. While innovative new musicians such as Wynton Marsalis and David Sanborn continue to extend the musical horizons, the African-American legacy of earlier styles remains the cornerstone upon which new performers build.

Rock Music

Like jazz, rock music is the audible history of the integration of African-based music into European-based American society. However, whereas jazz was essentially an instrumental music that originated at the beginning of the twentieth century, rock was basically a vocal style that originated in the 1950s. The African roots of rock are blues, gospel, jump-style jazz, and rhythm and blues, but the infusion of country music provided the final ingredient that caused the new style to explode sometime around 1954. It is impossible to point to the "first" rock song, but possible contenders include Jackie Brenston's "Rocket 88," Elvis Presley's "That's All Right Mama," and Bill Haley's "Rock Around the Clock."

Early Rock

In the early 1950s, the sound of rock and roll (as it was first called) included the rhythm and blues sound of performers such as Chuck Berry, Ike Turner, and Bo Diddley, and the rockabilly sound of country musicians such as Bill Haley and Elvis Presley. The two currents converged to create a sound marked by electrically amplified sound, blues-based harmonic progressions, a strong backbeat (accent on the off-beats), and a wild, spontaneous singing style. Rock and roll was music created both for and by youths. The lyrics reflected teen society and teen concerns—cars, sex, dancing, and love.

Rock Development

By the end of the decade, the pop music industry had absorbed and tamed the style (but not the content) of rock and roll. The smooth sound of "teen idol" singers such as Frankie Avalon and the well-crafted sound of the Brill Building "girl groups" such as the Crystals, had replaced the exuberance of the early rock performers. It took the "British invasion" of the Beatles in 1964 to restore the spontaneous feel of blues-based rock to America.

From its beginning, rock music had reflected teen society; by the mid 1960s, rock began to change society, as well. In the hands of musicians such as Bob Dylan (1941–) and the Beatles (1962–1970), rock music came to represent views on society. Instead of just boy-girl relationships, the lyrics explored such topics as racism, alternative lifestyles, and the Vietnam War. The music grew louder and more eclectic, drawing upon influences such as Indian meditation and psychedelic visions. Because the Beatles focused their energy on studio recordings rather than live performance, they produced some highly sophisticated albums including Sergeant Pepper's Lonely Hearts Club Band (1967). Huge musical gatherings such as that at Woodstock in 1969 asserted the power of rock.

Later Rock Styles: Disco, Punk, And New Wave

While the successful bands of the 1960s broke up, reformed, and continued to perform into the seventies, new developments in rock also took place. The *disco* style, with performers such as Donna Summer and the Bee Gees, provided a throbbing dance beat in a slick commercial package. In reaction, musicians in New York and Britain, such as Television and the Sex Pistols, created a *punk* style that rejected the smooth polished sound of popular music. The loud volume and anarchy of punk provided a new burst of creativity that asserted itself as *new wave* in groups like the Police, and laid the foundations for the alternative rock styles of the 1980s.

Rock Today

Today, rock music dominates the musical landscape across the world. The pop music industry has developed a wide diversity of styles appealing to all generations. From the nostalgia of "classic rock" to the "mall-walker" music of preteens, music is performed and disseminated internationally through television, satellite transmission, and recordings. Rock music is the popular music of our time.

Country Music

It has been claimed that "country music is America's music." Certainly, country music reflects the American experience. America is a nation of diverse ethnic cultures. Just as jazz, blues, ragtime, and rock styles developed from the interchange of these cultures, so country music emerged from a convergence of different musical styles.

Origins

Country music originated from the early traditional music—ballads, lyric folk songs, blues, and fiddle tunes—but it also incorporated popular music such as parlor songs and blackface minstrel music. Country music at the beginning of the twentieth century was simply the repertoire of rural people learned from oral tradition and performance of vaudeville, minstrel, and medicine shows. The term or concept of "country music" did not yet exist because there was no realization that this rural music could be equated with a single identifiable style.

First Recordings

The concept of country music, or "hillbilly" music as it was first identified, really came into being in the early 1920s with the advent of recording and radio transmission. The first country song to be commercially recorded and distributed was the fiddle tune "Sally Goodin," as recorded by Eck Roberts in New York City in 1922.

Radio Shows

During the 1920s country music consisted largely of folk tunes recorded by country musicians from the southeast portion of America. Musicians such as Fiddlin' John Carson, the Skillet Lickers, and Vernon Dalhart recorded and performed their music live on "barn dances," which were live radio shows that simulated old southern square dances. The broadcast of Nashville's "Grand Ole Opry" on WSM and Chicago's "National Barndance" on WLS spread this music across the country.

Evolution of Country Music

While country music was initially merely a regional phenomenon, it grew by the 1930s and 1940s into popular music with a more identifiable homogenized style. The image of the hillbilly was replaced by the idealized cowboy through films of cowboy actor-singers such as Gene Autry, and country music started selling all over the country—in cities as well as in rural areas.

Nashville

Because Nashville, Tennessee, was the location of the highly successful "Grand Ole Opry" show, the country music industry of publishers and recording studios eventually settled in Nashville. In Nashville, country music became big business and the country sound grew more commercial. The twang of the banjo, and the wail of the fiddle and steel guitar were replaced by the smooth sounds of strings in pop arrangements. Songs by the great country singer Hank Williams (1923–1953) were rerecorded by more "polished" pop singers, and country singers such as Eddy Arnold "crossed over" by adopting a smoother and less "countrified" style.

Fusion with Other Styles

In the early 1950s, a generation of country musicians reacted against this country pop style by charging their music with an infusion of rhythm and blues style. Centered at the Sun recording studio of Sam Phillips, musicians such as Elvis Presley, Carl Perkins, and Jerry Lee

Lewis developed the rockabilly sounds that characterized early rock and roll. The guitar picking and slapped bass were pure country, but the addition of drums, the blues progressions, and the heavy backbeat were borrowed directly from rhythm and blues. The fusion of country and rock was a marriage that continues to this very day.

Country Music Today

Current country music reflects both the legacy of the past and the trends of the future. Innovative performers are continually expanding the range of possibilities by drawing on contemporary idioms, while other entertainers stress the traditional grass-roots aspects of country style. Country music may be "America's music," but now it belongs to the world as well.

American popular music is based on a legacy of inherited folk music forms, but by the twentieth century these folk elements were recombined in new popular idioms. American popular music reflects the continuing cultural interchange of African-American and Euro-American culture through the development of such styles as blues, jazz, ragtime, rock, and country.

GLOSSARY

Absolute music   Music that expresses only itself and is not based on an extramusical program.

A cappella   A choral performance without instrumental accompaniment.

Accelerando   A gradual speeding up of the tempo.

Accent   An emphasis or stress on a note or chord achieved either through louder volume (dynamic) or greater duration (agogic). Accents are indicated as $>$.

Accidentals   Sharps, flats, and natural signs used to indicate raised or lowered pitches that occur outside the key.

Adagio   An indication for a slow tempo (between 66 and 76 on a metronome).

Additive form   Through-composed music in which new ideas are constantly stated without repetition.

Additive time   A temporal system in which units are added together to form rhythmic structures. Common in African and oriental cultures.

Aerophones	The family of wind instruments that encompasses both the brass and woodwind classifications.
Agnus Dei ("Lamb of God")	The last movement in the ordinary of the mass.
Agogic	An accent achieved by increasing the duration of a tone.
Akadinda	Melodic percussion music of West Africa performed on marimbalike instruments.
Alap	The rhapsodic introductory section of an Indian raga, performed in free time.
Alberti bass	A keyboard figuration characteristic of the classic period. Chords are broken up rhythmically in the left hand.
Aleatoric music	Twentieth-century music in which the element of chance controls composition and performance.
Allegretto	A moderate tempo indication between andante and allegro (between 100 and 120 on a metronome).
Allegro	An indication for a fast tempo (between 120 and 168 on a metronome).
Allemande	A duple-meter dance used as the opening movement of a baroque dance suite.
Altissimo	The high, penetrating register of an instrument.
Alto	The classification for the lowest range of the female voice. Also used to designate low instruments of certain instrumental families.
Amplitude	The size of a sound wave, determining the dynamics of a sound.

Andante	A tempo indication for a leisurely walking speed (between 76 and 108 on a metronome).
Answer	The second (and fourth) statement of the subject in a fugue; usually in the dominant key.
Anthem	A choral composition with English text similar to the motet. Developed to accompany Anglican worship during the Renaissance.
Antiphony	A musical texture distinguished by call and response between choirs.
Aria	A solo song in opera or oratorio whose text is reflective rather than narrative, thus emphasizing vocal virtuosity.
Arpeggio	The notes of a chord played in sequence rather than simultaneously.
Ars nova ("new art")	The fourteenth-century musical era that bridged the medieval and Renaissance periods.
Art song	Independent vocal compositions not attached to multimovement works, often lightly accompanied by keyboard; examples are the German *lied* and the French *chanson*.
Assai	An Italian term (meaning "very") used to modify tempo indications.
Asymmetrical meter	A meter containing an odd number of beats that can be subdivided into various groupings of triple and duple meter. For example,

$$\frac{7}{4} \quad \text{♩♩♩} \quad \text{♩♩♩♩}$$

Atonality	The lack of a tonal center; characterizes works composed according to Schoenberg's twelve-tone system.
Augmentation	The proportional increase in rhythmic values.

Augmented triad	A chord formed by superimposing a major third on top of another major third. The pitches C–E–G♯ form an augmented triad.
Balance	The fine-tuning of dynamic levels in a group of instruments so that no one instrument overshadows another.
Ballad	A narrative song generally preserved and transmitted through an oral tradition.
Ballade	A lyrical, narrative keyboard genre developed by Chopin during the romantic period. Also a late medieval song form characterized by three stanzas of eight lines each.
Baritone	The voice classification for the high range of the bass register.
Bar line	A vertical line drawn through the staff to organize metric divisions into measures.
Bass	The classification for the lowest range of the male voice. Also used to designate low-pitched instruments in some instrumental families.
Bass clef	The symbol 𝄢 used to indicate the lower range of pitches on a staff. The symbol designates the second staff line from the top as the pitch F.
Basso continuo (figured bass)	The keyboard and bass instrument accompaniment pattern in a baroque continuo texture.
Basso ostinato	A repeated bass pattern sounded continually throughout a composition. Also referred to as a *ground bass*.
Beat	The smallest unit of measurement of musical time; forms the musical pulse.

Bebop (or bop) A jazz combo style developed during the 1940s, marked by instrumental virtuosity and harmonic complexity.

Bel canto ("beautiful song") An Italian singing style stressing beauty of sound rather than dramatic interpretation.

Binary form A formal design consisting of two contrasting sections.

Bitonality Two different tonal areas sounded simultaneously.

Blues African-American vocal and instrumental style originating at the beginning of the twentieth century.

Blues note A slightly lowered note between regular scale degrees used in blues and other African-American styles.

Blues progression A twelve-measure harmonic progression that forms the basis for blues pieces (I–IV–I–V–IV–I–V^7).

Brass Members of the aerophone family in which the sound is created by the vibration of the performer's lips buzzing into a cuplike mouthpiece. Brass instruments include trumpets, trombones, and tubas.

Brass quintet A chamber ensemble consisting of two trumpets, French horn, trombone, and tuba.

Bridge A musical transition between sections. Also the *B* section in thirty-two-bar pop-song form (*AABA*).

Cadence A combination of melodic, rhythmic, and harmonic formulas that converge, leading the listener to a point of repose. A cadence concludes a musical phrase.

Cadenza	A virtuosic passage in a concerto, which displays the soloist's skill.
Call and response	A musical texture marked by dialogue between soloist and ensemble. Also known as *responsorial* texture.
Camerata	The Italian society in Florence that developed the concept of opera.
Cancrizans ("crablike")	A musical technique in which a melody is both inverted and played backwards.
Canon	The use of the same melody in different voices with each voice entering at successive time intervals. Similar to a round.
Canonical hours	The sacred observances in the Roman Catholic church held eight times each day.
Canso	A medieval strophic song form (*AB AB CD*).
Cantabile	In a singing style.
Cantata	An unstaged sacred or secular narrative sung with instrumental accompaniment developed during the baroque era. A cantata contains arias, recitatives, and choruses like the oratorio, but is on a much smaller scale.
Cantus firmus	An existing melody (often Gregorian chant) used as the organizational structure in a Renaissance mass or motet.
Canzona	A Renaissance instrumental genre in which the vocal chanson style was transcribed for keyboard.
Castrato	A male singer who was neutered as a child to preserve his soprano voice.
Chaconne	A musical form in which variations are built on successive repetitions of a harmonic pattern.

Chamber music Music designed for intimate performance with only one performer per part.

Chanson A Renaissance three-voice, secular song form. The text, usually an expression of love, was in rondeau form with a two-line refrain (*A B a A a b A B*).

Chorale A hymn tune with a vernacular German text set to music suitable for congregational singing.

Chorale prelude A short organ composition based on a chorale melody.

Chord The simultaneous sounding of three or more tones. The most usual chord is a triad.

Chordophones The family of string instruments.

Chord progression A formulaic succession of chords that determines the harmonic direction of a piece of music.

Chorus A refrain of repeated text and music between stanzas. Also a type of jazz improvisation over a repeated chord progression.

Chorus effect The "out of phase" sound quality resulting from instruments whose tuning is not in exact unison.

Chromatic A scale or melody constructed entirely of half steps. Chromatic harmony emphasizes the equal use of all twelve tones.

Clef A sign placed at the beginning of a staff to indicate the pitches that lie on the staff.

Cluster A chord constructed of successive half or whole steps.

Coda A concluding section appended onto a composition.

Codetta	A short concluding section of a composition; shorter than a coda.
Col legno	A string technique in which sound is produced by striking strings with the wooden back of the bow.
Coloratura	A virtuosic singing style that showcases the upper register of a soprano voice.
Common meter	A duple meter consisting of an accented beat followed by three unaccented beats; often referred to as march time. Indicated as the signature ℂ.
Common practice	The tertian harmonic system used for works generally belonging to the baroque through romantic periods.
Comping	A jazz keyboard accompaniment style that rhythmically highlights the chord changes.
Compound meter	A meter in which the basic beat is divided into three parts rather than two. A compound meter is formed by multiplying the top number of a simple meter by three. For example,

$$\begin{smallmatrix}6\\8\end{smallmatrix} \quad \text{♫♫ ♫♫}$$

Concertato	A baroque style that featured musical contrast expressed through different combinations of instruments and voice.
Concertino	The small group or soloist in a baroque concerto grosso.
Concertmaster	The first violinist in an orchestra, who serves as leader of the string section and is responsible for the orchestra's tuning.
Concerto	A genre contrasting a soloist against an orchestra; similar in scope and form to a

symphony, but usually containing only three movements.

Concerto grosso A baroque genre in which two groups of instruments, the concertino (small group) and the ripieno (full ensemble), are contrasted against each other.

Conductor The director of an orchestra or band. The conductor determines the overall sound by dictating tempo, shaping balance, and controlling dynamics.

Conductus A medieval homophonic song with strophic text.

Conjunct Describes a smooth melodic motion that proceeds by stepwise motion without large intervallic jumps.

Consonance Intervals in a harmonious relationship that creates a sensation of pleasant repose.

Continuo A baroque texture that featured a dominant soprano melody paired with a foundational bass voice. The soprano and bass were supported by an improvised keyboard harmony part also called the continuo.

Contour The characteristic shape of a melodic line.

Cornett A curved hornlike instrument made of either wood or ivory, which produced sound through breath blown into a cup mouthpiece. Originating in the Middle Ages, the cornett was widely used through the baroque period.

Counterpoint (contrapuntal) A technique in which two or more independent melodic lines are combined according to considerations of chordal voice leading.

Country music	American popular music built on a foundation of rural traditional styles. The earliest country music recordings date from the 1920s.
Couplet	Two lines of text verse that express a single thought; frequently rhymed.
Courante	A brisk dance in duple time, frequently used as the second movement of a baroque suite.
CPS (cycles per second)	A unit of pitch measurement. Also known as Hz (Hertz).
Credo ("I Believe")	The statement of faith that forms the third movement in the ordinary of the mass.
Crescendo	A gradual rise in dynamic level.
Da capo aria	A solo vocal form in ternary form (*ABA*) in which the return of the first section is ornamented.
Decibel	A unit of amplitude measurement.
Decrescendo	A gradual decrease in dynamic level.
Descant	A countermelody added above a melodic line.
Development	The middle section of sonata form in which the principal themes are expanded and explored through techniques such as fragmentation, modulation, and recombination.
Diaphony	A musical texture consisting of melody and drone accompaniment.
Diatonic	Encompassing scale steps within either the major or the minor scale.
Diminished triad	A chord formed by superimposing a minor triad over another minor triad. The pitches B–D–F form a diminished triad.
Diminuendo	A gradual decrease in dynamic level.

Disjunct	Describes a jagged melodic motion that proceeds by large intervallic leaps.
Dissonance	Intervals that create a sensation of tension and instability.
Divisive time	The Euro-American concept of time in which a whole note is subdivided into smaller proportional fractions.
Dominant	The pitch located on the fifth degree of a major scale. Also the triad built on this pitch.
Dotted note	Rhythmic notation in which a dot following a note increases that note's value by half of its original value. For example,

$$\text{♩. equals } ♫$$

Double escapement action	A piano mechanism that allows notes to be quickly rearticulated.
Double stop	More than one note sounded simultaneously on a string instrument.
Drone	A rudimentary harmony in which a single pitch is maintained below a melody. Bagpipes produce a drone accompaniment with their melody.
Duple meter	A rhythmic pattern in which an accented beat is followed by a single unaccented beat.
Duplum	The voice added above the tenor cantus firmus in medieval organum.
Duration	One of four basic elements of music; the aspect of time that determines how long each sound or silence lasts.
Dynamics	One of the four basic elements of music; the relative softness or loudness of the musical sound.

Electrophones   The family of instruments whose sound is generated, altered, or amplified through electronics.

Elite music   The art music of Euro-American culture, transmitted through written notation and generally performed in a concert-style setting.

Embouchure   The placement of lips, teeth, and tongue to produce a sound on a wind instrument.

Envelope   The characteristic dynamic shape, unique to each instrument, of *attack* (the time it takes for a sound to reach its full volume), *sustain* (the duration at which that volume is maintained), and *decay* (time it takes the sound to return to silence).

Episode   A thematic section of secondary interest. Also a section in a fugue in which the fugal subject is not present.

Equal temperament   A standardized way of tuning that allows performers to move freely through any key.

Etude ("study")   A work that explores a specific sonority or technical problem. The etude became a piano genre during the romantic period.

Exposition   The first section in sonata form, in which the principal themes are presented and then repeated. Also, the opening section of a fugue in which the fugal subject is introduced in each voice.

Expressionism   An early twentieth-century musical style marked by a subjective and emotion-charged approach represented through dissonance and disjunct melody.

Extended chords	Chords with additional thirds added to the basic triad; seventh, ninth, eleventh, and thirteenth chords.
Fantasy (also fantasia)	An improvisatory-sounding character piece that is loosely structured.
Fauxbourdon ("false bass")	A harmonic aspect of Renaissance style in which the melody is doubled at the interval of a sixth below the melody.
Fermata	A note held beyond its value, indicated by the sign ⌒.
Figured bass realization	In baroque practice, the technique according to which the keyboard (continuo) instrument improvised a harmony part dictated by the direction of the bass line and by notational symbols that indicated chords and voicings.
Flageolet instruments	Wind instruments whose sound is generated by wind directed over a narrow slit. Examples are recorders and organ pipes.
Flat	The musical symbol ♭ that lowers a pitch by a half step.
Flutter tongue	A coloration technique on wind instruments achieved by rolling the tongue while blowing.
Forte	An indication for a loud dynamic level.
Fortissimo	An indication for an increase in dynamic level beyond that indicated by forte.
Frequency	The number of sound waves per second; the determining factor in pitch.
Frets	Small metal strips inserted into the fingerboard of some string instruments, such as guitars, to make pitch definition more precise.

Frottola An Italian homophonic song of the Renaissance period based on strophic text depictions of love and courtly dalliance.

Fugue An imitative, contrapuntal composition developed during the baroque period. Fugue is a process in which a theme, or subject, is developed in imitation and contrasted with episodic material.

Fundamental The key note, or first harmonic, in an overtone series.

Fusion A jazz style featuring elements of both jazz and rock.

Galliard A dance in compound meter ($\frac{6}{8}$) frequently paired with the pavane in the Renaissance and baroque periods.

Gamelan The percussive orchestra and music of Java, Bali, and Indonesia.

Gat The developmental section of an Indian raga.

Gigue A dance form used as the final brisk movement of a baroque suite.

Glissando A rapid sliding across pitches, usually on piano, harp, or strings.

Gloria ("Glory to God in the Highest") The second movement in the ordinary of the mass.

Goliard A student musician-entertainer during the Middle Ages.

Grand staff The union of treble- and bass-clef staves to encompass a broad range of notated pitches.

Grave An indication for a slow tempo and somber character.

Gregorian chant The monophonic liturgical chant organized by Pope Gregory in the sixth century and used as the musical form of worship in the Roman Catholic church.

Half step The smallest interval between two tones in Western music (for instance, C and C♯).

Harmonics Pitches that sound in sympathetic vibration to a fundamental pitch. Harmonics are produced according to the overtone series.

Harmony The systematic chordal relationship of consonance and dissonance.

Harpsichord A keyboard instrument whose sound is produced by a mechanical action that plucks the strings.

Hemiola The rhythmic relationship of three beats to two, within a given meter. For example,

$$\text{♩.♩.} \quad \text{equals} \quad \text{♩♩♩}$$

Heterophony A musical texture produced when performers play different versions of the same melody.

Homophony A chordal texture in which the voices move together rhythmically.

Idiophones Members of the percussion family, whose sound is produced by striking, rubbing, or rattling the elastic material of which the instrument is constructed.

Imitation Musical "follow the leader"; a texture in which successive musical entries echo the original melody.

Impressionism A French-dominated musical style related to the contemporaneous painting style; it featured shimmering orchestral color, flexible rhythm, and extended harmonies.

Improvisation	Spontaneous composition and performance.
Intensity	Dynamic level or volume.
Interval	The musical distance between any two pitches. Depending on size, intervals in Western music are identified as major, minor, perfect, augmented, or diminished.
Intonation	The ability of a performer to maintain accurate pitch.
Introduction	A short section of a composition frequently used at the beginning of a symphony, concerto, or sonata to prepare the listener for the subsequent exposition.
Inversion	A chord in which the tones are placed in a different vertical order, so that the fundamental tone does not sound as the lowest note of the chord.
Isorhythm	A technique developed during the late medieval period that provided organization through rhythmic patterns (*talea*) and melodic patterns (*color*).
Jazz	An African-American style featuring improvisation and syncopated rhythms.
Jongleur	An itinerant professional musician of the Middle Ages.
Key	A tonal center based on the hierarchy of scale-degree relationships.
Key signature	Sharps or flats provided at the beginning of a work to indicate the key of the composition.
Krummhorn	A double-reed ancestor of the oboe. Its buzzy sound was produced by a reed set inside a cap.
Kyrie ("Lord Have Mercy")	The first movement in the ordinary of the mass.

Lai	A medieval song usually addressed to the Virgin Mary. The form consists of strophes of irregular length (*A A B B C C D D*).
Landini cadence	A cadence pattern of the early Renaissance period in which the leading tone moves down to the sixth and then leaps up a third to resolve on the tonic.
Larghetto	An indication for a slow tempo slightly faster than a largo (60 to 66 on a metronome).
Largo	An indication for a very slow tempo (between 40 and 60 on a metronome).
Leading tone	The pitch located on the seventh degree of a major scale. Also the triad built on this pitch.
Ledger line	A short horizontal line added above or below the staff to accommodate notes that are higher or lower than the staff.
Legato	An articulation term indicating a smooth connection between notes.
Leitmotif	A musical motive used to represent an extramusical character or idea. Leitmotifs were the basis of Wagner's music drama style.
Lento	An indication for a slow tempo between largo and adagio.
Libretto	Lyrics composed for an extended vocal composition such as an opera or oratorio.
Lied (plural lieder)	A German art song.
Lute	A fretted guitarlike instrument with a pear-shaped body and between seven and eleven strings; widely used during the Renaissance and baroque periods.

Madrigal	A Renaissance secular choral composition with vernacular text.
Major scale	The ordered succession of pitches formed according to the pattern of two whole steps, one half step, three whole steps, and a half step.
Major triad	The triadic chord formed by superimposing a minor third over a major third. The pitches C–E–G form a major triad.
March time	Common $\frac{4}{4}$ meter with a primary accent on the downbeat and a secondary accent on the third beat.
Mass	A celebration of the central rite of the Roman Catholic church; an important musical genre during the medieval and Renaissance periods.
Mazurka	A Polish dance in triple time. Also a romantic keyboard genre based on this dance.
Measure	A metrical unit of strong and weak beats. A measure, or bar, is marked off by bar lines.
Mediant	The pitch located on the third degree of the major scale. Also the triad built on this pitch.
Melismatic	More than one note per syllable in a text setting.
Melody	A rhythmic, ordered succession of intervals that constitute a coherent musical idea.
Membrano-phones	The drum family of instruments. Sound is produced by striking a stretched membrane.
Meno	An Italian descriptive word meaning "less."
Meter	The organization of accented and nonaccented beats. Meter is arranged in units called measures.

Meter signature	A fractional number that indicates the quantity of beats per measure and the quality of each of those beats. For instance, $\frac{4}{4}$ means that there are four beats in a measure and that each of those beats is a quarter note.
Metronome	A mechanical device invented in 1812 to sound the beats at various tempos. Modern metronomes are usually electric.
Mezzo	An Italian descriptive word meaning "medium."
Microtone	A step that is smaller than the half step of Western tonality. Microtones are frequently used in oriental music.
MIDI (Musical Instrument Digital Interface)	An electronic interface device that allows musical sounds to be stored and used as digital information.
Minimalism	A twentieth-century style distinguished by repetition of short melodic ideas, and slow or stagnant harmonic motion.
Minnesinger	A German secular musician of noble birth during the Middle Ages.
Minor scale	The ordered succession of pitches formed according to the formula one whole step, one half step, two whole steps, one half step, and two whole steps.
Minor triad	The chord formed by superimposing a major third above a minor third. The pitches C–E♭–G form a minor triad.
Minuet and trio	A compound dance form that is ternary at the sectional level and rounded binary within each section; frequently used as the third movement of a classical symphony.
Mixed meter	A type of rhythm marked by frequently changing meters.

Moderato	An indication for a moderate tempo (between 108 and 120 on a metronome).
Modes	Diatonic scales built on various patterns of whole and half steps; can be constructed by playing a seven-note scale based on each of the white keys of a piano.
Modulation	The shifting from one key or tonal area to another in a composition.
Molto	An Italian descriptive word meaning "very."
Monody	A solo song texture closely patterned after natural speech rhythm, with sparse instrumental accompaniment.
Monophony	A musical texture distinguished by one line of sound; melody without accompaniment.
Motet	A polyphonic, sacred, choral composition of the Renaissance period.
Motive	A short musical idea that can be used to generate and develop a longer idea or melody.
Movement	A complete and relatively independent section of an extended work such as a symphony.
Multiphonics	The artificial production of one or more notes in addition to the fundamental tone; performed on wind instruments or voice.
Music	Sound ordered in time.
Musica reservata	A Renaissance style of choral music emphasizing sensitive text depiction.
Music drama	A romantic opera style developed by Wagner featuring leitmotif organization, continually unfolding melody, massive orchestral accompaniment, and plots drawn from Nordic mythology.

Musique concrète	An early twentieth-century form of electronic music created by audio tape manipulation.
Mute	A device attached to an instrument that decreases the volume and alters the timbre.
Natural	The musical symbol ♮ which cancels a sharp or flat.
Neoclassicism	A twentieth-century style returning to music dominated by formal considerations.
Neoromanticism	A twentieth-century style returning to music marked by passionate expression characteristic of the romantic period.
Nocturne ("night sketch")	A short piano work featuring a singing melody over an arpeggiated accompaniment.
Noise	Sound that has no definite pitch and seems to lack order or coherence.
Notation	The use of written symbols to communicate musical expression.
Note	The sign indicating the pitch and rhythm of a tone.
Octave	The interval encompassing eight diatonic scale degrees.
Oliphant	A medieval musical instrument constructed from an elephant tusk.
Opera	A dramatic, multimedia genre fusing solo and choral singing with instrumental accompaniment, dance, staging, costumes, and scenery.
Opera buffa	Opera that developed out of the practice of inserting comic scenes in opera seria.
Opera seria	Opera featuring ornamented, virtuosic arias sung by both females and castrati.

Opera verissimo   A romantic opera style marked by plot realism and seamless and unified musical organization.

Opus ("work")   A number assigned in a chronological system cataloging a composer's output.

Oratorio   Unstaged opera based on a sacred (but not necessarily scriptural) text, created in the baroque period to replace opera during penitential seasons.

Ordinary   Movements of the mass whose texts remain constant each week. These sections include the Kyrie, Gloria, Credo, Sanctus, and Agnus Dei.

Organum   The earliest example of polyphony and harmony; developed during the Middle Ages.

Ornament   A musical embellishment such as a trill or grace note.

Ostinato   A short repetitive melodic and rhythmic pattern that is used organizationally in a composition.

Overtone   Secondary vibrations that are produced in relation to a fundamental pitch. The quantity and quality of overtones determines the timbre of a sound.

Overture   An orchestral introduction to a larger work such as a ballet or opera.

Parlando   Syllabically set, speechlike recitative used in opera buffa.

Passacaglia   A continuous variation form marked by a repeating bass line.

Passion   A musical setting of the Christian Passion story depicted through the text of one of the four gospels.

Pavane	A stately duple-meter dance paired with the more lively galliard during the Renaissance and baroque periods.
Pedal point	The use of an extended bass note held under changing harmonies in the accompaniment.
Pentatonic scale	A scale containing only five notes; for instance, that created by playing the black keys of a piano.
Period	A unit of formal organization represented by a pair of phrases and terminated by a full cadence.
Phrase	A single, complete musical thought analogous to a sentence of verbal language.
Pianissimo	An Italian word indicating a very soft dynamic level.
Piano	An Italian word indicating a soft dynamic level.
Piano trio	A chamber ensemble usually consisting of violin, piano, and cello.
Pitch	How high or low a sound is perceived. Pitch is based on a measured number of sound waves per second.
Pizzicato	A string technique in which strings are plucked by the finger.
Plainchant	A monophonic chant of the Roman Catholic church. Plainchant, sometimes called Gregorian chant after Pope Gregory, was the dominant musical style of the Middle Ages.
Poco	An Italian descriptive word meaning "little."
Polonaise	A stately Polish march in triple meter. Also a romantic piano genre based on the character of this dance.
Polyphony	A texture marked by rhythmically independent layers of melody sounded simultaneously.

Polyrhythm	Two or more layers of different meter sounded simultaneously.
Polytonality	Two or more layers with different tonal centers sounded simultaneously.
Pop-song form	A thirty-two-measure return form structured *AABA*. The opening eight-bar phrase is stated and repeated before a contrasting phrase called the "bridge" or "release." The original eight measures return at the conclusion.
Popular music	Music of a culture created and marketed with commercial intent and disseminated through mass media.
Portative organ	A small, portable organ of the Middle Ages. The keyboard was played by the right hand while the left hand worked the bellows.
Postlude	An organ composition played at the conclusion of worship while the congregation exits.
Prelude	A short introductory piece. In the romantic period, the prelude became a keyboard genre that subjected a motive or figure to various key modulations.
Prestissimo	An indication for an extremely fast tempo (over 200 on a metronome).
Presto	An indication for a very fast tempo (between 168 and 200 on a metronome).
Program music	Music based on extramusical considerations such as a story or descriptive idea.
Progression	The harmonic motion of chords moving from tension toward points of repose. Also certain common chord sequences such as the blues progression.

Proper	Movements of the mass whose texts vary daily. These sections include the Introit, Gradual, and Offertory.
Quadruple meter	Meters containing four beats in each measure; for instance $\frac{4}{4}$.
Quartal harmony	A type of harmony in which chords are built on fourths rather than thirds.
Quartet	A composition written for four performers.
Raga	In art music of India, ragas are scales of five to seven notes, used as the basis for melodic development. Each raga is specific regarding function, time of day, and means of development.
Ragtime	An American popular piano style developed about 1890, marked by syncopated melody against a marchlike accompaniment.
Range	The distance spanned by the top and bottom limits of a voice, instrument, or melody.
Rank	A set of organ pipes that are uniform in timbre.
Rebec	A gourdlike three-string bowed instrument of the Middle Ages.
Recapitulation	The third section of sonata form, in which the exposition returns.
Recitative	An operatic, through-composed solo song with light instrumental accompaniment used to advance the story line.
Recorder	A whistle-blown instrument widely used during the medieval, Renaissance, and baroque periods.
Refrain	Music and text repeated between stanzas of a song.

Register	The range of tones bounded by the highest and lowest notes of an instrument or voice.
Resolution	The musical process in which a dissonant sound is transformed into a consonance.
Responsorial	A musical texture distinguished by call and response between a chorus and a soloist.
Rest	A rhythmic indication for a duration of silence.
Retrograde	The backward presentation of a fugal theme or tone row.
Return form	A formal process marked by the repetition of large sections.
Rhythm	The ordered flow of music through time, measured by meter and tempo.
Rhythm section	Instruments (usually piano, bass, guitar, and drums) that maintain the harmonic and rhythmic accompaniment in a jazz ensemble.
Ricercar	A Renaissance instrumental form in which the imitative polyphonic style of a motet was transcribed for keyboard.
Riff	A short melodic fragment usually harmonized by brass or reeds in jazz style.
Ripieno	The full ensemble in a concerto grosso.
Ritardando	A gradual reduction in tempo.
Ritornello	A form used for movements of a baroque concerto grosso. The tutti sections are often referred to as ritornelli.
Rock (rock and roll)	An American popular music style based on country and rhythm and blues; originated approximately 1954.
Rondeau	A medieval poetic and musical form featuring a repeated refrain.

Rondo	A compound return form with contrasting episodic material interspersed with recurring statements of the initial theme (*A B A C A*); frequently used as the final movement of a classical symphony.
Rounded binary	A form that differs from simple binary structure by concluding with a brief return to the opening material.
Rubato	A flexible tempo characterized by a pushing and pulling of the melody against the accompaniment.
Sackbut	A medieval ancestor of the trombone.
Sanctus ("Holy, Holy, Holy")	The fourth movement in the ordinary of the Mass.
Sarabande	A stately dance form used as the third movement of a baroque suite.
SATB	A mixed chorus of soprano, alto, tenor, and bass voices.
Scale	An ordered succession of pitches that comprises the basic organizational structure of melody and harmony.
Scat	A jazz singing style using vocables rather than words to simulate the sounds of instruments.
Scherzo ("joke")	A return form sometimes used as the third movement of a symphony.
Scordatura	Changing the usual tuning of an instrument to alter the timbre or technique.
Score	Notated music in which all the parts of an ensemble are simultaneously represented, each on its individual staff.

Section	A large division of form somewhat analogous to a paragraph; often sixteen measures in duration.
Senza battuta	Rhythmically free, without direct beat.
Sequence	The repetition of a melodic idea transposed up or down.
Serial composition (serialism)	A twentieth-century system in which pitches (and possibly other elements) are arranged in a sequence that is maintained throughout the composition.
Sforzando	A strong accent on a note or chord.
Sharp	The notational symbol ♯, which raises a pitch by a half step.
Shawm	A medieval ancestor of the oboe, in which sound was produced through a double reed.
Simple meter	Duple, triple, or quadruple meter indicated by the number 2, 3, or 4 at the top of a meter signature.
Sine wave	A wave shape indicating a pure tone without harmonics.
Sitar	A long-necked, melodic Indian string instrument resembling a lute, with three to seven melody strings and a dozen additional sympathetic resonating strings.
Slendro	A five-note scale in gamelan music.
Sonata	A multimovement genre for a solo instrument, the first movement frequently being in sonata-allegro form.
Sonata-allegro form	A compound developmental form that contrasts a rhythmic theme in the tonic key with a lyrical theme in the dominant key. These ideas are subjected to an explorative development,

which is reconciled in the restatement of the opening material called the recapitulation. Sonata form is the usual design for the first movements of classical symphonies, sonatas, and concerti.

Song cycle
A number of art songs loosely bound together in a larger unity by a central concept or a single text author.

Soprano
The classification for the highest range of the female voice. Also used to designate the highest members of some instrumental families.

Sound
Vibrations transmitted through air and received by human ears.

Sprechstimme ("speech song")
A twentieth-century vocal technique in which pitch direction (but not specific pitch) is indicated.

SSA
A female choir with two soprano parts and an alto part.

Staccato
A mode of articulation in which notes are separated from each other by a brief silence.

Staff
Five horizontal parallel lines upon which notes are placed to indicate pitch. The *great* or *grand staff* is the combination of treble and bass staves, allowing a wide range of pitches to be notated.

Step
The intervallic relationship between two adjacent pitches. The half step is the smallest step common in Euro-American tradition.

Stile antico ("old style")
A term distinguishing the old practice of Renaissance polyphony from the newer baroque practice of clear text expression.

Stop	A device for controlling ranks of pipes on an organ or engaging courses of strings on a harpsichord.
Stretto	The use of close points of imitation in a fugal texture to build excitement.
String quartet	A chamber ensemble of two violins, viola, and cello. Also the genre of works written for this ensemble.
Strophic form (strophe)	A repetitive formal approach in which words change from one stanza to the next but the music remains the same. A strophe generally consists of four lines of text accompanied by four musical phrases.
Subdominant	The pitch located on the fourth degree of a major scale. Also the triad built on this pitch.
Subject	The theme of a fugue.
Submediant	The pitch located on the sixth degree of the major scale. Also the triad built on this pitch.
Suite	A multimovement instrumental work consisting of independent yet related dance movements.
Sul ponticello	A string performance technique in which the instrument is bowed near the bridge.
Sul tasto	A string performance technique in which the instrument is bowed over the fingerboard.
Supertonic	The pitch located on the second degree of a major scale. Also the triad built on this pitch.
Syllabic setting	The correspondence of one note per syllable in a text setting.
Symphonic poem	A single-movement orchestral work of the romantic period, based on an extramusical program.

Symphonic suite A programmatic, multimovement orchestral genre developed during the romantic period.

Symphony A multimovement genre originating in the classic period, written for an orchestra of strings, brass, woodwinds, and percussion. Classical symphonies often have four movements (an allegro in sonata form, an adagio song form, a brisk minuet and trio, and a lively concluding rondo).

Syncopation The displacement by unexpected accents of the regular metrical rhythm.

Synthesizer An electrophone capable of generating, modifying, and controlling sound.

Tabla A set of two northern Indian drums capable of various pitches.

Tala A rhythmic pattern, or cycle, in Indian music.

Tamboura An Indian string instrument that provides drone accompaniment for raga.

Tempo The rate of speed at which the underlying beat moves.

Tenor The classification for the highest range of the male voice. Also used to designate the analogous range of some instrumental families.

Ternary form A three-part formal design marked by a return of the opening material.

Terrace dynamics A sudden increase or decrease in dynamics, achieved through the addition or subtraction of instruments; characteristic of the baroque period.

Tertian harmony A harmonic system based on triads.

Tessitura The characteristic range of a singer's voice.

Texture	The relationship of layers of sound; monophony, polyphony, homophony, antiphony, and heterophony.
Theme	A melodic idea used as the basis of development.
Theme and variations	A keyboard form and genre consisting of a stated melody followed by a series of short episodes that vary elements of the original theme.
Through-composed song	A vocal form in which the text is set to continuously changing music.
Timbre	One of the four basic elements of music. Timbre is the tone color of a sound as measured by the characteristic shape of a sound wave.
Time signature	A fractional number representing the meter of a work, which is indicated at the beginning and subsequently at any meter change.
Toccata	A baroque keyboard genre with a free rhythmic feel and improvisational character, often used as a prelude to a fugue.
Tonality	The hierarchical relationship of tones in a harmonic system.
Tone	A musical sound consisting of a single pitch of constant frequency.
Tone poem (symphonic poem)	A one-movement orchestral work based on a program; developed during the romantic period.
Tone row	An organizational pattern of all twelve tones as the basis for composition in serial procedure in some twentieth-century works.

Tonic	The pitch located on the first degree of a major scale. Also the triad built on this pitch.
Traditional music	The folk music of a culture, passed on through oral tradition and performed in an informal atmosphere.
Tragédie lyrique	A French baroque operatic genre that developed a recitative style in French rather than in Italian.
Transposition	The performance of a composition in a key different from the original.
Treble clef	The symbol 𝄞 used to indicate the higher range of pitches on a staff. The symbol designates the second staff line from the bottom as the pitch G.
Tremolo	A quick pulsing in dynamic level. Also an instrumental technique (with string instruments) in which a single pitch is quickly rearticulated.
Triad	A chord consisting of three pitches, each of which is separated by the interval of a third; the basis of Western harmony.
Trill	A melodic ornament performed by rapidly alternating the original pitch with the one above or below it.
Trio	A composition featuring three performers. Also a contrasting section of a minuet or sectional ragtime composition.
Trio sonata	A baroque instrumental genre featuring two performers (often a flutist and violinist) above a keyboard and bass line continuo.
Triple meter	A rhythmic three-beat pattern in which an accented beat is followed by two unaccented beats.

Triplet	In rhythmic notation, three notes played within the time it would normally take to play two notes.
Troubadour	An itinerant secular musician of southern France during the Middle Ages.
Trouvère	An itinerant secular musician from the north of France during the Middle Ages.
TTBB	A male chorus consisting of two tenor parts and two bass parts.
Tutti	An Italian word meaning "all." Used to designate the full ensemble in a concerto grosso.
Twelve-tone system	A twentieth-century compositional technique based on the equal importance of all twelve pitches arranged in a predetermined sequence.
Unison	The performance of the same melody line by more than one performer.
Vibrato	A slight fluctuation of pitch. Controlled vibrato adds warmth to string or vocal timbre.
Vielle	A medieval ancestor of the violin, with four melody strings and one drone string. The word "fiddle" is derived from vielle.
Viol	A family of string instruments resembling the modern violin family but having a more subdued timbre than violins.
Virelais	A medieval song form with a refrain interjected between three different stanzas (*AB CC AB AB*).
Virtuoso	A performer with a high degree of technical skill.
Vivace	An indication for a quick tempo and lively character.

Voicing	The particular arrangement of tones within a triad. The use of root position and inversions to allow smooth voice leading in harmonic accompaniment.
Waltz	A dance in $\frac{3}{4}$ time.
White noise	All possible frequencies sounded simultaneously. Noise such as wind and waves.
Whole step	The interval encompassed by two half steps (for example, from C to D).
Whole-tone scale	A scale formed of successive whole steps.
Woodwind quintet	A chamber ensemble consisting of flute, oboe, clarinet, bassoon, and French horn.
Woodwinds	Members of the aerophone family, in which a column of air is set into vibration through wind directed across a mouthpiece or over one or two reeds.
Word painting	Musical representation of ideas generated by lyrics of a song text.

Index